ONITSHANESS

VOLUME ONE

ANCESTRAL VOICES

ONITSHA NAMES
AND
PHRASES TEASED OUT

OKEY MADUEGBUNAM
AGUNYEGO

ONITSHANESS

A compendium of published and unpublished
selected works on Onitsha matters

1995-2018

OKEY MADUEGBUNAM AGUNYEGO

TABLE OF CONTENTS

27TH NOVEMBER.
2016.

ONITSHANESS

"THOSE WE TAUGHT HOW TO RUN ARE NOW IN THE FOREFRONT AND THOSE THAT FOUND SUCCOUR WHILE LIVING IN OUR BACK HOUSES ARE NOW BUYING US OUT".

"THERE IS HARDLY A COMMUNITY WITHOUT CHALLENGES AND PROBLEMS BUT THE STRENGTH AND WILL OF THE PEOPLE ARE MEASURED BY HOW THEY CONFRONT THEM".

"ONITSHANESS IS ABOUT THE UNIQUE ELEMENTS THAT NEED TO BE REINFORCED IN ORDER TO BE RELEVANT, TO REGAIN OUR PRE-EMINENCE AND SUSTAIN IT".

"ONITSHANESS IS MORE OF STIRRING OUR COMMUNITY TO ACHIEVE MEANINGFUL DEVELOPMENT AND ZEST FOR THE TOWN.
ONITSHANESS IS AN OPPORTUNITY TO DO MORE FOR THE COMMUNITY THAN RESONATE TO PAST GLORIES".

"LET US CHARGE OURSELVES TO THINK BOLDLY AND SELL BRAVE IDEAS THAT WILL CREATE DRAMATIC RESULTS".

OPENING ANCESTRAL CHANTS

ELEGY I

OFU IFE BU ALILI
BU IFE ORA NA ASO
NYA KA OFOLU MEE
OTU ULA ATU UCHE
IFE SOLU OGBODI NA BU ALILI
ONE THING THAT CAUSES SADNESS
THAT WHICH THE PEOPLE DETEST
YET IT DARES US ALL THE TIME
AN ABNORMAL SLEEP THAT COMES
UNANNOUNCED AND UNEXPECTED
THAT WHICH IN ONE FELL-SWOOP
CARRIES THE INNOCENT INTO OBLIVION IS
GRIEF

ELEGY II

NWANNE ONYE
IFE DIKA NWANNE ONYE AMAZIA

OMALU ONYE
IFE DIKA NWANNE ONYE AMAZIA
OGOO OGO
IFE DIKA NWANNE ONYE AMAZIA
ONE'S RELATION THAT IS THE DECEASED
WHEN LAID IN STATE AND DURING WHICH
VARIOUS
RITES AND EULOGIES ARE PERFORMED AND
SUNG
IS OBLIVIOUS OF THE GOINGS ON
IT WOULD APPEAR THAT THE DECEASED
DOES NOT KNOW/REMEMBER
THE KINDREDS THAT MOURN HIM
A POINTER TO THE FINALITY OF DEATH
THE LAST AND FINAL AWAKENING
AN INEVITABLE ADVENTURE.

ELEGY III

ONYE EJINA OKWUTE KPA AMU
AWULE KA MMA
ONYE EJINA OKWUTE KPA AMU
AWULE KA MMA

IWELU OKWUTE KPA AMU
AWULE KA MMA
IFE MELU OGBODI EME YI
AWULE KA MMA

LET NO ONE MUCK THE INNER CAUCUS OF THE
ANCESTRAL SPIRITS. ALL SAID, THE GARB OF
THE SPIRITS (FIGURATIVELY) IS BETTER AND
EFFECTIVE. YOU DO NOT NEED TO BE
REMINDED OF THE AWESOMENESS AND
AUTHORITY OF THIS INNER CIRCLE.

IN OTHER WORDS, UNSHAKEN FAITH IS
BINDING. ANYTHING THAT IS CONTRARY TO
THIS FAITH IS SACRILEGIOUS. IF YOU DARE
MOCK OR VIOLATE THE TENETS OF THE SPIRITS,
THE EVIL CONSEQUENCES THAT VISIT THE
UNFAITHFUL WILL BEFALL YOU.
THE SONG IS A COUNSEL TO TENACIOUSLY
KEEP AND JEALOUSLY GUARD THE FAITH OF
OUR FOREBEARS.

"ORAOKWUTE IS A SECRET INNER COUNCIL OF
THE COLLECTIVE INCARNATE DEAD ALONG
WITH THEIR FEARFUL INCARNATION OF THE
ELDERLY DEAD-MUO AFIA. THE INNER CIRCLE
OF THE ELDERLY DEAD EMPHASIZES THE
PRINCIPLES OF HONOURING CUSTOMS,
SUPPORTING PUBLIC WELFARE AND LAW
ENFORCEMENT. THEIR VALUES IN THE PAST
ARE SIMILAR TO THOSE OF OGBO-NA-ACHI ANI
THE RULING AGE GRADE". OJINNAKA R.I.
CHUKWURA.

THE AUTHORITY OF MUO AVIA IS FINAL. THE
SPIRIT HAS THE POWERS TO SACK A WIFE THAT
IS WAYWARD AND/OR HAS BROUGHT OTHER
DISGRACES TO THE FAMILY. THE SPIRIT ALSO
IMPOSES FINES ON DEVIANTS AND CAN
DETHRONE A KING BY MERE ENTERING THE
PALACE OF THE KING AND SITTING ON THE
THRONE. THE SPIRIT IS GENERALLY REFERRED
TO AS "GOMENTI, ONYE NWE OBODO".

ELEGY IV

OBI .....OOH   OBI...... OOH
IMALU IFE MELU DIKE KA OJI KOLU AWOLO
IKOLU AWOLO

KWAYO   KWAYO   IKOLU AWOLO

ANCESTRAL SPIRITS, THE SPIRITS OF OUR
FOREFATHERS.
DO YOU KNOW WHAT INSPIRED THE BRAVE TO
PULL DOWN THE WOVEN GARB OF THE SPIRIT
OF THE DEAD THAT WAS HUNG ON A TREE?

HISTORY HAS IT THAT POWERFUL WITCHES AT
A TIME HUNG FOUR WOVEN GARBS OF THE
SPIRIT OF THE ELDERLY DEAD ON AN IROKO
TREE. THE CHALLENGE TO THE PEOPLE'S
SPIRITUAL BELIEF WARRANTED INVOCATIONS
AND AFFLATUS TO COUNTER THE WITCHES'
MACHINATIONS.

A SNAKE FROM THE CHAMBERS OF THE
VALIANT EMERGED, CLIMBED THE IROKO TREE,
BROUGHT DOWN THE WOVEN GARBS OF MUO
AVIA AND WENT BACK INTO ITS CHAMBER
WITHIN A TWINKLE.

THE MOVEMENT OF THE SNAKE IS EXPRESSED
IN A SONG AS OLILA OLILA.

DARING THE WITCHES AND DEFEATING THEM
WAS HEROIC AND THIS BRAVE SUCCESS CALLED
FOR JUBILATION, HENCE THE CHANT;

KWAYO   KWAYO   IKOLU   AWOLO
KWAYO   KWAYO   IKOLU   AWOLO

REFLECTIONS

Onitsha main market, otherwise known as Otu Nkwo Eze incontestably belongs to Onitsha Indigenous community. The market crises that reared its head forty one years ago resulted in whittling our franchise.

The then Administrator of East Central State Ukpabi Asika, later Ajie of Onitsha recommended 7.5% market revenue to be paid to Onitsha indigenous community against 15% the people considered. There was a grouse that the community was not adequately consulted. The 7.5% was only paid once. Questions have been asked why Onitsha's demand for 15% revenue derived from their land (market) is different from that of oil producing States/communities.

We may have lost this bid but I do not think that we have lost it entirely except we do not act. The Ruling Council is expected to advise on the facts on ground and then how to champion this case again. Our galore of SAN, reputable lawyers, civil right activists, and other professionals are expected to mount a serious campaign and support this challenge.

Our farm lands in Trans Nkisi are gradually and disingenuously appropriated. The former Anambra State government acquired the land for industrial projects only to allot them to people.

The manner of allotment was lopsided such that the

owners of the land were not given appropriate consideration and neither was compensation paid to them. This to me is another nursed strategy to weaken and make us irrelevant. It is essential to expose our people who may have compromised on this land matter.

Earlier hope placed on Ex-Governor Peter Obi in reviewing the land allocation was dashed. In an open letter to Governor Willie Obaino while highlighting the land issue, he was implored to readdress it dispassionately and also reminded that if such issue had been the case in other climes in the State many lives would have been lost. That we are not cut up rough should not be taken for granted.

But must we remain defenceless? We look up to the Ruling Council to advise the community of the true position of this case and how to challenge it.

Yet another uncertain crisis is boundary of Onitsha and her neighbours. Following the Supreme Court sitting in Abuja on 28th September 1995 in the suit no.sc./192/91:Chief P.O. Anataogu and 2 ors and H.R.H Igwe Isaac Iweka and 4 ors of Obosi, the judgement was ruled in favour of Onitsha indigenous community. In a chat with Late Onowu Iyasele, Chief Olisa Mortune he assured that the issue of boundary delineation has been finalized. No doubt, we have won countless boundary cases but we are yet to take possession of the land involved. How do we go? "Obu ama atu kobu na ube adironko? Is it that you cannot aim or that your arrow is blunt? Is it the case of barking the wrong tree or bucking responsibilities? This exhortation draws our people's attention to be alive with their responsibilities. It is also incumbent on us to have our finger on its pulse. .

So much has been written on how to marshal fund for community development; self-help.

One of them concerns mandatory contributions from every adult Onitsha person. One hundred naira -₦100- monthly contribution amounts to One Thousand, Two Hundred Naira -₦1, 200 – a year. If we use a modest estimate of forty thousand -40,000- Onitsha adults in Nigeria and in Diaspora, the contribution will add up to Forty Eight Million Naira. – ₦48m- a year. If the contribution is raised to Two Thousand Naira a year, it will add up to Ninety-Six Million Naira – ₦96m. At Five Thousand Naira a year and using the same population estimate, two hundred million naira – ₦200m – will be realized.This contribution can be paid through the family Heads -Diokpas or through Onitsha Improvement Union world - wide. The latter will necessitate every adult Onitsha person to be a financial card carrying member of the union, in other neighbouring towns; the penalty for not joining the town's union is stiff and stiffer upon death. It is needful for us to craft strategies that will sensitize our people to be committed to self-help. Our competitiveness also stands to be heightened.

The conferment of chieftaincy rests with Agbogidi. It is incontrovertible. A criterion one may suggest is the contribution to the town by aspirants prior to their conferment.

'Alo ka eji egbu okpa owelu gba mmee'; for a feat to be accomplished you require extra planned scheme. It calls for perception.

It is also no degradation to adapt practical strategies from others towns. They too, to a greater extent have benefited from us. Of importance is the fact that power stems from the ability to combine the knowledge and contributions of others with your own.'Ewele ife eji agwo nzu, gwo nzu ochake. The upshot of this narrative is that with a grand design in place, development and zest for the town stand to be stimulated. The earlier cited parlance concludes that such scheme will bring 'brightness', which is fruition.

It is also essential to honour our people that have caused development for the town without having a desire for chieftaincy. 'Eto dike ome ozo'; praise a man who has performed a feat and he would be glad to perform more feats.Some other ways to raise fund would include celebrating 550 years existence of the town. Sokoto caliphate celebrated 200 years of existence in 2004 and raked in much fund from Federal, State governments, Business tycoons Associations etc.

We can also come up with a special appeal launch for permanent residence for the monarch at Ime obi with guest houses/flats for distinguished guests.

'Ade enwesia nkwa na akwa ume'. This aphorism charges our people to use our bestowed resources, created resources and ideas effectively and wisely hence avoid stagnation and adversity.Finally, we must strive to lessen the disputes and quarrels in the families, villages and the town arising from Diokpaship disputes, land cases, Obiship etc. These disputes most often create wounds and leave scars. In many ways God is dishonoured by quarrels amongst His people. We must therefore strive for amity. All and sundry must embrace this olive branch and work for the development of the town.

Challenge is the basis of growth and development. We expect the Ruling Council to constitute Think Tanks that will address the militating issues against us.

May we keep the light lit by our forefathers over 550 years ago aglow?

OKEY AGUNYEGO
17/5/15

FOREWORD

The documentation of facts (in the form of book writing) as they effect a group of people for the sake of posterity is one of the most fascinating and modern inventions of the present age. It is changing the way we think and helps to avoid congestion of our memories. With the advent of information technology, this task has been made much simpler and it is now possible to record events as they occur, keep them in storage over a long period of time and subsequently produce same in book form. Such books can be distributed to important libraries throughout the world, thus ensuring that they can be easily accessed and used as and when required.

The Author Mr. Okey Agunyego has taken advantage of this development and has at great sacrifice both in finance and human labour successfully produced over five books on various issues. However, his writings are mainly based on what can be done by all to ensure the ancient Onitsha town regains and retains its glory which she lost as a result of rapid urbanization and the after effects of the three years civil war that badly affected this town.

Just as James the Apostle was nicknamed the "zealot" because of his zeal to get Romans out of Israel and have them replaced with a less oppressive government, I shall in this forward describe the Authors interest on his ancient town of Onitsha as that of a "Patriot". It is the same sense of patriotism that has led him to cleverly coin the word "Onitshaness" to denote any action taken or to be taken, any statement, any work that can be undertaken so that the once revered town of Onitsha, the pride of ibo people as a whole returns to the glory it once held among the comity of civilized towns within Nigeria in general and Anambra State in particular. And for the indigenes, it is a clarion call for them to wake up from slumber and develop their God's given talent for the good of her people. It is also a constant reminder to her people to stop chasing shadows and grab and retain what belongs to them, without encroaching on any other person's right.

Among the books he has written to explain the problems confronting the citizen of that town and proffering suggestion on what should be done to regain her glory include Ancestral Voices: Onitsha Names and Phrases Teased out.

Onitshaness: Practical Approaches Towards Renewed of our Fabled Town.
Onitsha Quest for Reinforcing and Sustaining
Pre-eminence
Ozanzediegwu
Ancestry and progenies
In search of Excellence: Synoptic Appraisals for the Development of Onitsha

Onitshaness: A compendium of selected works on

Onitsha matters 1995-2016.

The new project is a compendium of selected works, published and unpublished Onitsha matters 1995 to 2016. It is condensed into a single unit for easy reading and of a reference material. It calls for hard work, for honesty, for better interaction amongst the inhabitants of the ancient city, for the spirit of tolerance and forgiveness , for the adoption of "give and take" attitude, but above all for a humble and quick return to the teaching of Christ as the only way to overcome the problems created by ourselves.

Some of our children born abroad unfortunately know nothing or little about the customs and practices of our people. The hustle and bustle of city life makes it even more difficult for their parents to educate them on this. I see it as a duty on parents to teach their children on the happening within town of origin, hence the need to place copies of this condensed book on the shelves of their libraries and encourage their reading from time.

Time they say waits for no one; this is a truism and I urge all lovers of Onitsha town, Nwadianis, inlaws, friends and well wishers, particularly members of Obi's council to play greater role in implementing the several suggestions which the author has painstaking highlighted. I accept there are difficulties to be encountered, but the old maxim which says: mbido akwa naafiaaru, mana ebebe akwa mmilianya agbaba.

Which literally means that it is a difficult to start a cry, but once started tears starts to flow from the eyes this should serve as a source of strength in embarking on measures that would redeem the lapses of the past, however difficult and ensuring future for the generations yet unborn.

With this advice, I wish the Author well and pray that he shall live long enough to see his dreams come through and to the readers, a deeper understanding that something somewhere that engulfed the city in its present dilemma, but that is sure hope of getting things right if we place our trust in God and act with sincere hearts and combined efforts.

NWAKIBIE ORAKWUE P. EGBUNIWE
House of Gold
Isolo – Lagos
January 2015.

PREFACE

This compendium in essence is intended for easy reference. It contains selected write ups spanning from 1995 to 2016. The period 1995 to 1998 covers some articles I edited and contributed to Ado Focus; a magazine set up by Ado Circle Lagos, in the early eighties. I was the chairman of this magazine and during the period, four magazines were published and circulated. The articles include a chat with late Akunne Bosah President of Ruling Age Grade – Ogbo na achiani, an interview with late Akunne Fred Umnna, President of Agbalanze and many others articles.

You may find some issues repeated in another work with additional information. The point to note is that such representation accentuates the message therein and as well as stimulates the urgency to redeeming whatever might have gone wrong.The major theme that runs in this collection is on the urgent need for development of the town and her people.

Onitshaness defined, is all about the unique elements that need to be reinforced in-order to be relevant, to regain our pre-eminence and sustain it. Onithsaness is an opportunity to do more for the community than resonate to past glories.

At this stage, let me provide a brief rundown of this package and along the line highlight some issues that are worrisome. You will find a couple of letters to the Ruling Council on militating issues against our people with counsels on how to redeem them. The open letter to His Excellency, Governor Willie Obiano expressed our dissatisfaction on Trans Nkisi land matter and sought his dispassionate attention to enable us claw back our land.

Ancestral Voices, Onitsha Names and Phrases Teased out, is my attempt in unravelling the meaning of names and phrases. The initial attempt resulted in treating fifty names and fifty phrases in 1997 under the title; Curious Phrases and Names which was published in Ado Focus magazine in 1998. The first book form was published in collaboration with Ado Circle in 1999. This was followed with a revised edition with three hundred new entries in 2003. In the course of my consultations I found out that some people do not know the meaning of their names.Even though I consulted widely, the attempt, the first of its kind is not final. The names are listed alphabetically with their interpretations and counsels derivable from the names alongside. The phrases too have their literal and implied meanings listed and as well as counsels resulting from the phrases. There are some names that are peculiar to Onitsha. My prayer is that parents should name their children after circumstances experienced by the family or after the members of the family. Some people these days give names that have no bearing or reflection of the family antecedents.

The write ups, A wedge to Abyss and Restoration of

our value system provide enough insights and counsels. The outline of the glorious past, the present incubi, the why and wherefores and how to heighten our competiveness are carefully surveyed in both papers. The grand design intended to meet these noble tasks are treated in the text.Let me treat some of the worrisome issues raised In Search of Excellence: Synoptic Appraisals for the Development of Onitsha..Losing one's dialect is worrisome and tantamount to losing one's identity. Parents are to be blamed for this flaw but there are other factors that include the use of central Ibo in church readings and to some extent the influence of overwhelming population of non-indigenes on our youths. As against Ururu Anyasi, mgbede is now widely spoken by our people. The ways out of this debacle are tackled in the text.The Okpalaship of Onitsha comes next. Which quarters – Oreze / Isiokwe takes the saddle? What has happened to Oreze lineage that their nephews now come consider their turn has come? I know in recent past that both quarters performed that role at different times. My take is such that issues that divide us- and there are many -must be thrashed for posterity. We must bear in mind that we shape tomorrow's world by what we teach our children.Beautifying Monarchs' tombs and village shrines often engender serious contentions. A friend told me that Monarchs' burial places are shrouded in mystery but he failed to confirm his source of information. For those that are not in the picture, the tomb of Obi Eze Chima, Onitsha's first sovereign is decorated at Obior and signposted from the highway. Can we say that the tomb of Igwe Okwudili Onyejekwe buried at Okwueze is shrouded in mystery? I do not think so.Many would consider anything shrine as idolatry. That is fine but from another perspective, I see the shrines as historical endowments and when properly packaged will attract tourists. Take the case of pyramids in Cairo, Egypt with the mummies laid in there. This wonderful edifice was built by ancient Egyptians that were not Muslims. The sculpture of the sphinx adorning the main entrance pillar had its nose slashed by jihadist of later years. Today the pyramids are tourists' delights.It would not be out of place to construct a monument for our people that died during the 1967/70 crisis. This is another history book for generations unborn and beside it will attract both local and international tourists. Abroad, historical monuments including buildings are preserved. Some of the buildings are engraved with plaques indicating the personality that lived there. I cannot explain my passion when I cited the building that Shakespeare lived in London.I have in many write ups advocated commemorating our deceased brothers and sisters that caused many developments and assisted many of a people. It reminds us of courage and devotion of such people. It is inspiring.Although most of our old buildings were staffed and bulldozed during the war, I figure that the picture of some of the interesting old buildings can still be obtained from family members, for example that of Ozi Umera's house. The picture could be made in post cards with some history notes.

They can be sold as mementos during festivals. What about our masquerades? We have a good number of them to showcase in post cards. I would like to suggest a space be provided at Ime Obi where work of arts can be displayed and sold to visitors and indigenes as well.

Ozanzediegwu at the early years of settlement lived at Ojiba lane where the Obiefunas and Obelagus, both descendants of Ozanzediegwu reside. This is a historical place that can be signposted. There are many others; coronation ground, Ani Onitsha, Otumoye Lake Etc that can be signposted and turned into post cards. I am not sure about the final arrangement for the town to acquire the palace of Obi Okosi. The splendour of the palace lined with majestic grove is another endowment that can be turned into a museum. This definitely will attract droves of people; tourists, archaeologists, school children etc.I have included in this package pictures of rural background of Onitsha in the fifties and early sixties. It is nostalgic.I have made several cases of tree planting in Onitsha for many advantages they have. It would not be out of place for the Monarch or any of his representatives from the Ruling Council to flag off tree planting during World environmental day, Earth day or at any other auspicious period.

Another worrisome issue concerns the disturbing trend associated with the succession bids to Diokpaship which has dismembered many families. It is a harmful development that has to be checked. Late last year news filtered in that the Ruling Council has worked out modalities that will streamline the succession bids and other related matters. This blueprint if it is true cannot be further delayed. Doing what is right today means no no regrets tomorrow.

The book on Ozanzediegwu; – Ancestry and Progenies apart from tracing the author's larger family pedigree also shows the close knit affinity of Onitsha people. This revelation calls for remedying many ills we have caused ourselves. An anonymous quote reads. An offense against your neighbour is a fence between you and God.To mistreat or insult God's creation is to mistreat or insult the Creator.He who cannot forgive others burns the bridge over which he himself must eventually pass. –Hubert.The upshot of this narrative is that we must dampen down rifts in the families, villages and in the town than damper them. Afam Ogbotobo reminds us in of his songs that we are of one blood and umbilical cord 'Ofu Obala Ofuelili'. We have got to learn from our lapses or fail to learn.

Let me touch on some aspects of spirituality before I round off. Most religions uphold one God. It will interest you that Arch Angel Gabriel who conveyed God's message to Virgin Mary on her delivery of our Lord Jesus Christ as believed by Christians is the same Arch Angel the Muslim faithful believe who conveyed Allah's message to Prophet Mohammed, five hundred years after the birth of Jesus Christ. To some extent the

Ten Commandments compare well with the general rules on how Muslim adherents live their lives. The rules include; admonition on falsehoods, fornication, adultery, rebellion, trespasses of the eye, debauchery, and not swayed by passion.

In summary, there is one God but with different interpretations by various religions. What is important is that we live and survive by His Grace and not by our merit. We must trust Him to support our various projects, Onitshaness inclusive. It is said that there is no failure more disastrous than the success that leaves God out. We must not therefore forget to lay aside the sin that hinders us from pleasing Him. The power and complete knowledge of God is expressed in the following quote by Ackley.
His eye our secret thoughts behold
His mercies all our lives enfold
He knows our purposes untold
You cannot hide from God.

Let me conclude by hoping that the insights and counsels contained in this work will awaken our people towards redeeming Onitsha dreams-Onitshaness. May we be committed to offer that 'Extra' push which cumulatively will boost our competitiveness?

OKEY MADUEGBANAM AGUNYEGO
His Grace Lodge
Isolo Lagos
November 2014.

Please Note That Ideas Replicated In Various Write ups Are Deliberate.
They Are Intended As Constant Sensitization That Will Drive The Information Home.

DEDICATION

I thank God, for His gift of life, the strength and insight to set down this compendium. I would like to dedicate this project to our people late and alive, who have contributed in many ways to the development of our mother town.

To all the sick people in hospitals and at homes, I pray that God will heal them and also intervene in cases we think are hopeless. His power has no boundary known to men.

Life is a journey from womb to tomb.While death is inevitable the demise of my brother Osita, the wife Ngozi Agunyego and my cousin Nkiru Nzegwu – Danjuma touched me. I was also devastated on the death of Afam Ofoedu; a relation and a close friend May their souls and many others from the family, nephews, In-laws and friends rest in perfect peace?

This project is dedicated to them.

This work is also affectionately dedicated to my late parents, Mr. Alex and Rose Agunyego and to my immediate family Nwando, Obiora, Nonyem, Okey Jnr, Mbenyego, Myra and the entire Ozanzediegwu stock, comprising of Molokwu, Agunyego, Osaji, Nzegwu, Edeogu and Chukwuma.

EXALTATION

I will like to dedicate this compilation to my grandfather, Esesue Frank Akonobi Agunyego, a missionary trained carpenter. He took his trade to Zungeru where my father was born in 1916.Quite a good number of people that lived with their grandfathers up to early 1960's were opportune to imbibe   historical pasts and lessons there from. My grandfather narrated his successes, disappointments and betrayal by his cousin. A female relation of his who married an Asaba man was badly treated. My grandfather then avowed that none of his granddaughters will marry from Asaba. He testified against his close friend on land matters. His position was why his friend could not give his brother a plot land out of three plots of the family land. Amazingly the duo in the next morning sat on easy chairs discussing, snuffing, drinking palm wine while swathing flies. This is a rare happenstance these days.

He secured lands for his relations but failed to retain his choice plot. There was a dispute that claimed lives and arising from this my grandfather swore that he will not go back where blood was spilled – ebe egbulu ochu.
Over the time, he reminded us that his late father Mora predeceased his father Ozanzediegwu and as such we should not contest the custodianship of the statue (MUO) Ozanzediegwu. He cited other members of the larger family that cannot inherit this post.

At seven years, I was opportune to join him to his farm at Ufesi Nkisi. He often chose who will accompany him. I carried the drinking water. It looked a long trip because we had to descend the hill, cross the Nkisi stream and then ascend the hill before getting to the plain. It was an experience and fun too. During break time (Mkpulu) small round yam species were roasted with assorted vegetables and pepper and eaten with palm oil. It was a savory meal.

On the way back we washed our feet and faces on getting to the stream and after climbed the hill on our way home. He hardly used walk stick till he died at 84 years. He was a farmer and a carpenter of repute. He had a big yam barn at home. Obviously there was much to learn from grannies but wished they had been documented more in writing than oral.

Looking back, addled and with traces of anger, I wonder how we lost control of Ufesi Nkisi and likewise OTU Nkwo Eze. As I have often noted, I believe that we can still make our marks except we fail to act. That would be self-condemnation and destruction.

To my grandmother, late Madam Ifediba Agunuyego, nee Egbuniwe, I dedicate this work. She traded on kolanuts at Ose Okwodu. On Afo Igwe Market day at Ogidi, she took her trade there and in return bought assorted food stuff, cassava, plantain etc. She nurtured four of my brothers including me. She urged us to eat well and took delight when we did. She died at 85 years
This dedication is also extended to my late aunt, Mrs Agaegbu Ibegbu, nee Agunyego. I was gravely sick during my childhood. On each occasion when all hope were lost, she carried me piggy back to the local medicine man, Pa Audu who lived at lower Odakpu quarters. I was immersed in large pot of palm oil up to my neck. I survived. I believe that God works in diverse and mysterious ways, even through the medicine man to save me at the time. I remain appreciative to my aunt. She died at the ripe age of 85. I remain grateful to the goodness from God. All glories belong to him and may His dominion reign forever.

The last but not the least of those I dedicate this compilation is late Mrs. Agbakoba, nee Asika. She is the mother of Hyacinth Victor, Onyechi and Jumai. In

1986 we met at Willkinson – Bishop Onyeabo junction. No sooner I greeted her than she acknowledged my greeting and came up with the following remarks. Agunyego Nna, Isi Nwa. (Note Isi nwa refers to my father) " Arapu Kwolunu ebe unu ga alu uno".Did they leave for you people where to build a house. It was a question, an advice and a wake-up call, all rolled into one. It burned inside me and spurred me to eventually accomplish the task but not without the untiring moral efforts of my late aunt, Mrs. Agaegbu Ibegbu. She removed a pot filled with fetish objects from the plot.

I remain grateful to roles and influences on my life by these great characters. May their souls and the souls of others departed, through the mercy of God rest in peace? Amen.

ACKNOWLEDGMENTS

My interest in features was fostered in my University (University of East London previously North East Polytechnic) days with contributions to Applied Economics Department's Magazine; Applecom.

I must admit that the lecturer/student relationship during my time in London was genial, encouraging and helpful. I remain grateful to Dr Graham Wright, my personal tutor and other lecturers for their reassurances. This inspiration later manifested in my many write-ups while at Nigeria Airways. I delivered some of them as guest lecturer in Ground Training School, Lagos. I edited eleven magazines for the Marketing Department and I was a regular contributor to SkyPower News; Nigeria Airways Newsletter.

In another context, the germ of my interest on Onitsha matters was sown in my contributions to Ado Focus, a magazine of Ado Circle, Lagos, 1995 to 1998. Despite the fact that I was the Chairman, the Editorial Adviser, Odinigwe Onuora Nzekwu provided professional support and inspiration that blosomed my interest. He obliged me with a foreword to my first book Ancestral Voices, Onitsha Names and Phrases Teased out. My profound appreciation goes to him.

I remain thankful to Nwakibie Orakwue Egbuniwe who contributed to all my six books with foreword and articles. I would like to thank Nnabuenyi Obianeze Nzegwu, Akunwata Odi Ibisi and Chinyelugo Chudi Oranye for favouring me also with forewords to some of my works and also in sharing some useful ideas with me.

To others acknowledged in my previous works, I thank you all. It was by sheer chance that I stumbled across my late Dad's unfinished work in stencil, concerning Ozanzediegwu's family. It broadened my horizon. May his soul rest in peace?

My heartfelt thanks go to Akosa Jack Ikwueme, Anthony Osakwe – Ogo a.k.a. Nnukwu muo, Orakwue Ugbo, Adichie Agunyego and Fano Osaji for their various encouragements. It was pleasurable to have Okey Junior ask questions while I was compiling the manuscript. In a different circumstance, I am greatly touched by the thoughtfulness of Chike Onyejekwe. Ifeanyi Odili alias Diokpa joins others that played mid – wives during the birth of this compendiun

I praise and thank Almighty Father for supplying the power that boosted my willingness to tackle this project.

OKEY MADUEGBUNAM AGUNYEGO
His Grace Lodge
Lagos.
January

Ancestral
Voices
Onitsha Names
and
Phrases Teased Out
Okey Maduegbunam Agunyego
Revised Edition with 300 New Entries

ANCESTRAL VOICES

ONITSHA NAMES AND
PHRASES TEASED OUT

ISBN 978-060-662-9
2003

TYPESETTING
Andrew Ike Nwadu JP

ONLINE DIGITAL MARKETING
Marvtech Network Solution
21 Ikosi-Ketu
Lagos State

ONITSHA NAMES AND PHRASES TEASED OUT

ABOUT THE BOOK

A Practical guide for Onitsha families to use in naming their children unless prevailing circumstances dictate otherwise ....

The names and phrases exposition is a commendable cultural revival attempt.

Nwakibie Orakwue Egbuniwe.

A valuable book of names and phrases, besides it reveals the development shortcomings and offers a way forward on how Onitsha can regain her past glories.
Patty Mba

A welcome reference materials and a bold attempt at demystifying Onitsha names. Odinigwe Onuora Nzekwu.

LAMENTATION

The Nigerian crisis of 1966/70 occupies a major chapter in the history of the country. During the war, Onitsha came under the Federal attack from riverfront and from upland. The town was blitzed, strafed and much of it reduced to rubbles.

The people as a result fled in thousands to the hinterland as refugees. We lost a crop of the military offices; Colnel Sokei, Captain Okaka and many others. Many college kids that enlisted in the Biafran Army suffered the same fate. Following the withdrawal of Biafran Forces from the then Mid-West Region, Lieutenant Colonel Ifeajuna was labeled a saboteur and shot; a victim of power tussle and ideology. Following this allegation, many prominent Onitsha men and women were detained. The pogrom that took place in the Northern cities prior to the war claimed many lives of our people and Ibos in general. During the second reprisal coup, we also lost fine officers. The litany of unwarranted victimization continued after the war with a good number of Onitsha people in Police Force and Army were detained for over one year.

TRIBUTES

In grateful tributes to our forebears that gave us Onitsha Ado Na Idu and to numerous and other departed souls that believed and worked for the course of the town, I salute your courage and efforts. Grateful tributes are paid to our people that died during the civil crisis of 1966/70. Special tributes are paid to late Mr. Paul Ekweogwu, a dashing young accountant whose life was cut short during the 1966 pogrom in Kano, Lt. Col Theo Nzegwu, a fine pioneer military officer who was shot at Ikeja Cantonment during the reprisal second coup in 1966, Nnabuenyi Onwuseluka Egbuniwe, who though left mother earth on 28/12/97, he and other Police and Military Officers were detained after the war and to my late parents, Mr. and Mrs. Alex Okwudili and Rose Uzomaka Agunyego for their unwavering and self-sacrificing commitment in the training of their kids and wards.

FOREWORD 1

It has been my fate to read and vet manuscripts of many books on social and cultural subjects. This latest addition to the series of such books is a welcome development. Culture is one of the buzzwords today. To understand it, we must locate it within the traditions of thought and not merely treat it as a modern inventory of discovery. In writing his book, the author has completely chosen a difficult area to discuss. i.e. the identification and explanation of the meanings of various surnames and middle names which Onitsha people are identified with.

WHY WRITE ON NAMES?

It is a general belief in most African countries that the name given to a child at birth, to a certain extent, influences that child's course of events in his world. Without being superstitious, a quick reference to the scriptures will justify this assertion. Abraham who lived 2300 years B.C and who was the founder of Jewish Nation was called Abram in his early life. God promised him heirs and land for his people in Canaan and renamed him Abraham (Father of all Nations). Most religious adherents call him "Father of Faith".

In the book of Isaiah 7:4, it was prophesied: "The Virgin will be with child and will give birth to a son and he will be called Immanuel".

This prophecy was reported fulfilled by the Apostle Matthew in his gospel Chapter 1:21. 1:21. thus: "he will give birth to a son and you will give him the name Jesus because he will save his people from their sins".

Since the advent of Christ, who is the subject of this prophecy that was made over 2000 years ago, Jesus has always been on the lips of all believers.The Apostle of Gentiles, Paul was before his conversion called Saul. After his conversion, he rose to be the greatest of all converts.These scriptural authorities support the author's efforts in writing a book that will identify, explain and perpetuate the distinctive names which Onitsha people in particular and the Ibo race in general are associated with. Some of these names and phrases are going into oblivion because of our mad rush to adopt western ideas. We have the opportunity to tap and invest in the vast "cultural capital" but for the other reasons, especially in the quest for power and wealth accumulation, disharmony and betrayals are now the order of the day. In the process too we bastardize some of our cultural values. It would appear that we have forgotten the exhortation; "what you sow, you reap". We cannot completely disassociate ourselves from the consequences of our negligence.

A section of the book deals with some phrases which from time immemorial had formed the bedrock of our language. With the introduction of the central Igbo dialect which replaced the simple ibo language, spoken, written and easily understood by the Onitsha people a nail seemed to have been driven into the coffin of some of our beautiful and well meaning parables. Christ, during his life time taught with parables and so were our forefathers. Parables use few literal words but convey deep metaphorical meanings of what is intended to be said. The author should therefore be congratulated on his efforts to document some of these parables as contained in the phrases. His efforts should be seen as a sort of cultural revival which I must appeal to our youths to emulate.
We live in a dynamic world and we all must be prepared to adjust to changes resulting from this dynamism. Before the civil war, from Zik's Roundabout at Dennis Memorial Grammar School up to All Hallows Seminary was an exclusive preserve of Onitsha people. Economic circumstances coupled with self-interests have made us to lose this rare privilege. The powers we were then wielding in government circles have all been lost. With urbanization fast approaching on all nooks and corners of our great town and with intermarriage bringing us closer and closer with people, villages and town, bordering

Onitsha, we must be willing to accept the consequences for this evolution.

The author in his "Afterword" section of the book, lamented on the fact that Onitsha people are fast losing the position they once held in the scheme of affairs in the State. I share his views but as a Christian, living in a fast-changing world, we must not lose hope; rather we should reinforce our faith in God with whom all things are possible. With this renewed faith, all citizens both at home and abroad must try to relate our ethical, physical and social foundations to the adjustments of our resolve especially coming on the heels of the onslaught and ravages which event of the 30 years have brought upon us and for which one way or the other we must share the guilt. If we start now, to see facts and accept them as they are; if we can swallow our pride and condemn the moral decadence and truancies prevailing on the part of our children-the future leaders of this society – I believe all hopes are not lost. The adage – 'egwu kwusie nya lue uno' implies that we must remember home such that the necessary development of the town and her citizens are not neglected. This principle has made other town up-and-coming.

The last appendix in the book carried the names of the various annual festivities of Ontisha people. These are important festivals which have spiritual and cultural meanings. Unfortunately, the book is silent on the meanings and reasons why the festivals are held at that particular time of the year. I believe that there are still many elders living who will be willing to explain the purpose and importance of such festivals. The author and others may therefore wish to carry out a detailed exposition of these festivals.

I am aware that Ado Circle; one of the best-organized cultural clubs consisting of Onitsha elites working in Lagos is supporting the author in the publication of this book. I acknowledge their backing and express my thanks for this wise and timely decision. Such commitments should be copied by other clubs/societies.

In conclusion, I want to freely associate myself with this publication, having gone through the manuscript and offered necessary remarks. I therefore regard the book as the most practical guide for our families to use in naming their children unless other prevailing circumstances dictate- otherwise.

This book is therefore generally recommended to every Ibo speaking people and to Onitsha people in particular. I wish the author success and this book a wide readership.

OGBUEFI NWAKIBIE P.EGBUNIWE
House of Gold
100 Oshodi/Apapa Exp Way
Lagos. November, 1999.

FOREWORD 2

Ancestral Voices the first compendium of Onitsha names is the latest addition to the growing literature on Ontisha traditional life. In crafting this, his first publication which has over 850 entries (names) Mr. Okey Agunyego ventured into a field that has rarely been explored.

Names, among Ontisha indigenes, attest to the diversity of their origins – Edo,Ika, Igala, Igbo, Ijaw, Saro, etc. They sometimes define one's background and recognize the circumstances of one's birth. In a simple but clear and concise style the author explained what each of his entries that cover both sexes mean. He identified the roots of less than half that number, gave their derivatives, variant forms and pet forms and illustrate the circumstances that could attach a particular name to a particular person.

While congratulating the author on his pioneering effort and achievement in these areas, it is pertinent to observe that this volume would have transformed into a masterpiece if the painstaking research that yielded detailed information on some of the entries was extended to all others.

As a corollary, the author included in his volume over 250 saying and phrases just like S.I.Bosah did in his Groundwork of the History and Culture of Onitsha and Akunne Okey Alex Amuta in his The Ethos of Ontisha Ado n' Idu. In additional he included about 150 words and phrases that are rarely used these days by the very elderly. Then there are appendices into which are crammed various lists – ndichie positions, eze idi, Ontisha ebo itenani, ekene umuada, etc.

Mr. Okey Agunyego, author of this book, is the founding and current editor of Ado Focus, the five-year old publication of Ado Circle, a social club of Lagos-based Onitsha young men. His interest in things Onitsha started manifesting in that magazine which is devoted to news and comments about Onitsha affairs and about communities of Onitsha indigenes outside their homestead. It was as an editor of Ado Focus that Mr. Agunyego perceived a need to compile Onitsha names.

Ancestral voices is a welcome reference material that all Onitsha indigenes especially fathers and mothers, every Onitsha couple and anyone interested in Onitsha culture will find very useful because it is a bold attempt at de- mystifying Onitsha names.

ODINIGWE ONUORA NZEKWU
Lagos.
12th November, 1999.

PERFACE TO REVISED EDITION

Four years after the publication of Ancestral Voices, the demand of this compendium remains high. In considering a reprint, I have listed about three hundred new entries of phrases and names. The names also include a compilation of English Surnames of Onitsha indigenes. I also updated many of the previous names and phrases entries. The explanation Kame Ka Ime; let me do as you have done, I reckon is erroneously related to food. The new bent gathered form Onoli Oguda, Chief Okey Chude, I guess has more relevance. Please see page…. Some expressions are derived from village rites but their implied meaning have wider applications. Take a case of Ada Edebelu Onye Jelu Asaba Anu Okuku; you do not keep chicken for one that has travelled to Asaba. This is explained in page …. See also in page ….for the explication of Anu Muo Zue Oke Manya eju afo.

The expressions are written in Onitsha dialect, followed by their literal English meaning, implied meanings and other necessary explanations. This approach is intended for clarity and distinction. The names are listed in alphabetical order with their full names and English interpretation alongside. Other entries include exposition on Egwu Ota – Royal Drum, and Ufie – Royal Wooden Gong. Nwakaibie Egbuniwe called for the explication of Onitsha festivals in the foreword he obliged me. Having them inone cover I reckon would make for easy references. With due consultations, I have reproduced four articles on Onitsha festivals by Odinigwe Onuora Nzekwu and Obiora Obiogbolu that appeared on the back issues of Ado Focus Magazine in which I featured as Editorial Chairman. The remaining two major festivals, namely; Umatu and Owuwaji are lifted from the inspiring book – Groundwork of the History and Culture of Onitsha by Nnayelugo S.I. Bosah.

Many people would avow that one of the greatest gifts is that of learning. One major drawback is that our ethos was not finely documented by our progenitors, possibly because they were not exposed to printing then. But even post 1960 independence we relied to much extent on those that are vast in oral history. While it worked, some people harboured doubts on some representations they believe were bedeviled with biases. Many of these views are now hotly debated. Who performs the opening second burials rites – Ika Ozo? Is it the village political head – Onye

Iche Ume or the spiritual head – Diokpa. Are there other related roles that other Ndichie that are not "Umes' and Diokpa can play and at what stage? Another controversial issue, which has dismembered many kindred, is the contention on who is the custodian of the spiritual relics of the family – Ibu Muo. The case of who breaks kola nuts and who takes kola nuts first in different occasions is not without dissension. At what stage does age become a criterion amongst Ozo titled men in taking kola nuts or being served with drinks? Ignorantly or otherwise some of the salient aspects our various rites are neglected. In an outing of Ikwo Aka Ozo in America, not less than two hundred people attended it. It was grand but lacked a major rite. It was conducted in a hall and not in an abode. Perhaps the number of the attendees influenced the choice of this hall. The traditional rite of pouring water used in- Ikwo aka Ozo towards the abode of the host is intended to herald-'Olokoto' – which is abundant fortune, good health and harvest. The beneficiaries in this outing are foreigners that own the hall. This to my mind is a serious contradiction.

Reasons may also be advanced on why some Ozo initiates avoid going to the village Ani. While it is necessary to address the schisms that have dismembered many villages and families, the Ozo initiation without the initiate paying tributes to Ani is yet another contradiction.

In an article, Egwu Ota in Onitsha politics, the writer

Akunne Mbanefo Offiah cited instances from 1876 where an 'Ume' First Class Chiefs were deemed to have committed serious offences against the Monarch but the surrender of the paraphernalia of the Chief's office were never contemplated until the reign of Obi Ofala Okagbue. The vexing question is, does the jurisdiction the Obi has over the paraphernalia of the First Class Chiefs exclude the recall of them? I would like to crave the indulgence of Obi in Council, the Ruling Age Grade to call for submission of memoranda, not only on the issue cited but on others that would include burial, marriage, coronation rites, etc. the case of Inwu na Okpulu and Ipu Iba would also demand attention. The ratification of this exercise will provide a workbook that will also help in diffusing controversies/dissensions whenever they arise.

While recognizing the inspiring work of Nnayelugo S.I. Bosah, Odinigwe Onuorah Nzekwu, Ojinnaka Sam Ifeka, Akunne Amuta, Nnayelugo Ben Chukwudebe, Mr. Jerry Orakwue. Eke – Prince P.O. Ekwerekwu, and others, I believe that we need further works on Onitsha. Some of the works cited above are no longer available. The reprint and further works would engender some positive evolution. No effect is small as the cumulative effect stands to guarantee the posterity of the town.

I would like to use this opportunity to express again my profound appreciation to Odinigwe Nzekwu,

Nwakaibie Egbuniwe, Ado Circle and many others that were listed in the first preface for their contributions towards this compendium.

This reprint is dedicated to my late parents Mr. and Mrs. Alex Okwudili and Rose Uzoamaka Agunyeo, to my family Nwando, Obiora, Nnonyelum, Okey Jnr., Mbenyeogo, Myra and the entire Oza Nzediegwu stock.

Long Love His Royal Highness
Alfred Nnameka Ugochukwu Achebe Mni
Obi of Onitsha
Long Live Onitsha Ado Na Idu
Okey Agunyego
Ifediba Retreat, Ogbeoza Onitsha – June 2003.

PERFACE TO FIRST EDITION

Some historical books trace the origin of ancient Benin Kingdom which Onitsha was part of; from Ife. However, the history of Onitsha people is more hinged on their exodus from Benin in the mid-16th century, during the reign of Oba Esigie. That the Umueze Chima clan – as the family of the exodus clan and their descendants are known – can be found in Agbor, Iseleikwu, Isele Nkpitime, Isele Azagba, Obior, Onicha Olona, Onicha Ugbo, Onicha Ibabo, Ibusa, Illah, Ezi, Oguta and Obosi lends credence to this history. There are various accounts on what precipitated this exodus but their military preparedness was instrumental in routing and displacing the communities they encountered enroute to the periphery.

The exodus spanning over fifty years must have had its casualties and difficulties. The interactions that ensued over the period with the various communities must have also tremendously influenced Chima and his kindred to the extent that they began to lose their mother tongue. Having perfected a new dialect, Chima's kindred in turn influenced the Igala extraction of Onitsha during the later part of 17th century, so much that they – the Igala extraction – also dropped their mother tongue over the period. While there are traces of Benin, Igala and to a lesser extent some Yoruba (Ife) words, the culture of Onitsha people can best be described as a potpourri of Edo, Ika, Igala and Igbo.

This is not necessarily a history piece though by extension, historical background has influence on the language of the people as exemplified in the cases of Chima and his kindred and likewise the Igala extraction of Onitsha. This exposition is rather directed at unraveling the meanings of family names in Onitsha. Their lineage trace back to older and ancient names that are Edo, Ika, Igala and Ibo related, as in Okomanya, Ogbodogo, Agadagba, Ulutu etc. These much older family names are listed in Appendix i.

Generally names come about from circumstances at birth, death, good fortune, war and other family feuds. They are symbols, paragons, personifications and commemorations of these various circumstances. In fact most of them could pass as complete sentences, contracted a characteristics of most Onitsha names, a good number are curious. Take for instance 'Sokei' of which the full meaning is 'Obusona Okenye ka esi anwu' and Unegbu' which when stretched is 'Onye uno egbu onye isi achanya awo'. These contractions would not have been the influence of missionaries as the earliest contact with Europeans was in the mind 19th century; much later after Onitsha people had settled. There are however some names that have been anglicized with added h and r as in Arah, Boash, Mortune, Enwezor etc. The contraction characteristics of Onitsha surnames are also applicable to the names as in Okey, Eche, Osi, Chike, Chuka, Egbue, Uche etc. This may have been further influenced by the development of written language.

Part of this treatise is also directed towards unravelling some of the curious first names as in Ojebeta, Menofu, Ebili, Uketuonye Onu, Odera, Ekwulira, Bato, Bagii and many other first names. I have also attempted unravelling some common metaphorical phrases/expressions that are used in everyday conversation. Phrases/expressions like 'Uno Obogu' and 'Ife ano acho na isi ji bu awaya are commonly used but may not be well assimilated. The latter expression has been erroneously turned to – 'Ife ana achona awayi bu isi iji. These explanations are contained in the text. While putting the entries together, 'A matter of identity' – a book by Akunne Alex Amuta was published. It contains over a thousand entries of wise sayings. It was difficult not to compare notes and as a result I had to limit the entries on phrases/expressions in this publication. I however took interest in names of certain things and phrases, which though are often used but may not be fully appreciated by the young ones. The etymology of some of these entries dates back hundreds of years ago. They are not only typical but could be puzzling. They include Ile ebeletutu, Asumasu and ineline na ineline, etc. These and several others are included in the last pages of Exposition Chapter. Their meanings are matched against the words/phrases. I spoke with several people some who helped in teasing out the names and some others who confessed their ignorance of the meanings of their names. Even at that, names are better understood from the standpoint of the giver of the name.

Take for instance 'Ndidi'; which means Patience'. A baby named 'Ndidi' need not only be as a result of earlier child/birth problems of the parents but could also result from other prolonged obstacles. The name bearer is a symbol of 'Patience'. Take a case of a guy who for some reasons could not marry his sweet heart who at the time was pregnant. He named the baby 'Ndidi' and according to him, that was his consolation for not being able to marry the mother of the child. In essence, the import of any particular name varies with the leanings of the giver of the name. There are also babies that are named after their forebears and immediate parents. Seli and Diake are typical examples of names, named after the progenitors. These appear to have more historical pointers than other first names that are named after the father's or mother's first names. To represent all these leanings would be endless hence I have adopted a more general approach in unravelling the meanings of the names treated.

The names are listed in alphabetical orders with their full names and English interpretations alongside. The phrases/expressions have their literal and implied meanings listed as well. This attempt is by no means exhaustive. Any omission in the family names is by no means preclusion from Onitsha and for such and other errors I tender my apologies.

My interest in the project came about on the naming ceremony on my child in 1996 by Chief Arthur Mbanefo Odu, Akunwata Odi Ibisi, Col. Eche Chukwuma, Okey Omenye and Osoenyi Nzekwu were in attendance. In the discussion that followed, Odu wanted to know other variants of Bosa. We touched on other names and we were privileged to know the background of Odu's first name – Izuegbunam. Thereafter I considered fifty names and fifty phrases for publication in Ado Focus Magazine Vol. IV and over the time I put together over seven hundred names and over four hundred phrases for this publication. The Guinness Book of Curious phrases by Leslie Dunkling also inspired me. I made liberal and ample references to Ground Work of the History and Culture of Onitsha People by Nnanyelugo S.I. Bosah; Know Onitsha Families by Eke-Prince P.O Ekwerekwu and various other Onitsha traditional literatures.

My appreciation goes to Odinigwe Onuorah Nzekwu who not only obliged me a foreword but also read and helped in tidying the manuscript.

Nwakaibie Egbuniwe also obliged me a foreword of which I remain grateful. My appreciation also goes to Colonel Eche Chukwuma who provided the graphics for the front cover of this book. Mr Olisa Aguisobo and Nweze Obiora Amechi also studied the manuscript and offered some useful tips. To Fano Osaji, Charly Orefo, Akunwata Odi Ibisi,Ezennia Chuka Ifejika, Chike Ekweogwu, Nnabuenyi Uchenna Mbanefo, Ikenna Obiesie, Okey Omenye and many others with whom I discussed the meaning of various names and expressions, I give my thanks.

I would like to dedicate this project to various Onitsha personalities late and present who have contributed in various ways to the upliftment of our mother town. Finally, the dedication is extended to my immediate family; Nwando, Obiora Dozie, Mbenyeogo, Myra and the entire Agunyego family. If this attempt by any measure can increase the knowledge of our people, create further works on Onitsha and spur others to tackle the various development needs of the town then this exposition shall have achieved its purpose. You may wish to skip to Afterword Chapter in which I tried to provide an outline of the glorious past, the prevailing incubi, the why and wherefores and the way forward.

Long Live the Monarch – Obi of Onitsha

Long Live Onitsha Ado Na Idu

Long Live Ado Circle – Lagos

Long Live Ado Amaka Age Grade

Okey Maduegbunam Agunyego

Villa Abri La Rive

Owelle Ebo, Onitsha 1999.

FAMILY NAMES

ABADOM: Si Abadonalom: A reference is made to a situation that the family was traduced and chastised, hence a plea not to be chastised. The name bearer is wished well.

ABOKA: Aboka mbo; do not hold on too rigidly to your own standpoints. In other words, try to see other people's point of views; a commemoration of such disagreement and the bearer is seen as an epitome of flexibility.

ABOMELI: Abomelili; A commemoration of hostilities in which Abo was victorious and during the period the name bearer was born.

ABUA: A variant of Adibuah, and Onyeibo, signifying an arrival of a male child especially where the father has no brother. The name bearer is thus like a brother to him. The arrival of the bearer is extolled.

ABUTU: Abutu is of Igala origin.

ACHEBE: Anichebelum: A plea to Ani, the Earth goddess to protect the name bearer /family. An inference is made that previous births did not survive or that other calamities had visited the family hence a plea to be protected.

ACHIKE: Achuna ife uwa na ike: An advice not to pursue earthly affairs too fast. The corollary is to take things easy; A plea for the longevity of the name bearer/family.

ACHUKWU: Onye ajuna chukwu ajuju; let no one question God. The omnipotent knows what is good for the name bearer; a veneration to God as well as a prayer for the well being of the bearer.

ACHUSIM: Achuzinam: A plea not to drive me away, an inference that the bearer belongs to the kindred or has not faulted in any manner to warrant ostracism. The name bearer is a symbol of live and let live and an embodiment of strength of character.

ACHUTEBE: Achukalia mmadu, obe nofu: There is a limit one can be pushed around and messed about, an inference to such situation and a plea that the name bearer should have peace and prosperity or Achuta Obe; when a target is made, striving ends. The name bearer is this target. God is praised for this achievement.

ADAKA: Adaka is a chimp or an ape noted for its agility and prowess. The name bearer personifies these qualities. The name came about as an alias.

ADIBUAH: A variant of Abuah. (Lit-two of us) The arrival of a male child is welcomed. The bearer is seen as companion; A second male to the father.

ADINWERUKA: Adirom nweruka : I do not deserve to be displaced, A reference to a situation that the family's position was threatened. The arrival of the bearer is also seen as maintaining this rightful place of the family.

ADUBA: A variant of Anyaduba; Anya di uba. It refers to envy and resentment directed at the family detractors; a commemoration of such and plea that no evil should befall the name bearer.

AFAM: Afam efuna; a plea that the family name should not be extinct. The arrival of the name bearer is thus extolled and seen as a continuation of the lineage.

AFOAKA: Ife na eme aforo aka/ agbaro aka. There is a cause for the difficulties which the family had gone or is going through. God is pleaded with to stave off whatever evils that is behind these problems. The bearer named after such difficulties is expected to live a fulfilled life.

AFUBERA: Anya afubero/afunuro ife di otua; Not having seen a thing like this, the name bearer is this unique character. A priceless pearl, God is extolled for making this uniqueness, i.e. the arrival of the name bearer after a considerable long period/difficulties.

AGBAKOBA: Agbakoba ogalanya; Rallying around the rich or as in Agbakoba Emelie dike, rallying to defeat a fortified enemy. The bearer is named after such account. Both explanations tend to unity. The bearer is a paragon of unity, strength and progress.

AGBAPUONWU: Ka agbapulu onwu; to keep away from the pangs of death, an acknowledgement of the devastating effect of death and hence a longevity plea for the name bearer/family.

AGBOGU: Chukwu na agba ogu; God settles disputes/fights; A reference is made to hostilities prevalent at a time and a plea to God to protect the bearer and family from such hostility.

AGBU: Implies resistance to shackles, and other obstacles in life. The family by deduction faced such encumbrances in the past. The bearer is a symbol of resistance, courage and strong will power.

AGHA: Simply means war. A commemoration of such conflict, as in Agha eli nam; may the war not consume the name of bearer. God's help is sought.

AGHADIUNO: Aghadina Uno; War within the kindred; a commemoration of internal family conflict and the consequences are prayed not to affect the bearer.

AGU: Simply means leopard, a personification of agility and strength of a leopard. The bearer is seen to have these characteristics.

AGULEFO: Whatever happens, there must be somebody; a principal character that would be remembered for his good works. A reference is made to some kind of marginalization that the family experienced. The name signifies a better hope.

AGUNKWO: Death is here likened to a kite that carries away its prey at a fell swoop; A plea that the family is saved from incessant deaths. The bearer is wished long life

AGUNYEGO: Chukwu agunyego; a glorification to God in ensuring the safe delivery of the child. It is also a plea for the survival and longevity of the name bearer. By inference the family lost several babies at birth. The name bearer is thus dedicated to God. Or as in Agunyego; I have been counted; my place/right is incontrovertible.

AGUSIA: A variant of Agusiobo; Agusina obo

AGUSIOBO: Agusina obo; play down on vengeance. A reference is made to a volatile situation that demanded playing down on vengeance. The name bearer symbolizes this new turn from vengeance to forgiveness and leading to rapprochement.

AGUZANI: Agwuzani; Agwuzo ani; May the land be free from all blemishes and evils. By implication the world of the name bearer is prayed to be trouble free. The child is wished well.

AJAH: Ani ajagom Ike; The land was strengthened me with the arrival of the named bearer. As in Aja achulu chukwu; Sacrifice made to God; the name bearer is dedicated to God. Or Ajanuonwu; Death is not stopped by sacrifice. Death is ordained by God and only God's intercession can enable one to live long. A plea is thus made for longevity of the child. As in Ajakansi; See below.

AJAKA: Aja ka nsi; Sacrifice made to God is by far more effective than sinister means to achieve your aspirations/prayers. The arrival of the name bearer was a testimony of such belief in 'sacrifice'. God is praised

AJUFO: Ajugom ajo ufo; ajo ife etc. A rejection of vices/evils, bad image, and other associated wrong doings. The bearer is seen as an embodiment of virtue.

AKAYA: His hand. God's hand. This is an affirmation that God's presence / intervention guides and protects us. A case where the family was thankful on God's protection is explained by the name – **AKAYA**

AKANYA: Akana ife uwa na anya; Allow things to go by sequence or as in Akananya; Do not humiliate. Do not brag. Both sue for peace and humility. The name bearer is a paragon of peace and humility.

AKONOBI: Nwa akonobi; for the lineage to survive a male child is important. The bearer's arrival is thus extolled and seen as a guarantee for the continuation of the family lineage.

AKOSA: Aka Olisa; God's work is marvelous. The name bearer is seen as a hand work of God.

AKPABO: Akpabonam; Onye akpabonam; a plea here is made that the name bearer /family is not provoked; an earnest request to be left in peace. It signifies also the preparedness to challenge such provocation.

AKPALI: This is a title and alias. The name stuck as a family name over a period of time.

AKPOM: Onye akponam na onu; A plea not to be criticized unfairly. The name commemorates such a bellicose situation which the family has no hand in. The name bearer is wished well.

AMECHI: Onyema echi: Who knows tomorrow? Only God knows tomorrow. God is looked upon to guarantee good fortunes to the name bearer/family.

AMENE: A variant of Anyamene, Anyamene uwa; looking forward with hope. The name bearer is wished well.

AMESE: Amese Okwu; There is no need for dissension let there be peace; A commemoration of a disagreement requiring peace. The name bearer is a symbol of peace.

AMUTA: Amuta abo; Amuta nwa; Extolling God's gift of procreation. The arrival of the bearer, the second male child is joyfully welcomed.

ANAH:A variant form of Ani; Mother Earth, the source of all goddess. The name bearer is a product of this virtue. As in Anirah, it is an entreaty to protect and save the name bearer. The name is a pointer to previous births that did not survive

ANAKWE: Aniekwe; The Earth goddess has accepted the offspring. The benevolence of God is thus extolled.

ANALO: Anilo; let the earth contemplate the past and the future of the name bearer/family, variant of Anigekwu and Anikpe. Apparently untoward remarks against the family warranted a plea for God to intercede.

ANAMMA: Anidimma; extolling the goddess of earth. The bearer is a product of such benevolence made possible by God.

ANANTI: Anyazi na fa nti; Do not mind what people say, hence avoid obfuscation of one's pathway to progress; A commemoration of such vexatious comments is made. The name bearer is wished well. The name is a variant of Egenti.

ANATAOGU: Anataogu; having come back from war, peace reigns again. The name commemorates the end of this hostility. The bearer is wished well and prayed not to see hostility in his life.

ANAZONWU: Anizonwu; A plea to Mother Earth to save the name bearer from early death, or as in Anazonwu azo; nobody wishes or spoils for death. This calls for a restraint on unnecessary struggles in life.

ANIEBONAM: Ani ebonam ife m na amaro; Mother Earth is requested to absolve the name from the accusations. The name bearer is wished well.

ANIEGBOKA: A plea to Mother Earth to save the name bearer/family, coming from the litany of difficulties that included death that the family experienced. God is eulogized and the bearer is prayed to succeed in life.

ANIEGBUNAM: The plea to Mother Earth to save the name bearer/family. The plea could derive from a confession of guilt or an attestation that the parents are righteous.

ANIEKWEOGWU: As in Ekweogwu.

ANIEMENA: Another plea to Ani; - Mother Earth – not to invoke ills on the family/the name bearer. The bearer is thus wished well. The name also stands for ''God forbid bad things''.

ANIEROBI: Ani ada ero obi; there is nothing in life to warrant fright or a weakened heart. This implies strong will, boldness and determination required in life. The name bearer is symbol of this inner strength.

ANIEZE: Ani bu eze. The land is the king; Anikpe; an arbiter, Aniagolu; a witness, Aniemena; protector, Aniegboka; peacemaker, and Aniwetalu; source of livelihood. The various roles of Ani bestows him the kingship; A veneration of Mother Earth. The bearer is dedicated to Ani – Mother Earth.

ANIGEKWU: A variant of Anikpe; Let the Earth goddess intercede. Such judgment is seen to favour the name bearer/family that is deemed innocent.

ANIKAMADU: Earth as the source of life surpasses mankind. Extolling the benevolence of Mother Earth; the name bearer is the benevolence caused by God.

ANIONWU: Ana enye onwu enye; Death is not something you wish someone. A corollary is a plea for longevity and prosperity. The bearer is wished well.

ANIWETA: Aniwetalu; the product of mother Earth; the bearer is seen as such and the arrival of the name bearer is joyfully welcomed

ANUKA: Anuka ogu, a reference to efforts put in ensuring that the family's rights and place were maintained. The name commemorates this endeavor. Or in Anuka ogu ejie nya; after a prolonged fight restraint is sought. The name is a commemoration of this fight that was restrained for peace to reign. The bearer is a paragon of peace.

ANUMONYE: I am impervious to what you say. A reference to a circumstance where the family was forced to make unswayable decision; Turning a deaf as it were, the name bearer is thus seen as a paragon of single mindedness.

ANWA: Anwazi nam iburo Chukwu. Desist from tempting me because you are not my God. A reference is made to the strong will mustered by the family to counter such temptation. The name bearer is seen as a paragon of single mindedness.

ANYADUBA: Anya di uba: A variant of Aduba. The name refers to resentment and envy from one's kindred. A plea is made that family/name bearer is not affected by such envy.

ANYAEGBUNAM: May the uncomplimentary views of others not bother or affect me; A reference to such vexatious comment and a plea to be saved and protected from such. The bearer is wished well.

ANYAEJI: Ita ji nalum anya; Anya ejinofu; May the envy and malice directed at the family be stopped or not have any effect. A reference is made to such happenstance. The name bearer is wished well or as in Anya eji kwa nayi. Anyayi lue; May your eyes not be blurred. May your presence be felt? As in Anya oke, One's presence guarantees his right. The name bearer is wished to have a focus; A close supervision of events that will enable him to make his mark in life.

ANYAFULU: Ife anya fulu: What the eyes have seen. This could mean both difficult and pleasant times. The former is a commemoration of past difficulties the family encountered while the latter is a testimony of the good things i.e. the arrival of the name bearer of the name bearer-that has visited them family.

ANYAKWO: Anyi akwolu ndu? An older saying of of Anyi Ajukwolu ese ndu? Have we considered life; have we considered the implications in life for our various outbursts, for casting aspersions, hatred, betrayals, maltreatments etc. The deduction that follows is that any evil deed has a backlash. A reference is made to past circumstance in which the family was not giving fair hearing; A caution to family detractors; the bearer is named against this backdrop. The corollary is 'Onwero ife ka ndu'; there is no alternative to life.

ANYAM: My representation. The name bearer is the representative of the family/parents who is expected to protect the interest of the family.

ANYAMENE: A variant of Amene, Looking forward with hopes in life. Good things are wished to come by the way of the bearer.

ANYANNA: His father's alter ego, the view and wish of God. The name bearer is a gift from God. God is glorified.

ANYAOKE: Anya bu oke onye; your presence /representation guarantee your rights. The name bearer is seen as a cynosure of such right.

ANYAORA: Anyaka ora; at a vantage position you have a better view/right than others. The name bearer is seen as a paragon of a defender.

ANYOGU: Uwa ayaligo bulu ogu; the world has turned thorny; a reference to the difficulties by the family and God is looked upon to protect the name bearer /family.

ARAH: Anirah: A plea to mother earth to protect the name bearer from death and other evils, A variant of Chukwura. It could be deduced that earlier births were not successful. The baby boy is wished longevity.

ARAKA: Araba amaka, the bearer is named after a sojourn to Asaba which proved successful and beneficial to the family, a variant of Bini Amaka.

ARANYE: Aranye golum Chukwu ife nine na aka; Trust is placed on God. A plea is made for the protection of the name bearer. This prayer was as a result of past misfortunes the family experienced.

AREH: Ani erenitegom, Ani ewenitegom; A declaration of the benevolence of God, otherwise called Ani. In Ani ralum enye; May the goddess of the Earth testify for me i.e. the name bearer/family. A reference is made to a contentious scene and God is looked upon to deliver the name bearer.

ARIMA: Aribalu eze ama; Unique features/characteristics of a king are not hidden. The name bearer is a cynosure of all the princely characteristics.

ARINZE: Arinze Chukwu; by the grace, wisdom and power of God. The name bearer is a gift from God. This benevolence demands an unbridled praise to God, following earlier misfortunes.

ASIKA: Asika abulu; the name emanates from disagreement within the kindred but seeks solution to it. The name bearer is seen to bring about this truce.

ASOMUGHA: No reason to be full of regrets and bitterness. I abhor malice, a commemoration of situation demanding such frank talk. All untoward comments obstacles failures and unacknowledged efforts are now consigned to the past. The name bearer is an embodiment of vigour, new turn, straight forwardness and determination.

ATTOH: Ani eto; The land is praised. The Earth goddess-Ani-is commended for accepting the name bearer. The child is a product of God's benevolence and thus wished well.

ATUANYA: Given certain unfavorable circumstances, the arrival of the child- the name bearer –was unexpected. The joy it begot is bountiful; an appreciation of God's work is eulogized. A variant of Eyiuche (f).

ATUONA: Of special characteristics resembling that of a precious metal. The name bearer is a special gift from God.

AYALOGU: Ama eji mgbagbu yalu ogu- Wars are not avoided because death will result. A circumstance that was instrumental to not avoiding war is thus commemorated. The name bearer is a symbol of determination.

AZIKE: Azubuike; Ukuta azu; a variantof Azuka. A strong family link is a source of power. The name bearer is seen as a link/bulwark.

AZIKIWE: Onye nwelu azi enwero iwe; with good kindred background the room for anger and dissension is marginal. The name bearer is an embodiment of joy.

AZOKWU: Chukwu na azo kwu; prevention of hostilities/disputes is by divine intercession. The name is a commemoration of the cessation of such hostility.

AZOBA: Chukwuzoba; May God protect the name bearer/family. This is a pointer that the family was exposed to danger in the past.

AZUBOGU: Ukutaazu bu ogu; Kindred link is a good support/back-up/bulwark. The name bearer is seen as such.

AZUBUIKE: Ukuta azu bu ike; A kindred link is a source of power. The name bearer is part of this power and is wished well.

AZUKA: Ukuta azu ka ego; A strong family link is more valued than money. The name bearer personifies this link.

BALONWU:Belu onwu; Acknowledgment that death is inevitable and could strike unannounced; Hence a plea for longevity of the name bearer.

BOSAH: Belu Olisa, Reverence to God. His magnanimity is extolled. The name bearer is dedicated to God, and is part of God's munificence.

BELU: A variant of Bosah; Belu Olisa. Reverence to the Creator or Belu Onwu; acknowledging death which by implication calls for an entreaty for longevity.

CHIEKWE: Onye chiekwe lu gadi; if it is the wish of God the offspring will survive. As in Chiekwego: God has accepted the name bearer, after many hopes were dashed in the past. The name bearer is wished longevity.

CHIKEZIE: Chukwukezie; God is looked upon as the arbiter and as such the place and right of the name bearer are not in doubt.

CHIMA: Chukwuma; God knows why he created the bearer. God is looked upon to provide and protect the name bearer.

CHIOTU: Chi otuonye; an assertion that even if you are alone, God is there to protect you. The name bearer is wished well.

CHUDE: Chukwudebelu; Established of God hence let no one assault the name bearer; a plea to be left alone in peace.

CHUGBO: Chukwu gbo lum ogu; a plea that God puts a stop to one's predicaments. The name bearer is an answer to this plea.

CHUKWUDI: Chudi; there is God. God is omnipresent, omnipotent and omniscience. Here is a reminder that no one can hide from God. The name bearer is a beneficiary of God's intervention. Family detractors are warned that only God can judge human beings. The name bearer is thus wished well.

CHUKE: Chukwukelu; God's creation, and as a result the best in life is wished the name bearer.

CHUKWUEMEKA: Extolling God's benevolence. The name bearer is a product of this benevolence

CHUKWUDUMEKWU: God is my spokesman. Extolling the benevolence of God; the name bearer is part of this benevolence.

CHUKWUFO: Chukwufo; God is my judge, jury and witness; all in favour of the name bearer. The name bearer is dedicated to God.

CHUKWUMA: A variant of Chima. All knowledge belongs to God. He predestines what a child would be; a plea to grant the name bearer goodness of life.

CHUKWURA: A variant of Anirah; Seeking God's protection and longevity for the name bearer. It could be inferred that the previous child died at infancy, hence the plea for the name bearer to survive.

EBEZUE: Ebezue ogu; Rallying around; a commemoration of a difficult situation, which was followed with an unstilted support from the community. The bearer is named after such occasion and he is a paragon of strength.

EBO: Ebo zinam; A plea not to accuse one of what he knows not; A reference to such accusation and God is looked upon to intervene. The bearer is a product of this deliverance.

EBOSIE: Ebosinam; A variant of Ebo above.

EDEKOBI: Edekoro obi onu; the family- the heart of the family- is not together. A reference is made to dissension in the family at a time and hence a plea for unity. The corollary is, O bi edekogo; the heart is one for unity to be achieved. The bearer is named after such situation and prayed to survive.

EDEMANYA: Edenam anya; Adanam anya; Do not cast aspersion on me; A commemoration of the envy/resentment the family faced at the time. The traducers are warned to keep off the family /name bearer.

EDEOGU: Edegbue ogu anuba; Choose your battle line carefully for effectiveness. Here is a commemoration of a hostility/war that demanded careful planning. This compares well also with the phrase; Ebunu rie azu oso mpi. A ram makes a tactical retreat before attacking with its horns. Named after such scheme, the bearer is prayed to live a fulfilled life.

EDOZIE: Chukwu edozie okwu; God has interceded. The name bearer is a symbol of peace and unity. What was amiss before is now settled.

EGBOKA: Chukwu egbokalum or Ani egbokalum; through divine intercession all evil were barred. The name bearer came as a result of this benevolence from God.

EGBUCHE: Onwu ada egbuna uche; Death defies reason; an acknowledgement of such and a plea for the protection of the name bearer.

EGBUCHIEM: Madu egbuchinalum uzo; A plea is made that the progress of the name bearer/family is not blocked by the people, who had hitherto made things difficult for the family. The name bearer is wished well.

EGBUJI: Egbuji nyi lu okwa na agu; A renowned (yam) farmer that dared the bush fowls to his crops/harvests. Despite the incursion of the pests, and predators the crops/harvest remained plenteous. The bearer is named after the forebear's renowned avocation.

EGBUNA: Chukwu egbuna ; A plea to God to save the name bearer/family, especially coming against the troubles, envy, deaths and other difficulties experienced in the past by the family. The name bearer is wished longevity. Or as in Madugbuna; let no one kill another. This is a plea and a warning.

EGBUNIKE: The wrath of God on the people's misdeeds is pleaded for. His mercy is sought not to kill the name bearer. By implication the name bearer is wished long life. The bearer is dedicated to God.

EGBUNIWE: Another supplication to God to spare the name bearer though as human beings we may have offended God in several ways and attracted his wrath. This allows the family the opportunity to redeem the time. The name also is a plea to judge family fairly.

EGWUATU: Egwu atu onwu; death is never afraid. God's protection is hence sought to save the name bearer/family.

EJEM: Ejem be onye; did I visit or consult anybody? It is all happening by the power of God. God's benevolence is praised. The name bearer is dedicated to God.

EJIAMIKE: Ejirom amu ike; or Chukwu jamike; Do not try your devilish powers on me; a plea that no evil shall befall the name bearer, or a plea to God to invigorate and fortify the family. The name bearer is a product of this support.

EJIKEME: Ejirom ikem eme; it is not by my power but by divine power. The name bearer is a product of divine intervention.

EJIOFOR: A variant of Ejiogu. Ejim ogu na ofo; I am bestowed with righteousness and virtue. The name bearer is an embodiment of justice and fairness.

EJOH: Ejim ofo; bestowed with divine righteousness; a variant of Ejiofo.

EJOGU: Ejiogu; Ejim ogu ejim ofo; by this act one proclaims innocence/probity; A commemoration of a situation that demanded this proclamation. God's intercession is sought on behalf of the family. The bearer is named against this backdrop.

EKPECHI: Ka ana ekepluchi; Praying and thanking God for his mercies on the delivery and survival of the name bearer/family and for future progress.

EKWEOGWU: Ani Ekweogwu; the land forbids evil. A plea is made that name bearer be shielded away from all evils and devilish machinations. These calls for good wishes to the name bearer; a commemoration of a happenstance that demanded such rebuttal is made. The name is both a supplication and interjection denoting – God forbid evils.

EKWEREKWU: Okwu ekwerekwu; Disagreement that defies arbitration; A reference to such contentious scene that the family went through. God is however looked upon to settle this matter. The name bearer is a product of truce.

EKWUAJU: Rescinding one's former point of view; a reference to such happenstance, usually for peace to reign. The name bearer signifies peace.

EKWUE: Ekwueme; The power to propose and implement a favour with God. God's work is incontrovertible. The delivery of the name bearer is an attestation to God's command; or a variant of Emegoekwue. No matter how secretive or subdued an act is, it gets mentioned; a reference to such act. The bearer is dedicated to God.

EKWUNO: Ekwolo dina uno; Hatred and envy within the kindred; A commemoration of such feud and also a plea for good neighbourliness. Such feud is prayed not to affect the name bearer.

ELOSIEBO: Premeditated accusation. A reference is made to such wilful instance, but God's intercession is sought in favour of the name bearer/family.

ELUAKA: Umunna elurom aka; a reference to a contentious situation that warranted a major division in the family, hence the support of one's brethren was far reached. God's support customarily is sought for the name bearer/family.

ELU: A variant of Elumelu and Eluoka.

ELUMELU: One's rightful position in life is established. A plea is put to God to ensure that the name bearer maintains his rightful position in life. A variant of Ibelum, Iba elugom, my right to ascendancy to the family throne has come. The delivery of the name bearer is seen to guarantee this position; a commemoration of a circumstance demanding such proclamation.

ELUEMUNO: Having arrived home, the allusion is on the arrival of a male child. The name bearer is prayed to take up the leadership of the family and ensure the continuation of the lineage.

EMEAGAWALI: Ife mekata njo ogwalia mma; after a while that things get out of hand, a solution would be found. The name bearer is a symbol of a new positive development after the initial difficulties. Or as in whatever that is said has a reply; a commemoration of a circumstance that warranted a reply to untoward statements. The bearer is named against his backdrop and wished well.

EMECHETA: All favours, or denials and negative acts meted on one are not easily forgotten. The name commemorates an act most likely in bad faith. It is also a caution towards better neighbourliness. The bearer is a paragon of peace.

EMEJULU: Emejulu uwa odiba; Uwa bu onye mejulu ike ya odiba; putting in your best in one's lifetime and leaving the rest to God. God is looked upon to protect, reward and guide the name bearer/family in all their endeavours.

EMEGOKWUE: Emesiata aga ekwu. Ife mesiata aga ekwu; No matter how secretive or subdued an act is, it eventually gets mentioned. The name commemorates such happenstance and is paragon of truth.

EMEMBO: Emembolu; The name calls for retaliation when provoked; a commemoration of such attack in the past. The name bearer is wished the courage and strength to defend self in life.

EMENGO: Emena ngo; Madu emenam ngo; a solicitation not to testify unfairly against another or not to accept gratification to hurt somebody. A reference is made to such happenstance that family experienced. The name bearer is prayed not to be affected by this vice.

EMENIKE: Ife emenam na ike; An entreaty to God to save the name bearer/family from a sudden mishap, following the haunting experience the family went through in the past.

EMESIM: Emesinam; Another plea to check the calamities in life. The name bearer is thus wished well.

EMETA: Emetarom; A plea to be absolved from what one knows not of. The name bearer is a testimony of this exculpation.

EMODI: Eme odili gaba; One's good stride begets other successes. The name bearer is seen as a good mark made obviously possible by God's intervention and support. Or as in Ife onye me odibaluya; whatever you do, you beget; a counsel that good does not come out of evil.

ENEANYA: Ka ana ene anya; Looking with hope and high expectation. The future of the name bearer is thrust upon God.

ENEBELI: Ka ene bili uwa; Let us keep on living in his world and enjoy the bounties therein and for obstacles/problems, God is looked upon to assuage them. The name stresses on good neighborliness, and is also a plea for longevity and prosperity.

ENENDU: Ka ana ene ndu; Looking up to the future with hopes. The future of the name bearer is committed to God's care. It could be deduced that the family experienced early deaths in the past.

EROKWU: Agam erolu okwu; Must I take my life because of disagreement. The name commemorates past conflict and further seeks strength to accommodate such conflict. Such conflict is prayed not be affect the name bearer.

ENWEZOR: Onye newe uzo? Who directs destiny? Only God does; an attestation of God's power. He is thus looked upon to pave the way to posterity for the family.

ENWONWU: Onye nwe onwu? Who dispenses death or has death under his command. Acknowledging that all powers rest with God; His protection is sought for the name bearer/family.

EPUNDU: Epuendu atua alo; Where there is life, there is hope. The survival and longevity of the name bearer is prayed for. By inference the family experienced child deaths in the past.

ETUKOKWU: Etukona okwu igwe; Do not bother about the unpleasant things people say. A testimonial of such gossips in the past but the name bearer is wished and prayed to weather all obstacle in his life.

EZEDIUGWU: A prestigious king. The name bearer is wished royal prestige and clout.

EZEAZU: Eze azuka; Eze nwelu ukuta azu; a king that has formidable kindred support. The name bearer, a personification of royalty is wished the support the forebears had to enable him progress in life. Or Ezekpe azu; Lit the king that covers the rear. Both front and the rearguard kings protect the family from any invasion whether ahead or coming from the rear. The last male child in the family is referred to as the rearguard king.

EZEOCHA: Eze di ocha is white but signifies transparency/fairness; an attestation that the family was righteous. The bearer is named after the incidence that warranted such attestation. Eze i.e. King derives from Nwabueze; a male child is king. The name bearer is a symbol of fairness and probity.

IBEGBU: Ibegbunam; A plea is made for the deliverance from the antagonistic kindred; A reference to such incident. The name bearer is wished well.

IBEKWE: Ibe ekwego; The acceptance/agreement reached by the people is by implication seen as God's wish. The name bearer is wished the support of the people.

IBELUM: Iba elugom; my time to administer/occupy the family headship/throne has come. The arrival of a baby boy guarantees the succession of the lineage. The arrival is a source of joy and God is praised.

IBENEME: Acknowledging that one's kindred can be devious, hence a plea that nothing sinister befalls the name bearer /family. The family had earlier experienced such treachery.

IBEZIAKO: Ibezigom ako na uche; The insincerity of the people has taught me a lesson and made me wiser. The name bearer commemorates this new turn to wisdom.

IBISI: Nwabuisi; A male child is very relevant to the succession of the family headship and continuation of the lineage. The name bearer is prayed for to be knowledgeable and to administer his domain, successfully.

IBUZO: Nwabuzo; the road to posterity begins with a male child, or as in ibunauzo mem; Do not raise your hand on me first as the consequences may not be pleasant. A reference is made to such circumstance.

IFEAJUNA: Ife ajuna dibia okwe; the name refers to the cure-all attitude of herbalists; A reference to such circumstance, that the family had a recourse to herbalist.

IFEIRA: Ifeira kwulu: Ifedioramma, The wish of the people. The bearer is a product of general consensus of the people. The arrival is welcomed by all after a prolonged problem. As in Ifedioramma, That which pleases the people, the bearer is the subject and is joyously welcomed by the people. The name Ifeira may have resulted from an alias.

IFEKA: Ifekandu, Onwero ife ka ndu; There is no alternative to life. This acknowledgement pleads for longevity for the family that lost many children in the past. The bearer is wished well.

IFEJIKA: Ife eji aka bu nwa; Children are of prime values. They are sources of joy, pride, comfort and support. They are priceless gift from God. God is thus extolled for his benevolence. The bearer is wished the aforementioned traits.

IFEJO: Ife emejonam; May evils not befall on me; a plea that no evil/devilish machinations will affect the name bearer. This comes against the various malicious attacks in the past.

IFENU: Ife enu uwa ezu oke; Life never offers everything one desires; the name serves as a caution to be content with what one has and hence live long. Or as in Ife enu me; A reference to the obstacles and difficulties the family faced, but hope is mustered as things are bound to change. The name bearer is wished well.

IGBEGWU: Igbegwu atunam; May the dungeon considered frightful not bother me. This is an entreaty to be saved from diabolical trappings. A reference is made to a devilish attitude towards the family. God is looked upon to protect the name bearer; A variant of Udensi egbunam.

IGBO: Igboezue; Ebezue; A variant of Igbokwe below. Or as in Igbo egbunam; may the people not harm or kill me. The name bearer is prayed not to be affected by antagonistic attitude of the people; A variant of Ibemesi.

IGBOKWE: May the people (Igbo) have a general consensus; rallying together. This is a pointer to peace and support. The name bearer is a cynosure of this bond and assemblage.

IGELE: Igele is a title and an alias. It is named after a performer, a daring man, an achiever.

IGWEIKE: Igwebuike; (lit – unity is strength) the more, the more powerful; Eulogizing the arrival of a baby. The name bearer is an additional 'power factor'.

IGWEMMA: The more the merrier. The name bearer is born into this cream of people by implication is prayed to herald others to come.

IGWEZE: Igwe bu eze; Cumulative strength and power of a group of people is likened to that of a royalty. The name bearer is joyously welcomed as part of the larger group/royalty.

IKEAGU: Associated with the bravery of a leopard; the name bearer is a product of such characteristic and is wished well

IKEBUDE: Strength/authority is a source of pride; the name bearer is a product of this strength and is a pride to the family. The arrival is joyously welcomed.

IKEGBUNAM: May one's vitality not affect one's undoing imploring that one's efforts/commitments should not be in vain, and plea is made for such efforts to be fruitful and recognizable. The name bearer is a product of these efforts and is wished well.

IKEM: A variant of Ikemefuna.

IKEME: Ike Chukwu na eme; God's power is incontrovertible; extolling the powers of God. A corollary which is Ejirom ikem eme; It is not by my power or might. God is hailed for his mercies. The name bearer is one of such benevolence from God.

IKEMEFUNA: May my effort to bring forth a child not be in vain? The survival and prosperity of the name bearer is prayed for. Most probably, such effort in the past was not fruitful.

IKEMMA: Ike Chukwu di mma; God's works (power) are excellent; extolling the benevolence of God on the delivery of the name bearer.

IKENA: A variant of Ikemefuna or Ikegbuna above.

IKENGA: Strength, Might, Power. The name bearer is prayed to have these attributes that would propel him in life. Ikenga is also a statuette representing a man's spirit of fortune.

IKEOBI: Ike sina Obi; Force of character derives from purity of one's stock; Tracing or linking the name bearer to an aristocratic lineage as in Ike Obi-Daike. The name bearer is seen to have this link.

IKEOGU: Adequately armed (strong) to ward off any attack. A reference is made to such commitment and a plea that the name bearer is in position to protect himself.

IKEOMU: Ike omumu; the power to procreate comes from God; Glorifying God for bestowing one with this power. The name bearer is a testimony of God's benevolence.

IKOKWU: Nwa bu ike okwu; A child is a strong back up of the family. A plea is sought that the name bearer will play this support role for the family.

IKEPEAZU: Ekpe nam ikpe na azum; This refers to back biting, slander, defamation and other malicious utterances. A commemoration of such circumstance prior to the birth of the name bearer, who is also prayed, not be effected by such vices.

IKWUAZOM: Saved by one's kindred; A solicitation for support/protection from the kindred. The name bearer is a testimony of the support and protection given by the kindred.

IKWUEME: Ikwu na eme; A reference is made to the sometimes sinister role by the kindred. The name bearer is named after such malicious attack, and is wished well; a variant of Ibeneme.

ILOBUCHI: llolobu chi ka odili; Chukwu na elo; Life is as a result of God's considered thought/will. The family having gone through litany of hard times is pleased with the arrival of the name bearer; a jewel derived from God's intervention.

ILOCHI: llolo Chukwu; the considered thought-out-plan of God; the bearer is an outcome of this thought. He is thus dedicated to God.

ILOEGBUNAM: Ndi ilom egbunam; a plea to be saved from one's enemies. The bearer is wished all the protection. By inference there were harted and enmity in the kindred prior to the birth of the child.

ILOMUANYA: Ndi ilom mu anya; The name refers to the ubiquitous enemies being awake and alert. An entreaty for God's protection is sought for the name bearer/family.

ILOZUE: llolo Chukwu ezue; God's thought has materialized. The name bearer is a product of God's thought and is thus wished well. As in Ndi ilo zue; My enemies have rallied round. Surrounded by enemies, the name earnestly solicits for assistance and protection. A reference is made to such antagonistic circumstances against the family.

ILUKWE: llue ebeijeko ikwe; you are content when you achieve you aim; the arrival of the bearer is one these aspirations that is joyously welcomed. A variant of Achuta Obe; when a target is made striving ends. The name bearer is the target and the aim. As in Ilolo Chukwu kwe; God's thought has manifested, the bearer is the subject that has manifested and God is praised for his good works.

IMAGIE: Do you know him? God – "Chukwu nna" – is thesubject. Knowing God demands appreciation of and veneration for his benevolence. The delivery of the child calls for praise. A corollary of Imagie is Amam Chukwu; I know my God. The name bearer is dedicated to God.

INOMA: Ino na mma; In the midst of goodness. The name bearer was born when the family was buoyant and in high spirits. Or as in Ino Onuma; swallowing anger; Burying the hatchet as it were; a reference is made to such situation. The name bearer is an epitome of live and let live. A variant of Ifediba – Let by-gone be by gone. Or as in Inodu imalu; you know or you are in full picture of a happenstance when you are around; a reference to a polemic circumstance where the family detractor's dialectics were based on hearsay. A proclamation of righteousness is stressed. The name bearer is an epitome of virtue.

IREKWU: Ira ekwugo; a considered opinion of the populace. The name bearer is thus welcomed by all. The name is a commemoration of family consensus.

ISIMA: The headship knows all, implying that God knows all; a variant of Chukwuma. God knows the best for the name bearer.

ISITOR: Isitoruka,ofuruka; May the headship live long, an entreaty is thus sought for longevity of the name bearer, to acquire more wisdom and be in a position to offer advice based on experience.

IWEANYA: Iweanya ewenam; A plea is made to contain the wrath and envy that were resplendent prior to the birth of the name bearer. The bearer is named after such incidence and is wished well.

IWEGBU: Iwe naegbu. Anger destroys. Iwegbunam; an entreaty is sought for restraint on one's anger as not to hurt him the aggrieved; a reference to such situation. The bearer's arrival is seen to dampen this anger. By this restraint the nuance is such that one's sins would also be forgiven by the creator.

IWENJIORA: One's anger directed to his kindred. The incident that warranted such anger is commemorated. The name bearer is prayed to be free from the effects of the anger.

IWNEOFU: Enough of pent up anger. It implies forgiveness to those that have wronged the family. The arrival of the child is seen as a turn for reconciliation.

IWEOBI: Built up anger, that emanates from the heart should be contained. A reference is made to such anger, and God as usual is prayed to turn the anger into joy. All names with keyword iwe are a reminder that our wrath uncurbed will not fulfill God's perfect plan for us.

IWUCHUKWU: Iwu Chukwu ga eme; God's covenant is unwavering. The name bearer is a testimony of God command.

IWUNO: Home policies and guidelines; a plea that the laws of the land, which invariably is made possible God to protect the bearer.

IZUORA: Family consensus. The name bearer is welcome by all and is a cynosure of peace, unity and enduring nexus.

JIRO: Jiro na oba; A reference is cited to a period when the family's farm/barn mysteriously withered. A commemoration of this happenstance and a plea as well is made that the name bearer be spared from mysterious calamities.

KWASIE: Kwasie oku; to spill wealth. This is an alias. The family is considered opulent. The name bearer's progress and prosperity is prayed for.

KWENTO: Onyeilo Kwentoruka; A passionate plea to prevent the enemies from cutting short the life of the name bearer/ family; a commemoration of such vexatious and contentious scenes that required such request.

MACHIE: A variant of Madu adichie; a replacement of a lost gem. This is a case of the name bearer having arrived after the death of the father or brother, thus he is seen as a replacement/consolation.

MADUENU: Madu enu uwa; Refers to worldly beings and highlights the impermanency of life. One is therefore expected to be prayerful. A plea is sought for longevity in favour of the name bearer; Our Madu enu nam. Let me not be pushed around. The name bearer is an embodiment of strength of character.

MADUEGBUNA: Let nobody kill another; Vexatious relationship prior to the birth of the name bearer warranted this entreaty for restraint not to kill. The name bearer is wished well.

MADUEGBUNAM: A passionate plea to protect the name bearer/family. The name bearer is wished long life. The rancorous past and threats warranted this supplication.

MAKA: Ime mma amaka; eulogizing the advantages of goodwill. The bearer is a product of God's goodwill.

MAZAGU: Mazagu is of Igula origin.

MAZELI: Maluzelu; be wary; an advice seeking the protection of the bearer born in a topsy-turvy world. It is prayed that what inhibited the family should not affect the name bearer.

MBA: Onwu anu mba; Death defies admonition. An entreaty for longevity is made after several deaths had visited the family.

MBAJEKWE: Mbakwe; Mba ga ekwe; the populace will agree. A supplication is made for the name bearer to be accepted and supported by the people. The dissension in the past affected the family, hence the plea.

MBAMALI: Mba amalugo; Recognition from the people. A reference is made to such recognition given the family. The bearer is named against this backdrop. The name bearer is welcomed by all.

MBANEFO: Mbanefolum afa; Well wishes from the clan. For all the good work done by the family, the name is always remembered by the populace. The populace can also testify for the family in cases of accusations and disagreements; A reference of the above cited circumstance and the arrival of a child is welcomed.

MBANUGO: The people have heard and accepted. The arrival of the name bearer was well announced; A glorification to God for the delivery of the name bearer.

MBUNABO: Lit. First and Second; God's benevolence to the family the second time around is extolled. The name bearer is a product of God's benevolence and is thus wished well.

MBANWUSI: May the people/clan not be extinct. A reference is made to a calamity in which many people perished. God is placated to stave off such calamity. The name bearer is prayed to live a fulfilled life.

MEGAFU: Men Kam fu; an entreaty to discuss one in his presence and not at his back. A reference is made to slanderous comment against the family. The name bearer is an embodiment of boldness

MKPE: Mkpe Mkpe; the name has a connotation of complaints, accusation, grievance, grouse etc. and is a commemoration of the gripe the family encountered in the past. It serves as a warning to the family's detractors and as well as a plea for God's intercession in favour of the name bearer/family.

MELIE: Chukwu emelie; the arrival of the name bearer is seen as a victory on God's side. The bearer is a product of this victory. A glorification on the birth of the child is acclaimed.

MELIFEONWU: Emelum ife onwu; Onye melu ife onwu? Do I deserve death, does anybody deserve death? A plea is made for death to keep away. The name bearer is wished long life.

MEMKAMKWE: Melum kam kwe; If you extend your goodwill to me I would gladly accept it; a reference to a circumstance that some benefits/rights were denied the family. Any support to correct this anomaly would be appreciated. The bearer is named against this background and is prayed to secure all his benefits and rights.

MENKITI: Ife emenam buna nkiti; A plea is sought that all evils directed at the family should come to nothing. The name commemorates past antagonism against the family and the bearer is prayed to be successful in life

MENYUAH: Menyuam akwa; A plea to wipe away one's tears and sorrows is pressed. The arrival of the child is a break from this difficult and sorrowful past. God is thus glorified.

MODEBE: Muodebelu; A variant of Chukwudebelu; what God has put in place holds. A plea that no evil should befall the name bearer/family is made and the name bearer is wished well.

MODIM: Muodilim; May the grace of God be with the family and hence guarantee the survival and general progress of the name bearer/family.

MOKWE: A variant of Olisakwe; with God's consent all is well. The name is an entreaty for the well-being of the name bearer/family.

MOLOKWU: Mou naelo okwu; God determines all happenings; and settles all disagreements. A reference is made to a contentious past requiring God's intercession. The bearer is named after such case and is also seen as a product of God's intercession.

MORAH: Muo rapu; A variant of Chukwura; God's protection is sought for the survival of the name bearer. The name is a pointer that earlier offsprings did not survive. The bearer is prayed to live a fulfilled life.

MORTUNE: Moutune; Muonene; God's intercession is sought to protect the family/name bearer. It serves as a commemoration of disagreements that warranted God's intercession in favour of the family.

MOZIE: Muodozie; May God put right all that have gone wrong; a plea for a truce. The name bearer is an epitome of peace. As in Mouziem Uzo; God is earnestly asked to show the bearer/family the way to prosperity.

MOZO: Muo zoba; a variant of Azoba; Chukwuzoba; May God protect.

MUNONYEDI: Who is on my side? God is looked upon to support the family hence correct the injustice that visited the family in the past. The name bearer is seen as a future support of the family.

MOUEMEKA: The Supreme Being-God- has done well; a glorification to God Almighty for granting the safe arrival of the baby, perhaps the first child or coming after protracted problems the family experienced. The name bearer is God's reward and the perseverance put up by the family.

MUOFUNANYA: Extolling God for his love and mercies. The name bearer is a cynosure of love.

MUOMAOKWU: A variant of Muonweokwu below.

MUONWEOKWU: God has the final say, and knows everything. He is an overall arbiter. A plea is made for God's intercession to protect the family/the name bearer. With reference to such disagreement in the family, God is called upon to judge.

MUOWETA: Muowetalu; Caused by God, Established by God. The name bearer was made possible by God and is dedicated to God. There is a belief that what or who is ordained by God will live a fulfilled life.

NDAGUBA: Ndu aguba; a desperate need for life/good health. A reference is made to poor health that visited the family in the past. The new arrival is prayed to be healthy and to live long.

NDIORA: Ndiora egbunam; May I not be killed/hurt by the people. The name is a plea to save/protect the bearer from such antagonism. A commemoration of such hatred that the family experienced is made. The name bearer is prayed to have a fulfilled life.

NDIWE: Ndum di ufodu iwe; some people are not happy with my existence. This refers to envy and hatred from some quarters, hence God's protection is sought to contain this impediment, and the name bearer is wished well.

NDUANYA: Ndu afulu anya; Vivid existence. The name bearer is an epitome of fullness of life; a plea for the sustained longevity of the name bearer is sought.

NDUMMA: Good life made possible by God. The name bearer is prayed to live a fulfilled life.

NDULUE: Ndu elum; my turn for life-prosperity and joy- has come. God's approval is sought for the name bearer to live long and enjoy the bounties of life.

NGESINA: Ngo esina; Needless hedging a bet. Past disagreement is thus set aside and peace is sued. The name stands as a reference to a knotty situation requiring agreement of the affected parties. The name bearer is a symbol of peace.

NJAKA: Nkem jiaka; a variant of Nke akam. What you have by the dint of your hard work sustains you better than from other sources. The name bearer is seen as a resource and a pride to the family.

NJOTE: Njo gbate lete; May all the evils and lies not come the way of the name bearer/family. A plea for an upright life is earnestly sought.

NKPULUMA: Good seedling, such that guarantees good harvest. The name bearer is a cynosure of all that is good.

NNAMUA: Namulu; Delivered by Almighty Father. The benevolence of God on the delivery of the name bearer is extolled.

NNASO: Kosi so nna; as it pleases God. The name bearer is a product of God's wish. Previous malice and malevolence against the family are now put to rest by God's will.

NNEZIANYA: Looking forward for all the good fortunes from God. A plea is made for the name bearer to live a fulfilled life.

NNOBA: Nna bu Oba; God is the Alpha and Omega, the Omnipotent, Omniscient and Omnipresent whose command is incontrovertible. The arrival of the name bearer is a testimony of God's work and his benevolence is eulogized.

NNOKA: Ka nnoruka; a plea to live long. By inference previous children died in their infancy.

NNOSA: Nnebe Olisa; looking unto God for His protection and guidance. The name bearer is wished well.

NSOENU: Abstinence in life. Such self-denial prepares a man to adulthood; A reference to a situation that warranted such self-denial. The bearer is a product of such. God is praised.

NSOFOR: Abstinence required to be sanctified; circumstances requiring the family not to break her vow are commemorated. The name bearer is an embodiment of godliness. The bearer could also represent the purity which the people are expected not to defile.

NSONWU: Onwu enwero nso; No level of abstinence keeps death away. The name is an acknowledgement of the inevitability of death hence a plea for longevity and God's guidance of the name bearer.

NTEPHE: Onye ka enu tolu efe; Kedu onye uwa tolu efe? Who has all the contentment of life? A poser that calls for glorification to God for what one has. A reference is made to certain injustice meted to the family and a warning to the oppressor that no position is permanent. The name bearer is thus wished well.

NWABO: The name derives from an assumed name, an alias. Abo people then were noted for their decency, stylish and English mannerism. The name bearer was considered to have these Abo traits. The name further stuck after a family feud that warranted the family to take up the name 'Nwabo' against the main family name. It could as well mean that the name bearer was born in Abo, an equivdent of Bini Amaka.

NWAEBUBE: Nwa bu ebube Chukwu; A child is the blessing/glory from God; A resources to be proud of. The name bearer is an exemplar of various resources. God is glorified.

NWABUEZE: A child is a king. The importance of a male child is great as he guarantees the sustenance of the family lineage. The name bearer is a pride and pearl of the family and is wished well.

NWABUFO: Nwabu ufo nna. A child is goodwill from God. God is glorified on the arrival of the child. God is the Author and Maker of procreation. The family would have experienced some difficulties at early stage. The birth of the boy is seen as God's intercession and good will.

NWABUZO: A child is a pathway to progress. A solicitation is pressed for the well being of the name bearer.

NWACHUKWU: God's own child. The bearer is seen as a role model; an embodiment of virtues – prudence, justice, fortitude, temperance, faith, hope, charity and chastity. The bearer is dedicated to God.

NWADIOGBU: The comprehension of procreation is deep and rests with God. Eulogizing God for bestowing mankind with the power to procreate is sought. A plea to stave off difficulties of child birth is sought. The name bearer is a product of God's intercession and mercy

NWAGBO: A variant of Nwagbologu below.

NWAGBOLOGU: Nwa gbo lum ogu; the arrival of the name bearer has united the family and put a stop to untoward and vexatious comments. God's deliverance is extolled.

NWAGU: Descendant of a leopard; a personification. The bearer is wished the strength of a leopard to enable him defend his family/domain. In Nwa amulu na agu; The name bearer was born in the farm. God is praised on the successful delivery.

NWAMUO: Son of spirit/deity. This is another name given to reincarnated children. Having identified the tricks of the child in dying and coming back, a plea is made to Deity for the child to live long.

NWANODU: May the child stay. A plea for the survival and longevity of the bearer as pervious offspring died soon after birth.

NWANOLUE: A variant of Nwanodu; Let the name bearer live to ripe old age. An inference is made that previous issues did not live very long, hence a plea for longevity.

NWANOSIKE: May the child remain healthy. A plea is made for the general wellbeing of the bearer. Apparently previous children did not enjoy healthy life.

NWATAH: Son of Attah. Atta is said to be of Igala origin.

NWEJE: Nwa na eje; May the child go places. May the child's pathway be free to enable him attain heights. The name bearer is wished a fruitful and fulfilling life. It could be deduced that previous children had stunted life.

NWIBA: Nwa iba; A male child excepted to carry the family name along and preside over family functions. This is an acknowledgement that the family name has come to stay through the will of God.

NWIKE: Nwa ike; this refers to difficulties circumstances affecting the family prior to the birth of the bearer. The commemoration of this experience is made and God is looked upon to protect the bearer/family.

NWITE: Nwa Ite; A small cooking pot. As in Enenia nwa ite ogboyua oku; If you neglect a little pot it will quench the cooking light. The small pot by in is powerful; A reference to a situation that the family was neglected; and a warning too to the family detractors not to judge one by his looks. The name bearer is a symbol of clout; a variant of Odinfe anyi alo; small by size but heavy by weight.

NWAOCHE: Nwa echelu eche, a child that was eagerly awaited. The arrival marked joy for the family. Apparently the parents had earlier problems of childbirth.

NWAOFILI: Nwa eji fili akwukwa; a man who is married and meets his various obligations is said to be balanced. 'Ifi akwukwa'. The arrival of the child has further strengthened the parent's position in life.

NWOKEDI: Acknowledging the arrival of a male child, who is expected to carry the family name along; a plea for the family lineage not to be extinct is made.

NWOKOLO: Nwa okolo; Nwa okolobia; the son of an able-bodied man. Bravery, wisdom and strength are all sought for the bearer.

NWAONYUGBO: A variant of Ugbo. Nwa onye ugbo; son of a farmer/herbalist; the bearer is named after the profession of the forebears.

NWAORA: A child for all. This is made possible by God. The name beareris wished well; a variant of Obiora.

NWAOSISI: Nwa osisioma; a product of good seedling. The name bearer is seen as such or as in Nwa osisi; this is another name signifying reincarnation. The grave being marked with a stake makes it difficult for the reincarnated child to die again.

NZEAMAKA: An acknowledgement of spiritual virtue. God is good and beautiful. The bearer is a product of this virtue and is prayed for.

NZEAKOR: God is ever present; God is looked upon to judge. The name bearer is a product of God's judgement and is wished well.

NZECHE: Nze na eche; Guided by spiritual virtues; a plea is sought for the name bearer to be guided and protected by spiritual presence. The name is same with Nzekweche.

NZEGWU: Nze di egwu; Spiritual/divine power is deep and vast to understand. God is mysterious. The name bearer is a personification of the enigma.

NZEKWU: Nze na ekwu; Divine will orders; decision reached by spiritual/divine powers. God is in control. The name bearer, a product of divinity is wished well.

NZOBUIWU: A bet binds like the law. The name is a commemoration of such disagreement prior to the birth of the child. By this name, the attention of warring parties on such order is drawn. The name bearer is a personification of this order.

OBA: Nwa oba; Oba simply means a monarch, a king. God is looked upon as the Almighty King, King of Kings. The name bearer is thus seen as a son of God.

OBANYE: Having entered/been accepted/or secured; the arrival of the name bearer is joyfully welcomed. A plea for the survival of the name bearer is made especially as pervious conception was not successful.

OBECHIA: A variant of Obodo echina; May the world of the family not be extinct. The arrival of a male child is extolled.

OBECHE: Obe onye na eche ya; One's affliction, encumbrance and responsibility awaits him. Everybody carries his own cross. This is a commemoration of a polemic where the family was unfairly blamed. The name signifies a warning that for whatever omission, commission and liability a person commits the consequences will also visit the person.

OBI: The name refers to the family seat of administration; A heritage. The birth of the name bearer is thus seen as a guarantee to occupy/maintain this seat/family lineage.

OBIANWU: Obu onye ga anwu ka odili obodo mma; who is to die or be sacrificed to guarantee peace in the town; a reference of a contentious situation. The name bearer is a symbol of truce.

OBIEFUNA: One's heritage should not be lost. A plea is pressed for the survival of the name bearer who is expected to occupy his stool/heritage.

OBIESIE: Obi esiligom; accepting the challenges of life with equanimity and determination to succeed. The name bearer is a source of this strong will. God's benevolence on the delivery of the name bearer is thus extolled.

OBIEZE: Seat of royalty; the name is a personification of such stool and the name bearer is welcomed to this seat.

OBIGBO: Obidi gbo; an acknowledgement that the family lineage had a link with royalty. The name bearer is thus welcomed into the royal house.

OBINWA: The wish/quest for a child. The name bearer is an answer to the request. God is thus extolled.

OBINWE: Owned or under the jurisdiction of the royalty. The name bearer is dedicated to the royal house and is wished well.

OBIOGBOLU: The domain/dynasty that settled the hostilities/disputes at the time; A reference to a situation where ill-deeds were prevented. The name is seen as a symbol of peace and is wished well.

OBIORA: 'Vox populi' Voice of the people, the wish of the people. Such yearning is said to be the wish of God. The name bearer is dedicated to God. Such expectation could derive from problems that at a stage appeared insurmountable. The arrival of the name bearer is joyously welcomed.

OBIOZO: Obia na ozo; The delivery of the bearer coincided with the initiation into ozo of one of the members of the family; a commemoration of this occasion; Or as in Obi Ozo- Domain of priesthood. The bearer is seen as an epitome of priesthood.

OBODOECHINA: May the world of the family not be extinct. The arrival of the male child is gladly welcomed as his arrival will guarantee such continuity.

OBOLI: This is a title, which over the period stuck as a family name. The likes are ukpabi, Igele etc.

OBOSI: Obosisie; Lit. Something that uproots and upsets; A reference to a calamity as it were that caused the death of a good number of the family members; A commemoration and a plea to God to stave off such past calamity. The name bearer is wished well.

OBUMSE: Obum selu ogu; Am I the cause of the fight; disassociating one from the cause of hostility, hence a plea that the consequences should not affect the family. A reference is made to such situation. The female variant is Emetarom.

OBROTA: Oburota; the bad day is not today; a plea that the evil days are kept off. The bearer is wished well. By inference, the family was visited by a litany of troubles in the past. The name serves as an interjection-God forbid evils.

OCHEI: Oche yi; your stool; your heritage; the bearer's arrival is welcomed and seen as the realization of this stool.

ODAFE: Odafe is said to be of Benin origin.

ODELUGA: Udem edelugo gaba; My star is shining. The arrival of the name bearer-a star- is celebrated. The name bearer represents a new turn to posterity and prosperity.

ODIAKOSA: Odi na aka olisa; All depends on God. The welfare of the name bearer is thrust upon God. The name bearer is dedicated to God. This is also a reminder to detractors that God's power is supreme.

ODIAMMA: Odim mma; I am pleased. The arrival of the child is celebrated and well received by the parents. God is thus extolled and the name bearer is wished well. Or as in ife Chukwu emena di mma . God's work cannot be faulted. The name bearer is part of God's work that is joyously welcomed.

ODIARI: Odinari; Odina agbo, Odiatu; something unique and peculiar to the family. The name bearer is a pearl and pride of the family and the arrival is joyously celebrated.

ODIATU: Same as Odiari above.

ODIEGWU: Uwa di egwu; expressing the difficulties in life. A plea for the wellbeing of the name bearer is made. It would appear that the family experienced much harsh times in the past

ODIGBO: A variant of Obidigbo; tracing the family lineage to a royal lineage. The name bearer is welcomed into this ancestry.

ODIKPO: Odi na ikpo; Amongst the crowd; having distinctive features that identifies the bearer from the crowd, the name bearer is seen as first amongst equals; A pearl.

ODILI: Okwudili; Let us to rest all vexatious comments and let peace reign. Okwu dili Chukwu; God is seen as the final arbiter. The name bearer symbolizes peace. The female variant is Ifediba.

ODITA: A variant of Osita. Oditata odigbo, May the good fortune of today which is linked to past fortune extend to the future. A plea for good fortune is made for the family.

ODOBO: Harbinger of good fortune. The name bearer is seen as such and having arrived after past misfortunes, the road to progress and prosperity is opened. There is also a claim that Odobo is of Igala origin.

ODOGWU: A brave and successful man. The name is a personification of such qualities. The name bearer is wished well.

ODUKWE: Onye ka adulu odu okwe; who accepts advice easily; a reference to a serious disagreement amongst the people. The poser calls for truce. The bearer represents a new beginning.

ODUNZE: The paraphernalia of a monarch; a remarkable thing. The name bearer is seen as such and God is praised.

OFALA: Ofala is the yearly outing of the Obi of Onitsha. The name bearer is named after this day in which he was born. Igwe Ofala Okagbue was born on Ofaladay

OFILI: Same as Nwaofili; the arrival of the child has strengthened the parent's position.

OFFIAH: Offia aju; the forest rejects. This refers to early child deaths and the burial of the forest. The objection is a plea for the name bearer to survive and hence avoid the forest.

OFO: Divine righteousness; the name bearer is a personification of this power.

OFODILE: Ofokansi adile; Divine righteousness is far superior to magic and charms. A reference is made to such circumstance that the power was tested. The name bearer is a product of divinity and is wished well.

OFODU: Onye ka ofodulu; Uwa afodulu onye. What remains in life; an acknowledgement and inference that problems of life are universal? A reference is made to a desperate situation that warranted the name. God is looked upon to come to the aid of the name bearer/family.

OFOEDU: Ofo na edum; Divine righteousness guides me. The name bearer is an outcome of such divination and is wished well. God is glorified.

OFOELU: Ofoelum: Divine power has come my way. I have been bestowed with divine powers. The name bearer is a product of this divination. It would appear that family was denied of certain rights in the past.

OFOKANSI: A variant of Ofodile – Ofokansi adile.

OGALONYE: Ogalonye nya gali ibie: A plea that success should be widespread for all and sundry. The family/the name bearer is wished success in life especially coming on the heels of strings of failures. Or as in ilolo galu onye odika o jelu be Olisa: When one's plans are successful it would look as though one visited God. All good things come from God. His will is incontrovertible. The bearer is such manifestation from God.

OGAZI: Ogo adirozi: Benevolence is now hardly practiced. A commemoration of a circumstance where the family who had rendered benevolence services in the past is now not recognized or denied similar kindness. Despite such bad turn, the name bearer is expected to continue the benevolence of his forebear.

OGBUAH: Ogbu anu ukwu; a hunter of repute. The bearer is named after the profession/skill of the forebearer. He is prayed to be skillful.

OGBUE: A variant of Ogbogu; below.

OGBOGU: Ogbolu ogu, A variant of Nwagbo; Nwagbolum ogu; A child is a source of joy, peace and above all anti-friction. All the vexatious comments have been put to rest with the arrival of the bearer. The name bearer portends truce.

OGBOLU: Another variant of Ogbolu.

OGBOTOBO: Ogbu otobo; Hippotamus hunter. The bearer is named after the trade of the father/forebear. The name bearer is wished the skill, bravery of a hunter of such enormous sea animal.

OGBULI: Somebody who makes up with chica-uli-is a beautician and by refrence a do-good-man. The bearer is seen as such.

OGBUMUO: Something disheartening; It refers to 'umechi' early child deaths and similar travails. The name bearer having been identified to have reincarnated is thus requested to stay.

OGO: Ogo Chukwu, Gift from God. God is extolled on the delivery of the name bearer, coming on the heels of the problems encountered by the parents. The bearer is thus dedicated to God.

OGOEGBUNAM: Ogom egbunam; May my kindness not be used against me; a commemoration of the family's benevolence at a time, which was not duly acknowledged. The name bearer is seen as a comforter.

OGUEJIOFO: A divine guided fight; much is owed to God for His divination and intercession. The name bearer is the subject to be saved and dedicated to God.

OGUDEBE: Ogudebelu; Signifying that the bearer came into the world after a protracted hostility. With the feud over the name bearer is expected to live long.

OGUNO: 'Ogu uno egbunam; family feud.; the name is a commemoration of this feud within the kindred. The end of this feud is sought such as to protect the bearer. The name bearer represents truce.

OJEKWE: A variant of Onyejekwe; Onye ga ekwe. Who will agree? A reference is made to a disagreement defying solution. By implication God's intercession is sought. The name bearer symbolizes accord.

OJEMBA: Oje mba enwe ilo: a sojourner/traveler has no enemies; An entreaty that the family who has related with all and sundry is not befallen by evils/enemies. The name bearer is seen as a bundle of joy and represents friendship.

OJIBA: Oji iba, Oji ide, Onye ji iba; a person who holds the family together; a pillar of the family. The bearer is seen as a future resource centre, and a principal character.

OJIEGBU: Oji anya egbu: Oji anya egbu malu onwie; A poser that one who is filled with envy and hatred 'knows himself' or should be careful. By implication the family detractors are warned to keep off the family/name bearer; the name is a commemoration of an occasion where the family was visited with envy. The name bearer is prayed not to be affected by such envy and hatred from the kindred.

OJOGWU: The bearer is named after the forebear's black smiting trade.

OKADIGBO: Okika digbo; from time, some people's status are higher than others. The family is seen as an epitome of such higher status and the bearer is wished well and as well as to rise to high status in his life.

OKAGBUE: Odikasi gbue onye? Who deserves death; a poser that calls for restraint in human relations; a commemoration of a circumstance that pushed the warring parties to the wall? The name bearer is an epitome of truce and love.

OKAKA: Oke aka chukwu; God's special creation. A gift form God. Eulogizing God's will and hand work, the name bearer is the product of God's handiwork.

OKAFOR: A male child born on the third market day Afor, thus named after this market day.

OKALA: Okalais said to be of Igala origin

OKANI: Okanu melie; Okanu me; May the majority win; A commemoration of a deadlock that required such chancing. The bearer is named after such feud and is wished to thrive in good times and when there is chaos.

OKECHUKWU: Oke Chukwu kelu; God's special creation. There is no doubt about God's power which manifested in the birth of the baby boy. God is eulogized and the name bearer is dedicated to God.

OKIWELU: Obu iwe na elu; The height of anger and hatred is contemplated; A reference to a circumstance with anger and hatred at its peak. The bearer is named after this incident. Restraint/intercession is sought from God to keep tempers cool. The name represents this new turn to forgiveness.

OKOCHA: Okolo ocha; Okolobia ocha; a fair able bodied person. The name bearer is a product of an able person and is wished well.

OKOLO: Okolobia; A man of all season; Full fledged man; a man of importance. The name bearer is wished all these qualities.

OKONJI/OKOLONJI/OKOLOJI: Okolobia oji. The name bearer is of dark complex and product of able bodied parents. The emphasis is on complex. The name bearer is wished well.

OKOLU: Obuka olulu; Obu ka iwe lulu; the height of anger and hatred is contemplated. The name bearer is named after this incident. Restraints/intercessions are however sought from God. The name bearer represents this new turn for forgiveness; a variant of Okiwelu.

OKONKWO: Okolo nkwo; the name bearer was born on the fourth market day and thus named after it.

OKOSI: Obu ka osi so Chukwu: God's wish. The name bearer is seen as a gift from God;a product of God's benevolence. The arrival of the child is thus welcomed.

OKOSIEME: Obu ka osi eme: Kosi so Chukwu ka osi eme; A variant of Okosi; as it pleases God; A glorification of God's works. The name bearer is a product of such work.

OKPANKU: Lit. A collector of firewood; the character is seen as an achiever. The name bearer is prayed for to be industrious and successful.

OKWOSA: Okwu Olisa; Entrusting all conflicts to God's care; A reference to such disagreement and God is seen as the right arbiter to favour the family that is presupposed innocent. The name bearer is a cynosure of peace.

OKWUGBA: Refers to complicated conflicts; A commemoration of such conflict. The name bearer is wished not to be affected by such development.

OKWUEGBUNAM: A plea that disagreement should not hurt the family; A commemoration of such feud. The name bearer is wished well.

OKWUEZE: Disagreements arising from Obiship tussle. The birth of the name bearer commemorates this period.

OKWUDINKA: Oration or speech is an art. The name traces this artistic quality in the family. A reference to a circumstance warranting re-echoing this trait is made. Another version has it that-okwu-disagreement begets rancor. The name is a commemoration of such feud and the bearer is prayed to be absolved from the fall out of the disagreement.

OKWUAYANGA: Conflicts do not pass me by. There is hardly any comment that does not beget a rejoinder; A reference to such war of words. The name also calls for better understanding. The name bearer is prayed not to be affected by the fallout of such conflict.

OKWUAZI: The stand of the younger generation, especially in the face of opposition or other related conflict. A reference is made to such stand. The name bearer's welfare and protection by inference is sought.

OKWUMA: Relegating past conflict and looking forward to progress. The name bearer's arrival marks this new turn to forgiveness, rapprochement and progress.

OKWUSOGU: Okwu selu ogu; Words that offend give rise to fights; a reference to such happenstance. The name is also a reminder of the consiquences of disagreement thus it calls for better understanding.

OLEIGBO: Ka olelu Igbo; May good tidings visit our people for their commitments, unstinted support etc. A reference is made to such circumstance warranting the entreaty.

OLEHI: Onwu elie; Onwu na eli; Death devours; An acknowledgement of the powers of death to strike at will. A reference is made to past deaths that visited the family and a plea for longevity for the name bearer.

OLIMMA: This refers to reincarnation. The body of dead child is marked with knife in order to identify the child when it comes back to another life. Such identification prevents the trick of the child in dying and coming back. A plea that the name bearer, now identified, should live long is made.

OLISA: Olisa is God; Olisakwe God's consent. Nwa olisa is a product of God's consent; a variant of Nwachukwu. Belu Olisa; Reverence to God. The name bearer is wished well.

OMAME: Ima atu na ife melu; acknowledging that something spectacular happened. The name bearer is this phenomenon. God is praised; or in Oma me; bound to happen by the power of God. It refers to God's work which is faultless.

OMATA: Omalu dim ma tata nya dili gaba; May the good tidings prevail over the life time. The name bearer is the beginning of better times.

OMEGA: Melu gaba; Ka omelu gaba; Continue with your good works; a plea that the name bearer/family takes after the virtues of their forbear. This is also an attestation of God's benevolence and such bounties are prayed for.

OMEKAM: Oga emekam; a poser on whether the name bearer will emulate the parent. By implication the name bearer is wished well. An entreaty is made for the favourable antecedents to prevail for the family.

OMENAZU: Omenazu nnia; Refers to the instance where the father of a child died before the child was born. A reference is made to such birth, and an entreaty that the bearer would fit into the father's role.

OMENI: The female variant is Emengini. What have I done to warrant an attack/castigation? A plea is sought for God's intercession and protection; or as in Omenyi meaning a performer, an accomplished person. The name is a personification of an achiever.

OMENYE: Omenye golum. Chukwu emeyegolum, God has attended to my needs; Extolling God for his benevolence. The name bearer is a product of God's benevolence; or Omelu onye ka odi mma; onye ka ome ka odi mma? Who bears the burden/cross such that there will be peace. A reference is made to a vexatious circumstance during which the family was maligned. This is a poser calling for truce, fairness and good neighbourliness. The name bearer is a symbol of fairness; a variant of Obianwu and Ogbabu.

OMUTABO: A variant of Amuta. The delivery of the second child is commemorated. The birth is welcome. The variant is Adibuah.

ONIAH: Onini anwa; a plea to God for timely mediation in the injustice to the family; a commemoration of the incident. God's intercession is sought to protect the name bearer.

ONOCHIE: Madu anochie; A replacement; the arrival of a male child is welcomed and prayed for his survival as the prior child had died. The name bearer is wished well. The variant is Madu adichie.

ONONO: Onono is of Igala Origin.

ONONYE: Chukwu nonyelum ka Ononyelum; May god be with me. A plea is made for the survival of the name bearer. God is earnestly asked to be on the side of the name bearer hence, protect him.

ONUKWUBA: Onukwutelu uba; Success achieved by commitment, outspokenness and articulation; a commemoration of each success. The name bearer is an epitome of success.

ONUMA: Onu madu bu onu chukwu; the voice of the people is the voice of God. The name bearer is gladly welcomed after a protracted difficult period.

ONUMONU: The voice of all voices; Okwulu ora; the spokesman of the family; a man of all seasons; a personification of above characteristics.

ONUORA: Onu ora egbunam; May the unpleasant views from folk not affect the bearer. A plea is made to be saved from such view. The name bearer is a symbol of doggedness. Or in Onura; voice of the people; the bearer is the subject and is wished well.

ONWUALU: Onwu na alu enu; Death is malevolent and can upset the town; an acknowledgement of such and a plea for death to stay away from the name bearer. A plea for longevity is made for the name bearer.

ONWUATU: Onwu atu alo; Death does not reason with its victim. The name is both an acknowledgement of the powers of death and a plea for longevity of the name bearer.

ONWUATUMUO: Death does not strike the spirit/Deity. A glorification is given to the supreme power of Deity; the Creator. His immortality guarantees the procreation of human begins. The name bearer is dedicated to Deity.

ONWUAZO: Onwu Azolugo; Death has snatched another victim. An inference is made that the prior issue died; a plea that follows is for the survival of the name bearer; a replacement. The name bearer is wished longevity.

ONWUBUYA: Death begets sorrow hence a plea to lessen such sorrows by protecting the name bearer.

ONWUDACHI: Onwu bu odachi; Death is a stumbling block that can upset the family. A plea not to witness such death so soon is sought. The name bearer is wished long life.

ONWUDINJO: Death is malevolent; a variant of onwubu uya. A plea is sought by the family to be spared by early deaths. It would appear that the family had experienced several deaths in the past.

ONWUEGBUNA: A plea to be saved from death. The name bearer is wished long life.

ONWUEMEKA: Death has tried. A reference is made to an instance that death was within an inch in the life of the father or possibly the mother while pregnant. Having been saved and the baby delivered, death is thanked and God who decrees life and death is glorified.

ONWUEMELIE: Onwu na emeli uwa; The sorrow brought by death affects everybody. A plea for moratorium on death is made.

ONWUJEKWE: Onwu ga ekwe. A plea is sought for a respite of death and hence the survival of the name bearer. By inference the family was visited by death.

ONWUKA: Onwu ka dibia; Death when it wants to strike defies all medical/herbal attention. An entreaty for death to keep off from the family/name bearer is sought.

ONWULI: Onwudili; Onwudilu madu; recognizing that death is certain; people are expected to put their best while they are living in borrowed time. A plea for solace and doggedness. The corollary is MENYUAH; Wipe away one's tears and sorrows.

ONWUMA: Death knows when to strike its victim, God who gives and takes life is pleaded with to grant the name bearer and family a good life.

ONWUTA: Onwu talu ebo/uba; Death has claimed many especially one's kindered. A reference is sought to such debacle and a plea for a respite to death. The name bearer is prayed to have long life.

ONWUORA: Onwu na egbu ora; death is universal; an acknowledgement of this hence a plea for the name bearer to be spared till ripe old age.

ONWUZULIKE: Another plea for a respite to death; the bearer/family is wished long life.

ONYEABO: A variant of Abua. Welcoming a male child to the family where the father has no brothers. The new arrival is seen as a second factor; a support to the family.

ONYEACHONAM: Do not provoke me; A commemoration of such vexation. The name bearer is seen as a harbinger of peace and as well as a force to counter any provocation.

ONYECHI: Onye bu chi ibeya; is there anybody that is God to another. The poser calls for peace and good neighbourliness. A reference is made to a situation of high handedness that warranted the poser.

ONYEJEKWE: Onye ga ekwe; kedu onye ga ekwe; who will accept other people's views; a variant of Ojekwe. A reference is made to a disagreement defying immediate solution. God's intercession is thus sought. The bearer is an epitome of truce.

ONYENUCHIE: Everyman has his own direction (sense). The name is a warning /reply to the family detractors. A commemoration of such situation is made and bearer is wished well.

ONYENYEONWU: Who dispenses death; a variant of Anionwu, Ana enye onwu enye; an entreaty to God for the longevity and prosperity of the family/name bearer; or as in Onye nyilu onwu; who is beyond death; a reminder that we are all mortals; God gives and takes away life and nobody can challenge or counter his will. The survival of the name bearer is prayed for.

ONYIDO: Onyido ogbom; the burden rests on my mates. An instance is cited when the named bearer out-performed his mates. The name derives from a nickname. Onyido in this respect refers to an accomplished man. The name bearer is seen to be an achiever.

ORADIWE: A variant of Ndiwe; A commemoration of hatred meted to the family. The name bearer is wished God's protection.

ORAKA: Ora eji aka; Acknowledging the support from the kindred. The name bearer is named after this and is a product of such support.

ORAKPO: Ora akponam; a plea not to be castigated by the clan. A reference is made to unfair criticism meted on the family. Given this explicit request the family/name bearer is wished well.

ORAKPOSIM: A variant of Orakpo.

ORAKWUE: Orakwube; Let the people comment/judge. An attestation of the deliverance by God hence the people's negative comment/judgement is of no consequences. The bearer's arrival is a comfort to the family; or as in orakwubelum. Let the people talk on my behalf. A plea is sought for the people to testify for the family. A reference is made to a circumstance requiring the people to bail the family from an accusation. The name is also an entreaty to the kindred to join the family in announcing the arrival of the child.

ORAMALU: Ora amulugo; the news is known by all and sundry; eulogizing the arrival of the name bearer. The child is welcomed by all. The name bearer is thus wished well in life.

ORANU: Ora anugo; a variant of Mbanugo. The populace has heard about the family/child. The name bearer is thus gladly welcomed into the world.

ORANWUSI: May the people not perish; may the lineage of the kindred not be extinct. A reference is made to a war or other calamity that claimed many lives. The deliverance of the male child is welcomed.

ORANYE: Oranyelum; my mandate, fiat and glory has the blessing of the people. The bearer is named after this authority and is welcomed by all.

OREFO: Oranefo; Generality of the people has trust and love for the family hence the family is wished well and is much talked about. The bearer symbolizes this goodwill; A variant of Mbanefo.

OROBI: The family is undeterred; unperturbed and calm about past difficulties/obstacles. The arrival of the child is a source of joy and inner strength; a variant of Anierobi and Obiajulu.

OSADEBE: Olisa debelu; Under God's care hence let no one tamper/trespass. The name bearer is a gift from God.

OSAJI: Olisaji ndu; God is the source of life. The benevolence of God, exemplified by the delivery of the name bearer is thus extolled.

OSAKA: Osamaka; Olisa emeka; extolling the goodness of God. In Olisa emeka; God's support is hailed. The name bearer is a product of God's will.

OSAKWE: Olisakwe; God has agreed. The delivery of the child is through God's mercy. His authority is faultless. He gives and takes away lives. With the safe delivery of the child, a plea is made for longevity and general well-being of the name bearer.

OSANDU: A variant of Osaji; Olisa ji ndu; an attestation that God is the source of life, source of succour etc.

OSEGBUE: Olisa egbunam; May God not take my life. Admitting the erring and imperfect characteristics of human beings; a plea for protection and longevity of the family/ the name bearer is sought.

OSEKE: Olisa na eke; God creates. The name refers to infallibility and incontrovertibility of God's works. The name bearer is seen as God's special creation. He is thus dedicated to 'Olisa'-God.

OSEMEKA: Olisa emeka;a variant of Osaka. The name is an attestation of the goodness of God. The bearer is one of such example.

OSEMENAM: Olisa emenam; a variant of osegbue, Olisa Egbunam. May God not do me in; a plea for God's protection and deliverance is sought. The name bearer is wished well. God is compassionate and loveable, slow to anger and rich in mercy. The delivery of the name bearer is seen as God's mercy.

OSILI: A variant of Obiesie; Obi esiligom. My mind is made up, hence I have accepted the challenges in life with determination and equanimity. The name bearer is a source of this single mindedness.

OSOKOLO: He that comes next after 'Okolo' – an able bodied man. The name bearer is wished the qualities that would equip him to defend his family.

OSU: Osu uto. This refers to a case of – 'Umechi'- early child births following which the shrine was consulted, sacrifice made and followed with a request to grant the family a baby that will survive. The name bearer is delivered through the intervention of the deity as in Osu (Uto), Nwa (ogwugwu) or Nwa (Urai); A variant of Nwosu. The name is pleasant and is not related to a similar name osu that stands for an outcast.

OSUAGBADI: Osu Agbadi; see osu. The name bearer was delivered through the intercession of Agbadi shrine. This is similar to Osu Uto, Nwa ogwugwu, Nwa urai. The name bearer is dedicated to the shrine of Agbadi.

OTEKA: Ote aka odi njo, odi mma; Good days follows difficult and bad days. A plea is sought for more good turns. The name bearer is seen as a new turn to success and is wished well..

OTIGBA: Drummer boy. The bearer is named after the forebear's past time-drumming.

OTTOR: Ka otoruka; a variant of Isitor and Kwentoh. An earnest request for longevity is sought for the name bearer/family.

OZO: A variant of Obiozo, Obia na ozo; Having arrived during the ozo title occasion. A reference to such family status enhancing ceremony is made.

OZOBIA: Ozobialu; Announcing and ennobling the arrival of another male child. The name bearer is wished well in life.

OZOMA: Short form of ozomagala. See below.

OZOMAGALA: Ozomaogala is of Igala origin.

RALUM: A variant of Chukwura. A plea is made for the survival and protection of the name bearer, as previous issues did not survive.

SOKEI: Obuso na okenye ka esi anwu; is it only the aged that dies? Death defies age; an acknowledgement of the universality of death and a plea for longevity for the name bearer.

TAGBO: Tata bu gbo. It is never too late to make a start. Reminiscing past glories and wishing same now and in the future. The name bearer is a symbol of good things.

TABANSI: Tasia obi; perseverance, steadfast and patience. Given past difficulties God is earnestly asked to bestow these qualities to the family. The name bearer is seen as an epitome of these qualities.

UBAIKE: Uba bu ike: A variant of Igwebuike: The more the number the greater the strength. The name bearer is another source of strength.

UBADIGBO: Uba diba gbo; Tracing the wealthy status of the family to the ancestors. The name bearer is wished success in life.

UBILI: Ubili ka Nkwu: Both ubili and nkwu belong to palmaceae tree. The ubili is usually taller than Nkwu.The bearer of the name is seen as an outstanding person; an alias.

UDEAYA: Udeaya Egbunam: A references to an internecine war and a prayer for the family especially the name bearer that arrived during these hostilities; a variant of Ayaelinam.

UDEMBA: The pride of the people: The name bearer is this pride. He is joyously welcomed and God is glorified.

UDEMEZUE: My pride has blossomed with the arrival of the name bearer; usually a male child who is expected to carry the family name forward.

UDENABO: Extolling the benevolence of God, the second time around. The arrival of the name bearer; a second child is welcomed.

UDO: Udo Olisa; the abode of God. God is entreated to cleanse the name bearer such that God can reside in him. Udo also means peace. The name bearer is a symbol of peace.

UDOJI: Of formidable strength. The name bearer is wished this strength required to succeed in life.

UDU: Udu aku; Ite ego; Money/wealth pot. This implies affluence; an alias, denoting fullness and completeness. The bearer is seen as a man of wealth and influence.

UGBO: Ugbo dibia, farmland of herbalists. The bearer coming from this background is expected to live a healthy life. The bearer is named after the trade of his forebear.

UGOLO: Ugolo oma, Ugomma: A cynosure of beauty. The name bearer is seen as one. The benevolence of God is thus extolled.

UKPABI: Ukpabi is an alias, signifying an achiever. The name struck as a family name over a period of time.

UMEGBOGU: Umegbo, a variant of umebe (f) ikwa ume, May all that dissipates; envy, hatred injustice, etc be settled. It would appear that the family was plagued for a long time; hence a plea is made for God's intercession. The name could also be linked to prolonged travails of birth, especially where previous births did not survive. A plea is sought to end these pains and deaths. God is looked as the arbiter. The name bearer heralds rapprochement, new hope and better life.

UMERA: Umerali: All that dissipate one's effort is requested to cease. The name bearer is wished well. Or as in Umeomumu bezia nofu; an earnest request for an end to infant mortality is sought.

UMUNNA: Umunnakwe: A variant of Ibekwe and Umunnakwe. The consent of the kindred guarantees unity and support. The name bearer symbolises both. Or as in Umunna bu aya; the larger family often generates hostility/war. The name is a commemoration of such internal generated rife and prayed not to encounter such resentment.

UNEGBU: Onye uno egbu onye: where one is not killed by his kindred he is bound to live long. A reference is made to the treachery within the kindred and a plea for longevity for name bearer.

UWAECHIA: Uwaechina, A variant of Obodoechina; a plea to save one's lineage from extinction. The arrival of the name bearer is welcomed and is seen as a guarantee for the continuation of the family's lineage

UWAKWE: A variant of Umunnakwe: Family consent begets unity. The name bearer symbolizes unity.

UYAMASI: Uyamazikwo: Pains/sorrow knows why it afflicts people; consigning sorrows to the past especially with a good manifestation –the deliverance of a child or other good fortunes. The name bearer is an embodiment of resilience.

UYANNE: Uya nwa nne: The sorrows that losing one's relation begets; A commemoration of such incident. The arrival of the name bearer is welcomed as a replacement.

UYANWA: The anguish of losing a child and the desire-a-cry-to have another child. The bearer is named after this backdrop and is wished long life and virility.

UZO: Uzodimma, An acknowledgement of one's pathway t progress. The name bearer is an outcome of this adventure. Or Uzodimma aganya ugbolo nabo: When the road is prosperous it will be used again; an acknowledgement that the pathway to progress will always be revisited. The delivery of the name bearer is a manifestation of another beneficial pathway.

UZOECHINA: A plea that the road to procreation and prosperity is not blocked. God is looked upon to ensure that the lineage is not extinct and hence the plea for prosperity. The arrival of the male child is welcomed. The name bearer is wished well.

UZOKA: The road to prosperity matters most. A plea that success comes the way of the family and the name bearer is sought.

ENGLISH SURNAMES

ANDREWS
BOARDMAN
BOYD
BROWN
CAMPBELL
COKER
COLE
DENIS
GEORGE
HOLMES
JAMEISON
MCKINTOSH
MATHEWS
MICHEAL
MOORE
MORRIS
ROMAINE
SAINEZE
VENN
WALSON
WILSON

In old times names were summary of the purpose of one's existence on earth. Our surnames and to a great extent our first names fit into the above reasoning. Today many first names are named after popular names that are not linked to any event. Some Biblical names connote similar summary of one's existence. Abram was renamed Abraham and Sarai, Sarah. Jacob was also named Israel. God had to do these changes before the purpose of their lives could be established.

FIRST NAMES

ABIAGOM: (F) I have arrived. The worries, anxieties, doubts, bad words etc. are no more. The devil as it were has been shamed. The arrival is joyously welcomed. The name bearer is dedicated to God.

ACHUNA: Achufunam; Do not drive me away. A plea is thus made for the integration of the family and the guarantee of the name bearer's rights. In Achuna ife uwa na ike; Do not over- pursue earthly things. By implication, contentedness is advocated. The name bearer is an exemplar of peace.

ADAIBA: (F) The first daughter in a family home.

ADICHIE (M): Madu adichie: A variant of Onochie and Machie. A substitute/ replacement of loved lost one; a welcome and a prayer for the name bearer.

ADIKA: (M) Mba adika, Mba adiro ka nke anyi: Other towns cannot be compared with ours. A reference is made to circumstances that warranted the comparism in favour of Onitsha; a variant of Onitsha Amaka. The bounties of Onitsha are praised.

AFOMA: (F) Afoma Chukwu: Extolling the benevolence of God. God's goodwill (Afoma) is praised. The name bearer is a product of God's goodwill.

AFUNKEM: (F) Afugom nkem: I have set eyes on my desire. The name bearer is the subject. A variant of Nkem akonam: May what I deserve not elude me, Nkem dilim: May what is mine be for me. Nkem ji aka: What I have, I hold. In case where a woman who has been longing for a baby girl is blessed with such desire the name Afunkem fits. God is praised.

AFULENU:(F) Afulenu anya: Onyefulu enu anya? Who knows heaven? You cannot predict. Only God determines people's future; an attestation that God is in command and the bearer is wished God's guidance and protection.

AFULUCHIMANYA:(F) Establishing a close contact, rapport and love with God; The Omnipotent; the name bearer is dedicated to God.

AFUNURO: (F) Afunuro ife di otua: Anya afunuro: One has not set eyes on something similar. Relating to the birth of the child, the name bearer is priceless pearl, a unique child that is joyously welcomed. It could also be a commemoration of other benevolence enjoyed by the family especially when the expectations were dismal.

AGBODIKE: (M) Agbawo dike izu agba nya mgba nabo: you cannot make headway without the principal character. A reference is made to such neglect in the past. The bearer is named after this circumstance and is also seen as future principal factor.

AGBOMMA: (F) The name bearer is a cynosure of beauty.

AGHAELINAM; (M) A passionate plea is sought that the name bearer and the family are not killed in war. The birth of the name bearer during a war is commemorated.

AGEGBU: (F) Aga egbu onye? Who is to be killed? The poser calls for constraint; A commemoration of a persistent rancour within the kindred. The name bearer symbolizes truce and is wished well; a variant of Odika si gbue.

AGETU: (M+F) Agaetukoba: why overstretch the conflict; A commemoration of past rancor prior to the birth of the child. The arrival of the child is joyful; thus warranting forgetting past vexatious comment/rancour.

AGOM: (F) Onyeagom, onyega agolum who can testify or vouch for me? God is looked upon to absolve the family from such accusation. The bearer named after such denunciation, is a manifestation of exoneration; a new turn in life.

AJANUONWU: Death is not hindered or stopped by sacrifice. An inference that death strikes at will; an exit ordained by God. God's intercession is however sought to enable the name bearer/family live a fulfilled life.

AJUDESE: Onwu Ajudese, Onwu adiaju ese: Death needs no consultation before striking its victim. God's protection is therefore sought to enable the name bearer/family live a fulfilled life.

AKAEDO: (F) Eji aka edo; settling of disputes by the warring parties. The prolonged disagreement with its associated hatred, envy and antagonism reached a peak that the warring parties deemed it necessary to call it quits. The instance is commemorated. The baby girl is a paragon of peace.

AKONA: (F) Nkem akonam: whatever that is mine should not elude me. The name bearer is a part of this paraphernalia and is wished well.

AKUBUILO: (F) Wealth often attracts enmity. The bearer is named after this backdrop and is wished well.

AKUDO: (M) Aniakudo golum: The land has secured for me. I have made an imprint. The name bearer is this achievement and God 'Ani' is eulogized.

AKUZIE: (F) Akuzielumife, Azi akuzielum ife: Experience is a good teacher; A commemoration of past soured relations with the kindred and the determination to progress and prosper with the acquired experience. The name bearer is a source of strength.

AKWAKA: (F) Akwo aka ma eku: if you do not wash your hands you cannot handle/carry the bearer. By implication the name bearer is priceless and precious and hence must be handled with care. The name also is a plea to save the bearer from being contaminated by the blemishes of this world.

AKWAEKE: (M) A precious and priceless pearl that must be protected by all means and at all costs. A plea is made to God to grant the name bearer that sort of protection.

ALAZO: (F) Alazinam onu: Do not prompt or tempt me. Do not force words out of my mouth, hence do not disturb and provoke me. Let me have peace. A reference is made to a contentious circumstances that the family was about to be drawn into. The name bearer is an epitome of toughness, tenacity and non gullibility.

AMAKA: (F) Nwa amaka; A child is a pearl to be cherished/admired. God is praised. It is also a short form of Obiamaka.

AMANCHUKWU: (M) An attestation that I know my God; God's benevolence on the delivery of the name bearer is extolled.

AMANGBO: (M) Amalum gbo: Had I known, if I had known, I would have made my mark earlier. The corollary is that nobody knows what would have happened in past and future. God is looked upon to protect the name bearer/family.

AMAOGE: (M) Onye ma oge: Nobody knows the time for birth/death except God. An appeal for God's protection is sought for the name bearer.

AMEZE: (F) Nwa malu eze; A daughter that knows/associates/recognizes the king. God is the king; the Father Almighty. To know him or be the daughter is a key to life. The name bearer is dedicated to God. The male variant is Nweze.

ANAGO: (M) Ani golum: May the land hold brief/vouch for me. An appeal is made to be protected and saved from any accusation. The bearer is named after this circumstance.

ANALIEFO: (M) Analiefo afa: For all the good works of the family the people still remember and speak well of the family. The bearer is named after such recognition.

ANENE: (F) Anene uwa: Looking unto life with hope and good expectation. The name bearer is wished well.

ANIETO: (M) Ani etogom: The land has blessed me: The arrival of the child is a blessing worth praising.

ANIGBOGU: (M) Ani gbo lum ogu; an entreaty for the intercession of the goddess of earth to save the family /the name bearer.

ANINWETA (M) Aninweta: Begotten by the land. The name bearer is seen as such. The land, Earth goddess is praised.

ANOKWU: (F) Anu okwu: Onwu anu okwu: Death is impervious to counsel;an acknowledgement of the potency of death and a plea to God to save the name bearer/family.

ANYABOLU: (M) Anya bolu: May the eyes retaliate/revenge; a prayer for the secret machination against the family to be unearthed and countered. The name bearer is seen as the eye and representative of the family and he is wished the foresight and inner strength to protect the family. In Anya bolu dike ori; it is the eyes that accuse the strong man of theft. This implies that the eyes are more powerful than the brave man. The eyes are the representation of the family; the name bearer is a symbol of might. Akin to a saying: 'Onye ori na ezu onye ama na agba'. A person who commits mischief has someone stalking and trailing him. It goes to show how powerful the eyes are.

ANYANNA: (F) Anyanna lu: The delivery of the child is supervised by the Almighty father. God is praised.

ANWULI: (F) Anwuli ka: Immeasurable joy; the name bearer is the source of this joy.

AZINAFU: (F) A counsel and a reproof for the young ones to appreciate the works of God and hence be upright. With reference to benefits arising from being righteous, the name bearer is seen as a symbol of perseverance and hope.

AZODO: (M) Ani azodo: The land has safeguarded the name bearer; a variant of Ani akudo.The name bearer symbol of peace and comfort.

AZOGINI: Why did dispute; A commemoration of such contention and misunderstanding. The name bearer is a symbol of peace and comfort'

AZUBUIKE: (M) Ukuta azu bu ike: One's strength lies in one's siblings.

BAGII: (F) Okwu abagini? Of what use is disagreement. The bearer is named after a dispute and symbolizes truce, peace and good neighborliness.

BATO: (F) Benata okwu: Lessening contentious situations; a plea to reduce the disputes within the kindred. The bearer is named after this situation and also is seen as a new turn towards ending existing enmity.

CHETAONWU: (M) Remember death: if you remember that death strikes at anytime you are expected to live righteous life. A plea is made for the survival and longevity of the name bearer.

CHIEBONAM: (F) Chukwu ebonam ifem na amaro; A plea is sought that one is not accused unfairly. A reference is made to such development. The name bearer is wished well.

CHIBUOGWU: (F)Chukwu bu ogwum; God is my antidote, indicating a strong belief in God. The name bearer is a testimony of God's assistance.

CHIBUZO: (M) God, the Creator is in front. He protects guides and motivates. The birth of a child is a manifestation of God's benevolence. The name bearer is expected to walk in the righteous path and God's protection is also sought.

CHIEDU: (M) Chukwu na edum: God guides me. A plea is sought for God's guidance.

CHIDOZIE: (M) May God put in place all that was wrong. The birth of the name bearer is a symbol of peace and unity.

CHIEDOZIE: (M) God has interceded. Some past wrongs have been put aright buy him. God is praised and the name bearer is joyously welcomed.

CHIEJINA :(M) Chi ejibidonam: may darkness not overtake me. May my light not be extinct; a passionate plea for longevity and prosperity in favour of the name bearer/family. Or chieji ada kalu ubosi: If it is not night, the day is not over. The name inspires hope, optimism and non-desperation.

CHIGBATA: (M) God's presence is earnestly sought to protect the family/name bearer. The travails the parents experienced warranted this call.

CHIKA: (M+F) Chukwuka: The greatness of God is attested. The name bearer is a testimony of God's work and benevolence.

CHIKAODILI: (F) Everything is in God's care. God knows the best and His intercession are always cherished. The name bearer is wished well.

CHIKEZIE: (M) Chukwukezie; Chukwuekezigo; God has restored a certain balance in the creation of the name bearer. The name could also mean that God has apportioned the shares equitably. By implication both the balance and shares were hitherto not in favour of the family. The name bearer is a harbinger of this positive chapter in the dynasty of the family and is wished well.

CHINASA: (F) Chinasa okwu: God is looked upon to defend one who is wrongly accused. The bearer is named after such accusation and wished well.

CHINELO: (F) Chukwu na elo: Chukwu na elo ndu: Life is a result of God's considered thought/will. The name bearer is seen as a manifestation of goodness fromGod after some expectations/difficulties.

CHINWE(F) Chinwe ife enu uwa: God owns and presides over all earthly things. The bearer is part of God's accoutrements. The name bearer is dedicated to God.

CHINWENDU: (F) God is the cause of life and has power over life. God is earnestly asked to grant the name bearer well and long life.

CHINWEUBA: (M) God is the cause of wealth, procreation and prosperity. God's benevolence is extolled. The name bearer arrived when the status of the family was enhanced. The name is also a reminder that God can also strip one of such successes and hence calls for humility. The name bearer is an embodiment of success and humility.

CHIZOBA: (M) Chukwu zoba; May God continue to protect. A plea is sought for the protection of the family/name bearer.

CHUKWUDI: (M) Chudi; There is God. God is omnipresent, omnipotent and omniscience. There is a reminder that no one can hide from God. The name bearer is a beneficiary of God's intervention. Family detractors are warned that only God can judge human beings. The bearer is thus wished well.

CHUKWUKA: (M) Chukwu ka dibia: An attestation that God is more powerful than (native) doctors. The birth of the child is welcomed and God is praised.

CHUKWUNWEIKE: (M) God is omnipotent; all powers belong to God; acknowledging God's supremacy. The delivery of the name bearer is a manifestation of God's power.

CHUKWUNYO:(M) Chukwu nyo cha; God is earnestly asked to re- examine the family's case. A reference is made to such circumstance and the family is prayed to live a fulfilled life.

CHULO: M) Chukwulozie: God's contemplation is eagerly sought as He knows the best for the family/name bearer. Apparently the despondency the family went through warranted the hope in God.

DUAKA: (M) Chukwudumaka; a plea for God's assistance to a live a successful life.

DUBEM: (M+F); A plea is sought for God's guidance and protection.

DUMEBI (M) Chukwudumebi; i am living by the power of God. A plea for God's protection and companionship is sought.

DUMEKWU: (M) Chukwudumekwu; God is my spokesman; an attestation of one's faith in God. The name bearer is dedicated to God.

EBELE: (M+F) Ebelechukwu; by the mercy of God. The deliverance of the name bearer is through God's mercy/intercession. God is extolled.

EBILI: (F) Ka ana ebili na uwa: Let us keep on living and relating with each other in this world. A plea for longevity, prosperity, unity and joy is sought.

EBOKOSIA: (F) A female variant of Ebosie; having been accused unfairly by a majority of people, God is looked upon to redeem the family. The name is a commemoration of such happenstance and also a testimony that God has eventually vouched for the name bearer/family, with the arrival of the bearer.

EBUKA: (M) Chukwuebuka: God is great. The birth of the name bearer came as a result of God's intervention. By inference the family went through various difficulties in the past. The arrival of the name bearer is joyously welcomed.

ECHEFUNA: (F) Echefunaife Chukwumelugi; never forget the benevolence of God. God is extolled for the deliverance of the name bearer. The name is an avowal and a vow.

ECHEZONA: (M+F) A variant of Echefuna; 'Echezona aka oluChukwu', Do not forget the magnanimity of God.

EDEBEATU: (M) Something unique: The name bearer is seen as an epitome of uniqueness; a variant of Odiatu and Ifeatu.

EGBOKA: (M) Chukwuegboka; Chukwuegbokalum; A reference is made to past difficulties that is now sorted out with the arrival of the name bearer. God is extolled for his mercy.

EGODI: (F) Egodigbo; Tracing the family wealth (money) to the past. The name bearer is thus born in the midst of plenty; a variant of Obianujuaku.

EJIAKA: (M) Nkemjiaka or Ejiakaedo: My infallible expedient; my trump card. The name bearer is this advantage. Eji aka edo: This refers to family consensus to settle disagreements.

EKWUE: (F) Ekwunife: Do not say anything. The name suggests calmness and being calculated in the face of attacks. The name bearer symbolizes peace. Ekwuromife: withdrawal of unpleasant comments by a family detractor, especially after recorded success of the family. A reference is made to such circumstance.

EKWULIRA: (F) Ekwulukaaralu: It is not ordained that everybody should be equal. A reference is made to a contention requiring the above representation. The name bearer is also seen as first amongst equals.

EKWUTOSI: (F) Do not castigate, mock and bad mouth someone. The name is a commemoration of such occasion and a plea that such untoward comments should stop and not affect the family/name bearer.

ELEDIMUO: (M) The way it pleases God. The procreation and delivery of the name bearer is seen as a hand work of God.

ELOKA: M) ChukwuElokalum; Olisaelokalum: Reverence to God for his kind thought/ graces. The birth of the name bearer is a manifestation of God's considered will. God is thus praised.

EMEFIENA: (M) Do not transgress. Be upright hence lives a fulfilled life. A plea is sought for the bearer to have the fear of the creator and hence live long and prosper.

EMELIE: (M) Chukwuemelie: God has won. The arrival of the name bearer is seen as a victory over other people's dismal expectation.

EMENGINI: What have I done; a plea is made to be left alone in a peace to chart one's future. The name also connotes a warning to the family detractors.

EMENJO: (M) Emenanjo. Do not transgress, or go wrong. A plea is made for the bearer to live a model life and get the fulfillment of life.

ENEDA: (M) Kaanaenedauwa: Watching life go by; looking forward with hope. The name bearer's well-being is earnestly sought from God.

ENU BU ODA: (F) The vagaries of life; the name refers to varied circumstances in life with hearty times and grim and dreary times. A reference is made to such experience encountered by the family. The name also passes as a caution demanding that one should not forget God or be haughty when things are good as there could be bad times as well.

ENUKA: (F) Heavenly bounties are boundless. God is ennobled for his numerous mercies. The baby is wished well.

ENUMA: (F) Heaven knows what is in stock for everybody. God knows the best for the family/name bearer. A plea is sought for God's guidance.

ESSIA: (F) Ife mesia amalu; what transpired is now known. The name refers to past opinions or actions members of the kindred took and now subjected to review. The name bearer is named against this backdrop. A variant of Ifeme (m)

ETE: (M) Maduetenam, Onyeetenam: A reference to family feud with various camps casting aspersions and calumny on the other. A plea is sought not to be let down and likewise a plea to terminate such family disunity. The name bearer is a harbinger of truce.

ETUKA: (M) Etukobanaokwu; play down on disagreements and unpleasant things people say. A reference is made to such instance. The name bearer marks this new turn.

EYIUCHE: (F) Unexpected. Coming from background of certain position/problems, the name bearer was not expected. God is glorified for this deliverance.

EZELAGBO: (F) Emulating or taking after a unique character from an accomplished relation/member of the family. The name bearer is a pearl of the family.

EZIAMAKA: (F) Confirming that one's pathway in life is good. This is an attestation of God's benevolence especially on the delivery of the name bearer.

GBASIUZO:(M) Gbasiuzo: Follow the way which God has charted. A righteous life is thus sought for the name bearer/ family.

GBOLIWE:(F) Nwagboluiwe: The arrival of the child mitigated the anger borne by the parents against those that had derided the family .The name bearer is a symbol of peace and forgiveness.

GWAM:(F) Gwamnirum: Be bold and say it to my hearing (face). A reference is made to aspersion and calumny against the family that the family wants now to redress. The child is named after this incident.

IBEMESI: (M) Ibeemezinam: Folk should put a stop to their devilish and antagonistic attitude against the family. The child is named after this incident and is wished well.

IFEAKO: (M) Ife ako no obi: There is hardly anything that is lacking in the dynasty. The name bearer, a prince is prayed to live a fulfilled life of a prince.

IFEATU: (M) Ife atumelu: The delivery of the baby is a landmark. The name bearer is a source of joy and pride; A variant of Edebeatu and Odiatu.

IFEANYI: (M+F) IfeanyiroChukwu: Nothing is impossible for God. No problem is insurmountable for God. The delivery of the name bearer is an exemplar of God's mercy.

IFEDI:(M) Ifedioramma: A variant of Ifeira. The arrival of the name bearer is embraced by all. The long awaited has eventually come and the people are happy. God is praised.

IFEDIBA: (F) Kaifemelunu diba: Let bygones be bygones; forgetting the past. The bearer is named after such circumstances which mark a new turn to concentration, determination and progress.

IFEGBUNAM: (F) A plea is sought that no problem should reach a stage of killing another; acknowledging the struggles in life and passionately pleading that whatever problem that come the family way should be grappled/contented.

IFEME: (M) Ifemesia; ifemesia amalu: Taking stock after an unfavorable situation. The name refers to vexatious comment being reviewed to find out the roles individual played before deciding on what to do next. The bearer is named against this backdrop but no harm is meant against the family detractors.

IFEMENA: (F) A passionate plea that nothing sinister should befall the name bearer/family.

IFENJIORA: (M) A variant of Iwenjiora, something you hold against the people; A reference to injustice meted on the family that now warrants the comment. The bearer is named against this backdrop. The bearer is a symbol of forgiveness.

IFEUDE: (F) Something to be proud of. The name bearer is the subject. God is glorified for making this happen.

IFEYINWA: (F) Ife eyironwa; Onweroifeyili nwa: Nothing compares with a child. God is glorified on the delivery of the name bearer.

IFUNANYA: (M+F) Ifunanyachukwu: God's love and kindness. The name bearer is a product of God's kindness. God is thus extolled.

IGBEZE: (F) Igbandieze: The bearer is named after a musical outing that was dedicated to the monarch. The bearer was born during this period.

IGBOEGBUNAM: (M) May the people not harm or kill me. The bearer is named against the antagonistic attitude of the people and is thus wished well; a variant of Ibemesi.

IGWEZE: (M) Igwebueze: The power of a multitude is likened to that of a king. The name bearer is joyously welcomed as part of the multitude.

IKENNA: (M) A variant of Ike Chukwu: God's power; An attestation of the power and benevolence of God in the delivery of the name bearer.

IKPEDI: (M) The name refers to an outstanding case and is as well a commemoration of such outstanding case requiring judgment, which will favour the family. The bearer is named after this circumstance.

IKWEBA: (M) Ikwebuuba: Ikwe is a bulwark; A formidable defense. This defense is said to be the source of abundance. A family well protected, and not exposed to attacks will thrive well and have more children. The name bearer is a symbol of support and virility.

IKWUNNE: (M) From the mother's lineage: The bearer has features and characteristics of the mother's family; a variant of Ezeluagbo. As in ikwunne amaka; the mother's lineage is good. One often takes refuge in the mother's family. A reference to such event indicating the benefit of one's maternal link is established.

ILOANWUSI: (F) A prayer that the enemies of the family should not die such that they can retrace their steps and repent. The name bearer is a symbol of forgiveness.

ITO: (M) Itokili: This refers to being caged. This is a case of reincarnation of babies after death. The marks inflicted on them at death gives them away when they come back. With this identification the child is stopped from further reincarnation. The name bearer is thus welcomed to the world of the living.

IWEGBUNA: (F) A passionate plea that no provocation should kill one. A reference is made to various provocations the family was subjected to and followed with a plea for God's comfort. The bearer is named after such case and wished well.

IZUCHUKWU: (M) As a result of God's measured consideration; God is extolled for the deliverance of the name bearer.

IZUEGBUNAM: (M) The name refers to rancorous consultations; A commemoration of such meeting and an entreaty that the family/name bearer should not be hurt by the hatred generated in the meeting.

IZUKANNE: (F) Izukanan na nne: Confirming that agreement/concession can be reached easily by the children of a woman as opposed to different women. A reference is made to such circumstance, especially in polygamous homes. The child is wished well.

JIDE OFOR: (M) Whatever you do, be on the right. Reference is here made to untoward comments against the family. The name serves as a warning that further attacks would not be tolerated. The bearer is named after this family's new stand. The name also connotes a plea for God's guidance such that the bearer is fair in his dealings with others.

JUACHI: (F) Juba chukwu: God is my reference point. My creation and life is solely determined by him: The omnipotent. All questions about me should be addressed to God. The arrival of child is a testimony of God's good works.

KAMBILI: (F) Kwemkambili: A passionate plea for the family/name bearer to be left to live likes others. God is looked upon to keep the name/family out of the way of the detractors

KANAYO: (M) Kanayochukwu. God should be solicited and praised all the time. The arrival of the name bearer is glorified. This is an avowal for unbridled praise which God has poured on the family.

KANEBI: (M) Kanebinauwa: Holding on to life; Hoping that the fulfillment will come soon. A plea is made for a fulfillment in life of the name bearer; a variant of Ebili (f).

KAMME: (F) Kamelu: My disposition, My nature; my make-up. In other words, the way I am is the hand work of God. The name bearer is seen as God's special creation. Some difficulties prior to the birth of the child are inferred. God is praised.

KANODU: (M) Kanodunaeneuwa: Sitting and watching life go by; looking forward with high hopes. An entreaty is sought such that good things would come the way of the family/name bearer.

KAUWADI: (F) Obukauwa di: Is it the way life/world is? A reference is made to the injustice meted on the family. God is however looked upon to better the life of the family/name bearer. The bearer is named after such neglect and injustice.

KOSI: (M) Kaosi so chukwu kaosieme; God act as it pleases him. Everything that is or has been or will be, belong to him. His works are infallible. The arrival of the child coming after circumstances that initially proved difficult is a magnimous act of God. The child is dedicated to God. As in kosisoonye; kaosiso onyeka onaeme: It is the way that it pleases one that he acts. An entreaty is sought that family should not be antagonized. The detractors are also cautioned. The child is named after the circumstances warranting the family to act decidedly.

MADUABUROCHUKWU: (M) Human being cannot play the role of God; an inference that one's destiny can only be determined by God. Those that try to play the role of God are thus warned. The name bearer is dedicated to God and wished well.

MALUISIUWA: (F+M) Onyemaluisiuwa: Who knows the origin of this world. Who can fathom life? By deduction God alone knows as he is the creator. The poser calls for restraint of the wicked at heart. The name bearer is a symbol of live and let live.

MATAEFI: (F) A daughter that is adjudged accomplished and by marriage would bring a cow to the family when the need arises. Cow signifies wealth. By implication the name bearer is a harbinger of good fortune.

MBAM: (M) Mbaamaonyeukwu: Foreigners hardly recognize an accomplished man outside his town; A reference to the situation where the status of the family was neglected. The bearer is named after this backdrop. The arrival of the named bearer is highly celebrated.

MBENYEOGO: (F) Appreciation of a kind gesture. The name bearer is a kind gesture from God that warrants all our praise.

MEDO: (M) MedoluNwa; Meedebelu nwa. Ensure that adequate endowment is preserved for the child. Children are pearls and priceless gift from God. They are prayed also to sharpen their own endowments. The need for the name may have arisen because of past neglect by the kindred, thus requiring correction. The bearer is a paragon of support, stability and maturity.

MEMNOFU: (F) Memnofu: A plea for the travails of birth/other difficulties to pass by quickly; An inference of such difficulties during the birth of the name bearer. The child is wished well.

MGBOJIKWE: (F) Omemgbojikwe; Chukwu naeme mgbeojikwe; God acts as it pleases him and timely too. God's power and benevolence on the safe delivery of the name bearer is thus acknowledged and appreciated.

MMABUEZE: (F) The beauty of royalty. Beauty associated with royalty. The name bearer is seen as a cynosure of such beauty, and is joyfully welcomed. God is glorified.

MMAMELU: (F) A glorification on the arrival of the bearer. The name bearer is a bundle of goodness and joy.

MUKA OSO: It is my choice. It pleases me. Apparently the untoward comments on marriage and other issues against the family were burdensome. However, the delivery of the baby girl brought happiness and boldness to dismiss the earlier comments. The name bearer heralds new hope for the family.

MUKOLU: (M) Mukaolulu: It is my turn; my turn/chance has arrived. A testimony of God's deliverance on the family/name bearer is made. The name bearer represents this new turn and is wished well.

MUONYELU: (M) A variant of Mouweta: Caused by God.

NCHEKWUBE: (M) Kanchekwube Chukwu: Let me place my hope on God. A plea is made for the survival and well-being of the child.

NCHEZO: (M+F) Echezona; Do not forget God's benevolence; a variant of Echefuna.

NDALAKU: (F) The name bearer's arrival coincided with when the status of the family had improved considerably; a variant of Obianaujuaku. The name bearer is expected to have an advantage with the resources in place.

NDIBULUM: (F) What if other people are like me; a poser soliciting for good neighborliness, and unity. The bearer is an epitome of peace and progress.

NDIDI: (F) Ndidiamaka: Patience. The name is a reflection of the perseverance that leads to success and joy. The name bearer is the end product of this success and joy.

NDU: (M) Ndumma: Good life; Good health; such is prayed for the name bearer. An inference is made on the past poor health that visited the family. The power of God to provide one's needs, to protect, to guide, to forgive etc, is acknowledged. God is praised.

NDUBUILO: (M) The name refers to hatred associated in life. It is an acknowledgement of such and a plea that the family/name bearer is spared from such hatred and envy.

NDUBUISI: (M) Life provides grounds for future hopes; a   variant of Epundu. A plea is made for survival and longevity of the child.

NDUKA: (M) Ndukaaku: The life of a child surpasses other resources. A plea is sought for the survival of the name bearer.

NEBOLISA: (M) KaenebeOlisa; Looking unto God for the well-being of the family/name bearer.

NEBUWA: (M) Kaenebeuwa; watching life. In looking forward to prosperous expectations, the name bearer is welcomed and wished well.

NGOZI: (M+F) Ngozichukwuka; God's blessing is supreme. A plea for God's blessing. The name bearer is a blessing from God.

NKAKA: (M+F) Nke aka onye: Nkeakam; what you have sustains you. Be content. The arrival of the name bearer is welcomed and is seen as a source of contentment to the family. The name represents hope. God is glorified.

NKACHUKWU: (M) Nke aka chukwu: God's special creation. The name bearer is a gift from God that is well appreciated.

NKASI: Nkasi obi chukwu: God ameliorates, pacifies, and soothes. He is glorified. The name bearer is a product of perseverance.

NKECHI: (F) Nkechinyelu; Given by God. The name bearer is a gift from God. A glorification of God's benevolence is thus sung.

NKEM: (F) Nkemakonam: May what is mine not elude me. By inference all that is due the family is earnestly requested to come through. The name bearer is part of this paraphernalia and is wished well.

NKEMEFUNA: (F) May my efforts not be in vain or lost. A passionate plea is sought for the survival of the name bearer.

NKILI: (F) Ife nkili: An admirable subject. A cynosure of beauty; God is thanked for her arrival.

NKEIRU: (F) Nkeiruka; the best is yet to come. This refers to the family's faith in God. A passionate plea for the realization of these hopes is made. The baby is wished well.

NKOLI: (F) Nkolika; Consigning the past obstacles, vexatious comments etc. as bygones that are better told as story , especially when the family has been delivered from all those misdeeds. The name bearer is part of this deliverance.

NNAEMEKA: (M) A variant of Chukwuemeka; God has done well. The works of God on the arrival of the name bearer is thus appreciated.

NNAIFE: (M) Nnabuife; the Father is supreme; Praising God for his mercies. The name bearer's deliverance is the handwork of God.

NNAGOZIE: (M) May God bless? A plea is sought for the blessing of the name bearer and God is glorified.

NNAMDI: (M) Nnamu di: An attestation that my God is awake and by my side. God's mercies on the family and the arrival of the name bearer are extolled. Nnamudi could stand for a situation where the bearer is named after his grandfather; this is an attestation that the grandfather has come back to life or a replacement of the grandfather.

NNONYEM: (F) Nonyelum; Chukwunnonyelum; May God be with me. A passionate plea is sought for God's protection and guidance for the family/name bearer.

NONSO: (M) Chukwunonso: God is near/close by to the family. God's benevolence is praised for being close by and ensuring the deliverance of the name bearer from other obstacles that the family had faced.

NWADI: (M) Nwadinafo; A child is in the womb; an avowal of great things God had done in ensuring that the parents could procreate. God is glorified.

NWAFE: (M) Nwafenna; Nwafennaobuluisinka: Obedience to the father begets wisdom. A plea is thus made for the name bearer to be reverential and hence live good life. Father in the name represents both God and paternity.

NWABUILO: (M) A child often generates controversies/enmity. A reference is made to such contention against the family prior to the birth of the child. God is requested to ensure that such hatred does not affect the name bearer/family.

NWAIZU: (M) The name bearer is seen as a manifestation of God's consideration/consultation /grace; a variant of Izuchukwu.

NWAKA: (F) Nwaka ego; A child is more valuable than money. God is praised for meeting the family's desire for a child. To them the child is more than a pearl. God is magnified and glorified.

NWAMAKA: (F) A child remains ever important. God is extolled for the deliverance of the bearer. The attestation of the benefits of a child is made.

NWAKALO: (M) Nwaka alo; a male variant of Nwaka ego. A child is more valuable than the acquisition of a title. God is praised for the delivery of the baby boy.

NWANDO: (F) Nwabundo; An attestation that a child is a source of shelter, peace and joy. God is praised for these benefits.

NWANKIE: (M+F) Nwabiankie; the child came on his/her own. The child has his own life/world. A plea is sought that no negative influence would detract the child's progress.

NWANNEKA: (M+F) The bond in having blood relations is highly priced; the name bearer adds to this bond.

NWANNA: (M) God's son; the child is dedicated to God; a variant of Nwachukwu.

NWAMALUBIA: (F) The child knows the circumstances on ground and came. The circumstances could be assorted difficulties of which the arrival of the child ameliorated. The arrival is joyously welcomed.

NWAGAZIE: (F) A passionate plea is made for the travails of birth to pass by quickly and for the child to survive. The name bearer is thus wished well.

NWANYIFE: (F) Nwanyibuife; acknowledging the importance of woman. The arrival of the baby girl is welcomed and God is praised.

NWAOGWUGWU: (M) A child that came through the intervention of deity. Prayers are often offered to 'ogwugwu' shrine for a child. The birth of the bearer is seen as an answer to such entreaty.

NWAUFO: (M) Nwabuufo; Nwabuufonna; A child is a goodwill from God, the Almighty father. God is glorified on the arrival of the name bearer.

NWESE: (M) Nwaeseokwu; Nwadieseokwu. There is no dissention. The name bearer is an epitome of peace, truce and tranquility.

NWAINYA: (M) Nwabuinya; A child is a resource to show off; a variant of Nwabude. God is praised for making the bearer, the show piece to happen.

NWOBU: (M) Nwaobuora; A variant of Obiora. The name bearer is welcomed by all and God is glorified.

NWUDE: (F) Nwabuude; A child is an object of pride. In acknowledging this pride made possible by God, the name bearer is wished well.

NWUME: (M+F) Nwaume; Refers to travails of birth. The birth of the name bearer came with much difficulties; a reference is made to such pains. God is looked upon to see the name bearer/family through difficulties in life.

OBIAGELI: (F) Obialugeliaku; having arrived to enjoy life. The bearer arrived when the status of the family had considerably improved. A passionate plea is sought that the baby will survive and enjoy this status/wealth.

OBIAGWUNCHA: (M) The lineage thrives; the lineage is not extinct. The delivery of a male child guarantees the continuity of the lineage. The birth is celebrated.

OBIAJULU: (M+F) Obiajulugom; my heart is at peace. The arrival of the bearer cooled off the anxiety of the family. The name bearer is seen as a symbol of comfort.

OBIAMAKA: (F) Obi Chukwuamaka; the wishes of God are glorified. The bearer is the wish of God.

OBIANAMMA: (F+M) Obialunamma; arrived when things are good. The name bearer is prayed to enjoy this new found wealth; a variant of Obiageliaku.

OBIANEZE: (M+F) the bearer arrived during coronation and is thus named and wished the best in life.

OBIANUJU: (F) A variant of Obianamma. The bearer arrived when the family's status/wealth had considerably improved. The name bearer is wished longevity to enjoy this new found wealth.

OBIEKWE: (M) Obi Chukwuekwego; God has consented. The name bearer is seen as result of God's determination and ordinance.

OBIDI: (M) Obidigbo; Tracing royalty to the forebear. The bearer is seen and wished to possess royal traits like his ancestors.

OBIDIKE: (M) The heart of an accomplished man. The name bearer is this 'heart', the pride and pearl of the family and thus is wished well.

OBIDIMMA: (M) The family's lineage is proclaimed well hence the arrival of the bearer. A plea that the name bearer lives long to enjoy the bounties of this world is sought.

OBIKWELU: (M) Obi Chukwukwelu; confirmed by the seat/domain/kingdom of God. The name bearer is seen as a product of God's confirmation. He is thus dedicated to God.

OBINNA: (M) Obi Chukwunna; the father's wish. The delivery of the name bearer is seen as such and God is glorified for his benevolence, despite earlier doubts, worries and castigations that the parents experienced. God was on their side.

OBIOZOR: (M+F) Obianaozo; the arrival of the child was during the ozo initiation in the family. The name bearer is thus named after this family status enhancing occasion.

OBUME: (F) Obumumelu; A variant of Obura below.

OBURA: (F) Obumramebeife; Obumramebeajoife: Did I create a precedent? I am not the only transgressor. In making it bold to ignore other people's negative views on the family errors, God's forgiveness is sought, and the name bearer is wished well.

OBUSOM: (F) Obusom me; A variant of Obura.

OBUSOME: (F).Obusom me: A variant of Obura.

OBUZOME: (F) May whatever comes first be. An overstretched disagreement defying settlement within the kindred warrants this articulation. But let there be peace. Let by-gone be by-gone. The name bearer is a harbinger of truce.

ODAFE: (M) Odafe is said to be of Benin origin.

ODERA: (M+F) Chukwuedera: What God has ordained. The name bearer is a product of this ordination and is wished all the protection from God. The name originally was a title name but is now a general name.

ODIAKOSA: (M) Odinaka Olisa: Everything is left to God. Committing all the family's cares to God; God is looked upon to be the fortress and refuge for the family /name bearer.

ODIATU: (M) Something unique: The name bearer is seen as something unique and made possible by God; a variant of Edebeatu.

ODIESE: (M) Odieseokwu: There is no disagreement. Whatever that happened, for the rancorous past, the family's position is neutral. The name bearer is a source of joy and peace.

ODIMOKIKO: (M) I cannot express my heartfelt appreciation enough. The arrival of the name bearer warrants such appreciation. God is glorified.

ODINFE: (M) Odinfeanyialo; Looks light but is heavy; a case is pressed not to judge someone by his looks. The name bearer is thus seen as a man of substance.

ODINKEMALU: (F) I am ignorant of all that had happened, especially the alleged accusations. God is seen as all knowledgeable and by His wisdom the family expects to be exonerated and to live a fulfilled life.

ODINACHI: (F) Odinachi; Odin aka chukwu: Everything depends on God. The welfare of the name bearer is prayed for despite the negative machinations from the family detractors.

ODISA: (F+M) Odiisaokwu? Odiro isaokwu: Is it necessary to react to provocation. There is no need for such reaction. A reference is made to past vexatious comments against the family. The arrival of the name bearer was an instrumental testimony in not reacting to the vexatious comments. The name bearer represents wisdom.

OFOBUIKE: (M) Right is might. God's power is extolled. A reference is made on a situation where shame was brought to the enemies of the family. The name bearer is a paragon of tenacity.

OFUCHI: (F) Ofuchinaenye: Acknowledgement of the uniqueness of the Almighty; the power of procreation comes from God. God is thus extolled for his benevolence for the delivery of the name bearer. Or in OFUCHI: Ofo Chi Odi: God's goodness no doubt supports our exsistences. An opportunity to see a new day reflects the meaning of the name. It further follows that the blessings, successes and victories gained counter the past difficult situations. The name bearer is wished calmness, composure, good health and longevity.

OFULUZO: (F) Someone who has missed his way. This is another reincarnation related name. Upon identification of the coming again of the child, an earnest plea is made to God for the child not to go back to early death. A plea is made for the longevity of the name bearer.

OFUNNE: (F) Ofunneka: The solidarity of children from one mother is affirmed, a variant of Izukananne. A reference to such circumstance that confirmed this solidarity is established.

OGABU: (M) Ife chukwukwulugabu: What God has ordained would be. The name bearer is a product of God's ordination and is wished well. Or ogabu onye kaome lu kaodimma; who would calamity visit such that there would be peace in the family? A reference is made to some dissension within the kindred that defied immediate settlement. The poser calls for life and let live. The name bearer is a symbol of peace.

OGADI: (M) A passionate plea for the survival of the name bearer. Apparently, the family experienced child mortality. As in Ogadimma; all is well. The bearer is seen to herald good fortunes.

OGANUSI: (F) Oganwusi; when we are all dead; is it when we are all gone? This is a poser calling for right things to be done while we are alive; a poser to be fair when we are living in a borrowed time; a poser for salvation. The bearer is named against the background requiring that truth prevails.

OGBENYEANU: (F) The name bearer is a pearl out of reach for marriage by poor people. The name bearer is highly priced and favoured by the family; A treasure rich and rare.

OGECHUKWU: (F) Ogechukwuka. God's time is the best. The arrival of the name bearer is seen as an ordination from God. It could be inferred that the family had some encumbrances but continued to hinge their faith in God.

OGUGUA: (M) Oguguoam akwa: My comforter. The name bearer is seen as a comforter and answer to the family's problem/difficulties/sorrows. The name bearer represents a new positive turn for the family.

OJEBETA: (F) Ojebeta kwudoluonye nya: A sojourner that meets up someone that started yesterday. The name is associated with reincarnation. No sooner the subject is identified, he/she is pleaded with to stay back, that is to stop reincarnating and hence live a full life.

OJINI: (F) Ojinika: What you have and hold is an advantage. The child is the subject who is likened to a treasure. Children are seen as priceless gifts from God. The male variant is Ifejika; Ife eje aka bunwa.

OKOLOMA: (M) Nwokolooma: the bearer is a cynosure of handsomeness and is wished all the virtues that will make him a model. God is praised.

OKUBUILO: (M) Wealth often attracts hatred. A reference is made to such happenstance. A plea that such hatred does not affect the family/name bearer is also sought.

OKUE: (M) Okomuefuna; May my share/place/right not be displaced. A plea is sought such that the bearer's right in life is secured.

OKWUDIBA: (F) Okwudibaluonyekwulie; forgetting all the contentions/disagreements. A plea is made that such contentious circumstances should be put to rest. The bearer represents a new turn to forgiveness.

OKWUEGBUNAM: (F) May rancor not hurt me. The rancorous past animated so such schisms. The name bearer, a female is prayed not to be hurt as is seen as a harbinger of truce/peace.

OKWUONICHA: (F) The name refers to a particular Onitsha dispute. The bearer is named after the dispute.

OKWUTULU: (F) Unresolved disputes abound: A commemoration of unresolved problems of the family. A plea however is sought that no negative effects resulting from these disputes should affect the family/name bearer.

OLILI: (M+F) Ife olili melu; something so savor. The arrival of the name bearer warrants all the entertainment and God is praised.

OLOKPO: Nwaolokpo; Ripe and blossomed. The name bearer is a cynosure of beauty.

OLOLO: (M) Ife lo ma oloro: Whatever happens, life must be cherished. The name pertains to reincarnation. The subject is pleaded with to make his/her case known. That is whether to stay or not.

OLUCHUKWU: (F) The work of God. The bearer is seen as such. The name bearer is dedicated to God.

OMEDIKE: (M) Omelu dike: Ife melu dike. A good thing has happened to a war lord. The child is the subject and the arrival is joyously welcomed.

OMULUZUA: (F) Whoever that brings a baby into this world should train the baby. A reference is made to non-acknowledgement of the family's efforts in training other children that are not theirs. The name bearer is named after this happenstance.

ONUILO: (M) This is another reincarnation related name. The remains of children are normally buried in the village square-onuilo. The child believed to have reincarnated is named onuilo. By this identification he is solicited not to depart as soon as his design is now known.

ONUONICHA: (F) The voice of Onitsha people; the wish of the kindred. The birth of the child was the yearning of the people and by deduction, the marvellous work of God.

ONWUEMENA: (F) A plea is made for death not to strike. The name bearer is wished long life. By inference the parents had experienced deaths, hence a plea for death to stay out.

ONWUATUALO: (F) Death does not reason with its victim. An inference that death strikes at will: hence a plea for God's intercession to save the name bearer/family.

ONWUELINGO: (M) Death defies bribe: Acknowledging that death strikes at will and could not be checked by gratification, it is a prayer that death shall not visit the family/name bearer too soon. A plea for longevity is sought.

ONWUNACHU: (M) Death is on the hot pursuit. God, the giver of life is prayed to save the family/name bearer from the pangs of death. A plea for longevity is sought.

ONWUSELUAKA: (M) A plea for death not to lay its hands on the name bearer. The bearer is wished long life: The corollary is Chukwura. May God spare the life of the baby?

ONYEARI: (F) Onyearinam. May I not be chastised; a reference to contentious circumstance which the family wishes to be absolved. The name bearer is named after this and he is wished well.

ONYEIBO:(M) A companion: Usually the first male child of a man without brothers is named Onyeibo. The name bearer is seen as the second person as the name explains.

ONYEKWE: (M) Onyekwelu: who will agree? A reference is made to disputes with warring parties taking opposing views. God's intercession is sought. The bearer is named after such circumstances and represents a new turn.

ORAFU: (M) Orafugo: The populace has seen and witnessed the delivery of the bearer. God's benevolence is extolled. Vexatious comments are laid to rest with the delivery of the name bearer.

ORAME:(F) Oraname: Devilish machinations are prevalent in the society- the populace. The name is a commemoration of a particular evil design against the family. All hope is thrust upon God to protect the name/family; a variant of Ibeneme.

OSEKA: (M) Olisaeloka; Olisaelokalum: God's considered thought. The name bearer is the subject and God's contemplation is praised.

OSITA: (M) Ositatadimma odigbo: It is never too late to mend. The name bearer is the beginning of the better times.

OTITO: (F) Otitochukwu: God's praise; the name bearer is seen as such and God is praised.

OYIBOKA: (F) The advent of Europeans brought in its wake civilization. Medicine is part of it. The bearer's deliverance was facilitated by modern medicine. The bearer is named after this and other life saving measures brought by Europeans.

OYILIEZE: (F) Regal in appearance. The name bearer is seen as such and is thus wished good fortunes and other distinctions of a king.

SELUOGU: (m) Obumseluogu: Was I the one that caused the fight; a reference to a hostility which the family would like to be absolved from. The bearer is named against this backdrop and seen as an embodiment of truth.

SOMUADINA: (M) May I not be alone. The plea could derive from untimely past deaths in the family or arrival of the first baby. The troubles the family went through is compensated with the birth of the baby boy who is prayed not be alone and to maintain the dynasty.

SOMKWUE: (F) Solumkwube; an entreaty is sought for the kindred to join the family in proclaiming the good works of God. The name bearer is this showcase.

SOMTOCHUKWU: (M) Solumtobe Chukwu: Join me in praising God. The arrival of the bearer is welcomed and God is praised.

TOBECHUKWU: (M) Praise God. The arrival of the bearer is welcomed and God's benevolence is praised.

UBAKA: The more the merrier. The name bearer is thus welcomed into the large family. This is an attestation that the people are priceless resources.

UBANYIONWU: (M) Uba anyiro onwu: Death defies wealth and multitude. A reference is made to a circumstance whereby many deaths were recorded despite the wealthy states of the people at a time God is looked upon to save the name bearer.

UCHEANU: (F) Ucheanuife: One's preoccupied thought often is shielded away from advice. A reference is made to a circumstance where advice was not heeded by warring kindred. The name bearer is a counsel to be sensible and the bearer is a symbol of discernment.

UCHENNA: (M) Uchechukwunna; God's considered thought. The name bearer is a result of such opinion. God is praised for this benevolence.

UDEKWE: (M) Udemekwe; my pride and glory have blossomed. This is a case of one's efforts come through. The arrival of the name bearer is the pride that is glorified. The parents are thus happy to see their offspring.

UDENNA: (F) Udeegbuna; A variant of Udensiegbuna or may my pride not hurt me; the latter call for humility. The bearer is an epitome of humility.

UDENSI: (M) Udensiegbunam; A plea that diabolical trappings should not affect the family and the name bearer. A reference is made to hatred, rancor and devilish attitude against the family prior to the delivery of the name bearer. The child is thus wished well.

UDEZULU: (F) A variant of Udemezue: My pride has blossomed with the arrival of the name bearer. God is extolled.

UKETU: (M) Uketuonyeonuozuenyaaru; When a man has waded through many difficulties he becomes impervious to difficulties. He is undeterred to problems. This is likened to may your road be rough. This makes a man. The name bearer is wished well.

UMEBE: (F) Ume nwaebego; the difficulties of procreation are over with the arrival of the name bearer. God is praised. The name bearer is seen to open way to other births.

USOBU NANDU: (M) Good neighborliness is better cherished when the parties are living. A reference is made to family contentious circumstances warranting the assertion that good relationship are better savored when the people are alive. A plea for fraternity is thus sought and the bearer represents peace.

UWADI: (M) Uwaadinchekwube: The world is not firm to be relied upon. This is a pointer that life is ephemeral. A plea for longevity is thus put to God and the bearer is wished long life.

UWAOMA: (F) Good life. The bearer arrived when the family problems had been considerably reduced. A plea is sought that the name bearer will enjoy the bounties of life.

UZOAKA: (F) Uzoamaka; an attestation that a sojourn undertaken by the family was fruitful. The name bearer is part of this bounty. God is glorified for this.

UZODIMMA: (M) The male variant of Uzoamaka above.

PHRASES

KAME KA IME: May I do as you have done. This is erroneously associated with food and that Onitsha people do not sincerely invite people to join them while eating. This aphorism is better explained as follows:

It is customary for the head of the family to break kolanut and pray over it in the morning. Where a man visits another in the early hours of the morning – 'igba uzo' the friend being visited will naturally ask if all is well. Upon answering by the visitor, the host would come up with the expression – 'kame ka imelu' – signifying, 'let me do my morning rituals as you did before coming to my place'. It is only after the prayers that the visitor introduces his mission.

ONWERO IFE NTI NU KPOCHI: There is hardly anything heard by the ear that would make it go deaf. The speaker is unmoved and impervious, to the litany of woes. In taking up the gauntlet the speaker has also thrown down the gauntlet. Further inference stresses the fact that those with the courage to act can overcome the most daunting obstacles.

OKUKU EGOLU OFU NA EJI OFU UKWU AKWU:A newly bought fowl stands on one leg in the new abode. Standing on one leg implies instability. When related to humans, the person in a new environment studies it before he becomes streetwise and stable. It also serves as a counsel to look before leaping.

OKE GBABALU NA ONU CHOLU OGU OKWU: The rat that runs into a hole provokes the use of hoe. What you consider a safe action when the subject has erred is often visited by another unpalatable action. The phrase serves as a warning to miscreants that no matter how much they run/hide, the long arm of the law would sooner catch up with them.

ONYE NYULU NSI KA OJEKO UYI/NKISI GA EKWUDO MA ONAKO IMILIKITI IJIJI:A man who defecates on his way to the stream will meet the nuisance of flies on his way back. By implication, one cannot run away from his guilt. This serves as a counsel to be judicious.

IMA AKWOM NA AZU UKWUM ANA AKPU NA ANI: You do not give me a piggy back with my feet dragging on the ground. Piggy back is likened to support whereas feet dragging on ground implies compounded problems. Here is a case of ineffective support/solution to an existing problem. The speaker expresses his disdain for half measures.

IFE AFULU NNE EWU NA ORU KA AGA AFU NWAYA: What you observe in a she goat's private part is similar to that of her female siblings. This is a case of all tarred with the same brush and sharing the same characteristics. The negative connotation infers that young ones are most likely to take the bad habits of their parents.

MMA NOKWO NA UKWU UDALA LACHA ICHUCHU: How would I be around the sherry tree and eat unripe sherry. By connotation, a person in midst of plenty need not suffer. The speaker objects any benefit that is not commensurate with his status/position.

NKITA GA EFU ADI ANU UKPOLO OFIFE DI NTA:A dog that will go astray will not heed the whistle of the hunter. This is a caution to miscreants on the consequences of obstinacy.

NWANYI DI IME AMAGO NA OMARO NWOKE:A pregnant lady cannot claim virginity. This refers to things that cannot be denied or covered, thus it serves as an exhortation to young ones to be of good behavior. A variant of Ada ekpudo afo ime aka: You cannot cover up a pregnancy.

ONYE MELU AJO IFE NA ATULU AMUMA EGWU: One that commits grievous offence is afraid of lightning. This is a case of a person fretting about his guilt. The speaker by the expression absolves himself or points out the guilt of another person.

IYO NWANYI NA AMU NWA OTU: Asking for sex from a woman in a delivery room. Asking for something from someone in pains, distress or from one that is incapacitated is bound to fail. This is an off-colour aphorism that urges people to make reasonable demands.

ONYE ASI KWANA NA NWUNYE NNIA JELILU AKWA NA IRUE, ARU YA WE KWULU OTO: Let no one say that his father's other wife adjusted her wrapper in his presence hence he became randy. This is a case of giving a lame excuse to justify one's desire. It serves as a counsel to be principled.

ADA EJI AKPATA ETUFU ABU OGALANYE: You do not build up resources, misuse them and then expect to be rich. This serves as a caution not to be wasteful.

AGADI AKA NKA NA EGWU OMALU AGBA: An aged person that still relishes on his past youthful desires (dancing). The desires range from lewdness, obstinacy, crime, back-biting etc. Such a person is considered unashamed. This is said derisively to the addressee.

OBU EZIOKWU NA ODUMODU BI NA AGU MANA ODI ATA AFIFA: Even though a lion's abode is in the grassland, it does not eat grass. Lions undoubtedly are carnivorous and their dominion in the wild is not in doubt. The corollary is that a person endowed with such prowess of a lion need not be hungry to the extent of eating grass. By this expression the speaker is unequivocal about his state of satisfaction contrary to what others may think.

OFU AKA EJI PIA NWATA ITALI KA EJI AGUGU YA: It is the same hand with which you use in spanking a child that you use is patting him. By inference, one is expected not to be too harsh.

AGA AFUSIA IKPU KPONYA ERE: You do not mistake a vagina for groin. One is expected to be unquivocal. It has same meaning with, call a spade a spade.

OKILIKII KA ANA AGARUBE UKWU OSE ADA ALIA ENU: You go round the pepper plant as you cannot climb it. By inference, the person referred to as pepper plant is firm, strong and powerful and any action against him is bound to fail. This expression is often said in a boastful manner.

NKPI SI NA OBULU NA OBURU IJE OJELU NA IKWU NNEYA, OMA AMUTA ETU ESI ESU IMI: The he goat says that but for his sojourn to his mother's clan, he would not have learned how to stick up his nose and upper lip. This is an act which the he goat employs in attracting female goats on heat. Learning this act from his maternal clan infers heredity. The subject asserts that it is no fault of his/hers.

ENE GBANARILU ONYA ANWULI KWANA MAKA OFIA DI OGBU: An antelope that escapes the trap should not rejoice because the forest is vast. A rogue that escapes arrest for now is likely to be caught in the near future. The expression serves as a caution on the consequences of crime. It is also an expression that life is not bed of roses as reflected in the adage – the forest is vast.

IKPOCHI OGIGE MA EWU GBAPUSIA: Locking the stable doors after the goats have bolted away. This is a case of late action and by implication one is expected to be alive with his responsibilities.

OGBU OJA NA EFICHA ONUYA:A flautist wipes his mouth. This is a case of one helping himself while performing a given task. It is often said in lighter mood and such act is not considered as a serious graft.

OKWUKWU BELU NA ANYASI, NWATA NWUA NA UTUTU: The owl cried in the night and the baby died in the morning. This is a case of premeditated action as against that of coincidence.

OTULU UKPOLO NA AFIA NA EKWO EKWO MALU KWO NA NWANNE YA NWELU IKE ISO NA NDI OGA EMULU ARU: He that throws stone in a crowded market stands a chance of wounding his relations. This serves as a caution to be careful, and to be pragmatic.

EGWU NA OGENE YI: The drum is together with the gong. Being together implies harmony and in agreement. This is said by the speaker to assure the addressee that he is alert. This is same as to have one's wit about him or to have a finger on its pulse. There is therefore no cause for alarm.

OKENYE SOSIE OCHELU IBEYA: The growth of adults is said to stall at a stage for young ones to catch up. Here is an admonition not to oppress a young fellow who over time could be in a strong position. One therefore is expected to be sensible.

EGBUSIE OKE/OKWA DI NA OFIA, OYILI OKE/OKWA AMALU NA ONWU FA ELUGO: When there are no rats/quails to be killed, their look alike figure that their death are imminent. This premonition calls for caution against wicked acts. It calls also for preparedness and circumspection at all times.

IGBA NJA MMANU: Producing superfluous palm oil. A child, perhaps the only issue is prayed for to produce "excessive oil" which infers progress, virility and good health.

NKU NWOKE KPATALU NA OKOCHI KA OGA EJI SI IFE NA UDUMMILI: It is from the set of firewood fetched by a man in the dry season that he will use during the rainy season. By implication one is enjoined and charged to work hard, as not to lack in life – any season.

ONYE NOTE AKA NA UKWU OSISI NNUNU ANYUA NYA NSI NA ISI: If one stays under a tree for a long while, the chances of the bird defecating on him is high. One therefore needs to get the lead off his arse in the sense of stop wasting time. This is an exhortation to be active.

EKILIBE IKE NWANYI EGBUE LUYA EWU: If you admire the buttocks of a woman for long, you kill a goat for it. This is a pointer that lust has a price. It also serves as a warning to control one's sexual desires.

ONYE AJUJU ADE EFU UZO: One who asks for direction to a place does not miss his way. It is better to seek clarification on issues before taking decisions. This is an affirmation that seeking counsels is not weakness. It is thus better to ask than to wallow in ignorance.

OMAKALU UTU OKPODO ISI NA ANI: Is it well for the phallus to hang down. Hanging down implies dejection. Things may not be that well, the speaker seems to say, but all hope is not lost. The upshot of the expression is that in any difficult situation perseverance is necessary.

UZELE ENYELUGO NTUFIA AKA: Yawning has aided sneezing. A situation that is presumed mild but triggers to something sinister is expressed by this byword. This is lamentable but it also calls for circumspection and restraint.

ODIGO KA ONYE NWENU GA AMA: It is enough for the owner to know. This is another case of going to the top of one's bent; a situation where one can no longer tolerate overbearing oppression, and antics. The addressee is thus warned to retract from his/her bad attitude or face the wrath of the speaker.

NWANZA NA AGBA MME KA ARUYA RA: The canary bird bleeds in relation to its size. When related to people, one is expected to act within his capabilities. The corollary is that one should not take more than one can handle. The speaker asserts by this expression that he is doing his best.

EKWE EKWE NA EKWE NA UTE EKWELE: Not agreeing all the time, lands one in a mat made of coarse ribs of palm frond. This is against a mat made of soft treated raffia. The pun is on ekwe ekwe and ute ekwele, which is not agreeing and rough mat. The aphorism implies that a stubborn child is more likely to be involved in bigger trouble.

EKWUE EKWE DI NKENU NA ISI: To much acquiescence is said to be associated with head nodding 'nkenu' bird. The addressee is seen to abase himself to a point of being foolish. This is an exhortation not to be gullible.

IFE ILI ADE EME AKAKPO: Ten things (encumbrances) do not happen (affect) a dwarf. With a height disadvantage, having other nine disadvantages is a killing. On the contrary as the saying goes, God would not allow those things to happen. By this expression the speaker asserts sometimes boastfully that he cannot be found wanting.

IFE NKWU GBATA KA DIOCHI GA EKOTU: The palm wine taper brings down whatever wine that the palm tree yields. What is realisable at a given time is what you use. In essence one is expected to plan with what he has. This serves as a counsel to be realistic.

DIOCHI ADE AKOSI IFE OFOLU NA ENU NKWU:
The palm wine taper does not disclose all he sees
while tapping. Apart from the fact that the volume
cannot always be guaranteed, he encounters wasps,
rodents, and at the near top of the palm tree he
surveys the surroundings with feelings of vertigo at
some stages. Definitely not all the experiences are
pleasant. In life, there are some things you ignore.
Some divulgences can easily offend others. The
expression thus calls for guarded utterances.

**NWATA LIE IFE ONA AMULU ANYA OLARU
ULA:**A youngster realising the desires that kept him
awake then sleeps. This is often associated with
lasciviousness. It is an admonition to young ones to
restrain lewd desires until they come of age.

EFI NA AGBA ONYE GA EGBUE ANA AGBA: As
the cow grows bigger the owner/butcher gets big too.
By implication, when a problem appears overbearing,
there is usually a matching strategy to counter it. A
stubborn child's attention is drawn by this adage, that
his obduracy will be matched by the same degree of
punishment or problems he will face later.

IKE NOMALU ANI AGBISI ADA AGBAYA: In
mastering the act of sitting, the ants do not sting the
buttocks. If you are well acquainted with the
circumstances, methods and opportunities in any
sphere, one is not likely to make serious mistakes. This
is a counsel to be alert.

ENE SI NA ONA AGBA OSO NA AWUNI ENU MAKA OMARO EBE ONYA DI: Antelope says that it runs and jumps because it does not know where the trap is laid. By inference, cautionary measures in whatever one does are very necessary.

OJI ONU EGBU OJI: He that cuts the iroko tree with his mouth. Such a person is a blunderbuss mouth. He could be a charlatan and as such should never be taking serious.

NNUNNU UGBENE YA NA AGALA ONU ADA EFE NSO NA ANI: The bird whose feather is highly prized does not like flying low. By implication, one ought not to expose himself to the enemy. He is expected to protect what gives him a cutting edge. This generally is to be wary.

ONYE ALA NA AKU NGBANU MAKA AGBA ITE EGWU ONWE NA AFIA: The mad man hurries because he is always having a dancing engagement at the market place. As the mad man knows his way to the market, the expression is a counsel not to underestimate anyone, even the mad man. A variant of onye ala na uche ya yi; The mad man has his senses.

OKOKOPLO MA OSO MA ONA ESI NNI MALU NA INU NWUNYE ATUNYEGO NA UKWU: If a bachelor sighs while cooking you better know that his getting married in near. Though self explanatory, the expression is an exhortation to do things at the right time is one of things to consider when one is of age.

MBOSI ONYE TETALU ULA BU UTUTU YA: Whenever one gets up is his morning. This serves as a consolation that all hope is not lost. This philosophy is now challenged by postulating that one who gets up by midnight stands the chance of being alone. In other words one has to be abreast with what is happening around him and take timely actions.

AKPURUM MMILI NA ONU:I am not holding water in my mouth, One who holds such water does not express himself well, whereas who one does not, is clear in his expression. This aphorism is said with all seriousness to the addressee. The decisiveness of this phrase serves as a warning to the addressee to mind his business.

ANU NA ENWERO AGBA ATAGBUKWANAM:A plea that an animal without jaws should not devour one. By inference, minor problems are not expected to weigh one down. Likewise something undignified and unbefitting ought not to ruffle one. The speaker of the expression is thus bracing himself.

OYA BENATA OFEKE OCHEZO DIBIA GWOLU YA: When an ailment is mitigated, a fool/scallywag forgets the herbalist that treated him. There is a general tendency by people to forget past problems as soon as they are sorted out. The addressee is considered an ingrate.

UGO EGBO NA MGBAGBU: The eagle has perched where it can be easily be killed. By inference, the die is cast. The fat is in the fire. The phrase signifies that a great deal of trouble has been incurred or great efforts have been put, and there is little now can be done but rather wait for the result.

KEDU KA OKUKU GA ESI NA EWELU ITE EJI ESI YA IWE, KAMA NMA EJI WELU GBUE YA: Surprising that the chicken holds grudge against the pot in which it is cooked than the knife that is used in killing it. This is a sheer case of misplaced anger.

AGADI NWANYI NONA EBE AKPALU NKATA OKPUKPU NA ELO NONYA KA ANA EKWU MAKA YA: An aged woman who is close to where bones are discussed figures that she is the subject. The old knowing that she is frail is bound to worry. This is said of one with guilty conscience.

OKUKU NA AKPA NNI NA ANYASI IFE SO YA:A chicken that feeds in the night heralds bad omen. Chicken come to roost in the evening.The foreboding expressed by the speaker, calls for caution and wariness.

ITALI EJI PIA NWUNYE IZIZI EDEBELU NA AKPATA KA EGEJI PIA NWUNYE OFU: The cane with the senior wife is flogged and kept in the ceiling would be used on the new wife. The addressee, often a stubborn child is warned on the scourge others before him had experienced. He is thus expected to be of good behavior.

ASO SOLU OKWA MAKANA NNIAFA SO NWELU OFIA: Benefit of doubt should be extended to the quail as his progenitors are amongst the owners of the bush. This is a case of seeking reprieve/exempt for someone when such reprieve was previously granted to another. This is a counsel is to be fair to all. What is good for the goose is also good for the gander.

ONYE NA AMARO ONYE KALILUYA BU EWU: He that does not know who is stronger than him is a fool. This is a cautionary phrase to size your opponent before spoiling for a fight and as well as to know one's limitations.

NNE EWU NA ATA NNI UMUYA ANA AMUTA: As the she goat chews the curd its offspring's watch and learn. The phrase usually has negative connotation that children are likely to pick up bad habits from their parents.

OKUKU NYUA ARURU ANI ACHUBA YA OSO:A chicken that farts is pursued by the land. This is another case of a miscreant with guilty conscience. The addressee is reminded that his ploys are known and as such he cannot get away with them.

DIBIA LIJUE AFO OBUA MMKPOLOGU NA AJO OFIA: A well fed herbalist uproots the plants in a dangerous forest without worries. The case of the higher the remuneration, the higher the risk/services is highlighted. Those seeking thorough services of an agent are reminded of the high bills they attract.

EKWUKA OKWU NZIZO, ONYE CHILI NTI ANU YA: When so much of the talks are made in low voices, the deaf hears them. A miscreant who is impervious to several private counsels is bound to run into bigger troubles. At the stage it would be too late to correct his ways. This is a warning that stubbornness does not pay.

OFU MKPISI AKA LUTA MMANU, OMETU TA NKPISI AKA NDI OZO: When one finger is daubed with palm oil, other fingers get smeared. By inference, one's action often affects other members of the family. The expression serves as a caution to the recalcitrant 'one finger' to be of good behavior.

ANYA KA EJI AMA OKA KALU AKA: By mere looking you can know a ripen corn. Looking in the phrase is associated with experience. With such experience one can decipher a stronger character in a man – a ripen corn.

IJU OGIGA IJU OCHICHA: One who baulks to move and also refuses others to pass him. By inference, the person is a spoiler; a dog in the manger.

CHINCHI SI UMUYA NA IFE DI OKU GA EMESIA JUA OYI: Bed bug told his kids that what is hot would be cold. The same turn of events is applicable in life. After the rain comes the shine. Obstacles may come in litany but are sorted out over time. The phrase enjoins all to be patient in adversity.

KWA MBOSI BU NKE ONYEORI MANA OFU MBOSI BU NKE ONYE NWE UNO: Everyday is for the thief but one day is for the owner of the house. Miscreants by this expression are advised that the long arm of law would sooner nab them, hence they should be of good behavior.

ANYA LISIE ONU EWELU LIE: The eyes feast first before the mouth eats. By implication one is expected to be circumspect and also to re-order his priorities.

MBEKWU SI NA NSOGBU ONWELU AMA ANYIGBUE MAKA IFIE KA OJI EBU FA NA AZUYA: The tortoise boasts that no matter the magnitude of his problems, it cannot crush him, hence he chooses to carry them on his back. By inference people are enjoined to persevere in their troubled times.

OBU EZIOKWU NA EWU ADA ATA ALU MANA EMEKPA NYA ARU OCHICHA PULUYI EZE: Granted that goats do not bite but in a state of desperation they bare their teeth. The goat in this aphorism has exhausted his capacity of endurance, A warning therefore that you must be careful about the fury of a patient man. You should also desist from deliberately hurting others.

IKE NKWUCHA ABURO UJO: Being circumspect cannot be alluded as cowardice. The speaker wants to establish his relevance and the addressee is warned not to take any undue advantages.

ANU ANA AGBA EGBE ONA ATA NNI: An animal who despite being shot at keeps on feeding. The subject, a man by implication is strong willed and single minded.

UZO DI MMA AGA NYA NGA NA ABO: If the journey is good, it attracts a second outing. This implies that any venture that is successful should be maintained.

EGWU RUALIA UDE ERUALIA: When the music (rhythm) changes the chorus also changes. Here lies a pointer that when the condition changes a different approach/strategy is sought to tackle it.

OJI NMA JIDE JI: He that holds the knife and the yam. Such a man is endowed with authority.

NKITA NINE NA ELI NSI MANA NKE AFULU NSI NA ONUYA BU OLI NSI: Though all dogs eat human waste, it is the one found with the waste in its mouth is the culprit. The phrase is an exhortation for kids to stay out of trouble and hence avoid the consequences of being caught fomenting trouble.

AGBISI GBA IKE OMUTA AKO: When an ant stings the buttocks it becomes wiser. When one goes through litany of trials/obstacles he becomes more careful. Experience is thus the best teacher.

ONYE KWE CHIYA EKWE: If one consents, his God would also consent. This is said to embolden people in despair. It heralds optimism.

ONYE NWE NWA ORU NA ALA: Who has the child being sexed by a slave, The slave as it were has gone beyond bounds. This is said in a fury about those not qualified but are trying to challenge the aggrieved speaker.

ONYE NA AMORO EBE MMILI SI MABA YA AMA AMA AMANI OKWUSILI: He who does not know when the rain started beating him is not likely to know when the rain stopped; a curious experience that signifies a state of confusion faced by the subject who is advised to know the facts on ground which will enable him to act wisely.

ADE EDEBELU ONYE JELU ASABA ANU OKUKU: Chicken is not kept for someone who has sojourned to Asaba. When the village shrine is propitiated – ilo ani – a chicken is singed and roasted and then eaten on same ground. Nothing is saved for anyone not present; an expression used in lighter mood that if you are away, you miss the action/fun/feast.

OGEDE NTITI ABACHIE OGEDE OJOKO:A situation where banana has outgrown and overtaking plantain. This appears unthinkable. The expression however refers to a case of neglect or sheer aggression thereby warranting a lower caste to appropriate what is meant for the higher caste. This is said with concern.

AKWUDOM ORI BU ORI: Aiding a thief is tantamount to being a thief. This is said as a counsel that no excuse will get you free in such instance. The addressee is thus expected to be of good behavior.

ADE AKPU MMILI NA ONU WELU NA AFU OKU: You do not hold water in your mouth while blowing flames. Such exercise leads to futility. By inference, the addressee is cautioned to be more committed.

AGU LOTE IFE OLILU OLA CHA MBOYA: When a lion recollects what he devoured in the past, he licks his nails. Remembering earlier successes makes one happy/content and hopeful even when the present condition is not favorable.

MMILI EKWE ONYE LIGO OGA EKWEYA LIDATA: If a tide is too swift for a man to move upstream, it will at least enable him to get back to where he started. This is a pointer that there is always a way out in any given difficult time, especially when a person has given his utmost best.

MBULU AYALU ONYE IRU MA ONYE AZU:A club thrown misses someone in front row and hits one at the back. This is said of an innocent being maligned. It serves also as a caution to people to be reasonable.
ONYE NDIDI NA ELI AZU UKPO:A patient person eats the best fish. A patient person also stands to be rewarded. The expression is an encouragement not to lose hope in any adversity.

DI NA NWUNYE DI NA ALO OFU IBE JI ABULU FA NNI: Where husband and wife are in harmony, one piece of yam could serve them as a meal. The emphasis is that, understanding, trust and love in any relationship is bound to be fruitful. The expression is also an advice for people to be patient and prayerful in adversity.

AMAKA NNI ESI IKE AGA EJI AGBONO WELU NOFIGAYA: No matter how hard the pounded yam is, the 'ogbono' draw soup will aid in swallowing it. This is a pointer that with support, the toughest obstacle can be surmounted.

OLAGIE NA EKU ANYA: One's eye brows being laden with specks/blinders. The phrase is directed to an errant/mischievous child who defied several cautions and as a result got himself into serious trouble. By his act, he is put to shame. He has therefore to bear the consequences of his guilt.

OKUKU CHUBAYI NA UTUTU, GBABA KWO MAKA NA IMARO MA OPULU EZE NA ANYASI: If a chicken pursues you in the morning, you would better run away because you do not know if it grew teeth overnight. One is expected to be wary at all times and should not take chances.

IKPE MA ONU AGBA ERULU: When the mouth is declared guilty the jaw collapse. The mouth and jaw are associated. By implication the shame/infliction caused by a family member (jaw) will affect other members of the family (mouth). The phrase is thus a counsel to contain a deviant's case before it becomes out of control.

NWUGO NA AGBU: The eaglet in chains. A phrase is used by the speaker to show that all may not be well but he is managing.

ATUNYE IFE NA OZO: Not contributing to the money used for 'ozo' title taking. The addressee would like to benefit from the efforts of others without his own contributions. He is seen as selfish and lazy.

ONYA NASIA APAYA ADA ANA: When the wound heals, the scar remains. The addressee, a rebel/an errant is cautioned on the lingering consequences that awaits his nonconformist attitude.

IGBA UZO NWUNYE ABURO IGBA UZO NWA: Early marriage does not mean early procreation. That you started a project/venture much earlier does not guarantee success. The expression by inference calls for commitment from inception to maturity.

DUGAM OLU ADE ENWE UGBO:A hired farm hand cannot claim ownership of the farm. The essence is that people should know their limitations and places in the society; a warning therefore to the addressee not to bring himself to shame.

NGWELE SI UMUNNEYA NA OKA MMA NAFA JI ODU WELU AKPA NKATA MAKA IFE ONU KWULU AJOKA: Lizard is quoted as telling his kindred that it would be better to discuss by wagging tails because what the mouth utters is awful, and besides the walls have ears. This means that discretion is paramount in discussing sensitive matters.

ADA ASI NWA MALUIFE PUTA NA ANWU: You do not advise a reasonable person to come out of the sun. The upshot of this expression is that if the reasonable fellow fails to do what is right, he bears the consequence of his action. It serves as a caution to kids to be of good behavior and to keep away from crimes.

ADE ANU ONU OFUONYE WELU ARA OLO: You do not hear from only one person and overrule/take decision. The expression calls for fairness of judgment.

NSI NZA EPU OSE OPUE ANUNUNGWE: Out of the waste of small variety of canary bird springs either pepper or small variety of garden egg. As this bird feeds on such fruits the outcome of their waste is determined. By implication, the consequence of bad behavior is obvious. The expression thus serves as a caution to brats to be of good behavior or else they will live to regret the consequences of their action. This could also be said by someone who is indifferent to whatever happens – good or bad.

IGBUE NWATA ODUDU NA ARU IGOSI YA MMEE MAKA ODIKA IKPACHA ANYA PIAGBANYI AKA: When you kill a fly that perches on a small boy, you should show the person the blood or else he thinks that you deliberately smacked him. The corollary is that there is the need to justify one's actions.

AGWO NA ADIRO ILE ACHILIYA NA AKA: The snake that has lost its bite/sting is easily taking by hand. When related to people, when a man loses relevance he is neglected and ridiculed.

MADU AMA ENWUSI OKE NA ELI OKE: You do not have the likes of rats and eat rat (elsewhere). Why bother to eat a lesser grade rats. By inference one should maintain his dignity. This is often said in fury by a speaker that felt insulted by young fellow (rats) having enough of these insults calls for disassociation from the rude young ones.

AYA AKALU AKA ADI ELI NGWULO:A war that is planned does not consume the (lame) weaklings. This simply means that if you are forwarned, or deeply involved in a particular task/exercise many catastrophe can be avoided and likewise all the necessary effort would be put in for the success of the exercise.

ATUCHAPUBA AKPU DI NA AJI, AJI AGBALU OTO: If you insist on removing all the rough edges (spots) on the skin, the skin becomes plain (naked). When you overdo things perhaps for perfection, there is always some drawbacks. A counsel therefore to be realistic and modest is advocated.

OBURO OKPOLU ONYE AFE OJI NA EMELI: It does not follow that he that calls in the police, wins the case. The addressee having high hopes of success/justification is cautioned to look before leaping and to assess the situation critically.

AGANA AGANYE AKA NA ANYA YA: Threading the corals/bracelets through their eyelets. This requires painstaking efforts. The expression is an exhortation to be careful and in doing proper things.

AZOTASIA ANI EWELU WE ZOTA UTE: Securing the land (floor) first before contesting for the mat. The corollary is that one ought to get his priorities right.

EJIRO UTUTU AMA NJO AFIA: You cannot assess the viability of the market in the morning. In fact the fate of any venture cannot be known at the initial stage (morning). This calls for perseverance.

ADA ENWESIA NKWA NA AKWA UME: You do not have high hopes/support and yet be depressed. A well placed person is not expected to suffer in the midst of plenty. By inference the addressee is charged to use the resources bestowed on him wisely.

ICHE YILU ENYI KA EJI ATU ENYI:A stone whose size is compared to that of elephant is used in throwing at the elephant. This is intended to have result. The expression implies that commensurate honour/respect/relevance ought to be given to someone's effort. It is a counsel to strive for success.

ITI IGWE NA ACHA ACHA: Smelting when the metal is not red hot. It connotes premature action. Meeting a woman who is seeing her period and believing that she would conceive is an example. The phrase serves as a counsel to be sensible.

JIDE KA IJI: Hold on to what you are doing. By inference the addressee is doing well.

MALU KWULU: Mind your stance. The addressee by this expression is not doing well. The phrase is a gentle caution to be alive with one's responsibilities.

ADE ANO NA MKPA NA AKPA AKWU: You do not pluck palm nuts when you are in a disadvantaged/distressed position. The pun is on mkpa (need) and akpa (pluck). This is an assertion by the speaker that he cannot get a work done because it is not convenient for him. This could also serve as a counsel for people not to undertake ventures that they are not prepared for.

AGE ELI MBEI MA CHI GA EFO: Mbei is a special prepared cocoyam that is cooked for a long time. Just like any other food, you cannot savour it until it is cooked. By extension, one ought not to rejoice until success is achieved. The expression also underscores the need for perseverance.

AKU AGU NA NTI, NTI ADE EZUIKE: If a mouthful of nuts is not finished, the cheeks do not rest. This serves as a counsel not to rest on your oars until you achieve your goal.

AJA EGBU EDI: Sacrifices eaten by deer does not kill it. One who eats something considered harmful and is spared is considered to have a clear conscience. The speaker wants to make it known to the addressee that any devilish machination fashioned against him will fail as he has not done anything wrong.

ADA AGBA AKA ALI OJI: You do not climb the iroko tree without aid. A feat of this magnitude – iroko climbing or other ventures calls for an assistance. This is an exhortation to a person dabbling into a venture without preparedness, to seek necessary counsels.

ACHUA EWU NA UBI OGA NA OBA:A goat that is chased out of the farm gets into the barn. This is a case of rascal ending up as a hardened criminal. The expression serves as a reproof and admonition that crime no matter the scale does not pay.

JI EJI MMA, MMA EJIE JI: If the yam does not cut the knife the knife cuts the yam. This is said in a do or dies situation. Having reached one's endurance capacity the speaker does not care what happens after.

KA EZE NWE IRA KA IRA NWE EZE: As the king has sovereignty over the people, the people also has right to be heard. This calls for sensitivity of the monarch on the yearnings of the people and the need to mobilize and carry the subjects along. Where the call is not heeded, there are statutes; the people can invoke to isolate the king.

MAPU ADE EGBU AWO: The toad is not hurt by its leaping. The aphorism suggests that a man should be daring to achieve feats, by the expression the speaker would like to justify his escapades.

ONYE KUCHILU NWUNYE NNAYA AMA AMA NA INU NWUNYE GALALU ONU: He who inherits his father's widow does not realise that marriage is costly. A person that enjoys freebies hardly appreciates the labour in making wealth. The expression is said of someone who does not appreciate the opportunities bestowed on him.

IFE UDENE JI ABU ONA AYI NWUNYE YA ONA ETI MKPU BU KA UWA MALU NA NYA NWELU UTU MAKA APURUBA NWUNYE YA AKOLU UWA NA OBURO NWOKE:A vulture is quoted as saying that when he makes love to his wife, he makes her to shout. This is employed to show the world that he has functional penis else the wife tells the world that he is a eunuch. This is a risque adage which by inference, one tries to establish a strong proof that a deal exist between him and the person, lest the partner reneges.

NCHI NA EGBU ONA EZE: As the grasscutter feeds, he is on the lookout. There could be a hunter or predator around; hence the grasscutter has to be wary/alert. By inference, circumspection is called for in all we do.

NWOKE NWANYI NA AFULU OJA NA AMA EGWE MUO:A man whose wife plays flute for ends up scaling the imaginary walls of the dead. The corollary is that a man that is controlled or manipulated by his wife is destined to be a failure.

IGA ANUSIA OGU KA NWOKE BIA BEBE AKWA KA NWANYI: WOULD you after fighting as a man then end up crying like a woman. Crying detracts from feats/bravery, but translates to dismal failure. One should call it quits before the failures set in. This is equivalent to quitting when the ovation is loudest.

NWATA JI ONOKO NKU AMA AGBANARI ANWULU:A child that holds a bunch of burning sticks must be ready to contend with the smoke that comes out of it. Who dares to take any risk must be prepared for the consequences if it fails. An exhortation to be careful is conveyed by this aphorism.

NWATA NA ATA AKARA NA ATA EGO YA: A child that eats beans cake is also spending (eating) his money. This is said as a reminder that anyone that relishes in any past time has a price to pay. The expression calls for pragmatism.

OJI AKA NA ABO ELI NNI AMARO AKA METOLU AFEYA: He that eats with both hands would not know which one that soils his dress. Such a person is not careful. The phrase serves as a warning to young ones to be careful otherwise they would face the consequences of their actions, connoted as 'soiling their dresses.

IFE KWULU IFE AKWUDEBEYA: Where one thing stands, another thing stands besides it. In Chinua Achebe's interpretation, the world of the Ibos is a world of dualities. There is no one way to anything. While there is one point of view, there is another. It is good to be brave but also remember that the cowards also survive. There is therefore no absolute anything.

UDENE GA ABU OYI EGBE KA OWELU MALU EBE OFIA NA AGBA OKU: A vulture must remain friendly with the kite in order to be acquainted with the latest bush burning incident. The guide offered by the kite is thus beneficial to vulture. This is a case of one riding on another one's back for personal benefit. The person is thus considered selfish.

OFU ANYA JI ISI UGWO: One eye is indebted to blindness. A person who is handicap as in having one eye, has no backup if the only surviving eye is blinded. By implication, lack of backup in any endeavour is not likely to be successful. The speaker thus harps on the need for a backup.

ANUALIA DI AROLIA UKA: When a woman remarries, her manner also changes. The new mannerism/attitude is intended to suit the new bridegroom else the earlier problems that marred the first marriage may come up. In general application, new strategies are paramount in a declining/comatose undertaking.

KWEM LA MMILI DEBE IKO: Allow me to drink water and keep the cup down. This is said by someone who is pestered by another, usually a child, to be spared some rest.

ORI NA EZU AMA ANA AGBA: While robbery is on, intelligence report on the robbery is also on. This is an exhortation that a thief is always trailed; hence the addressee is warned on the inevitable consequences of theft.

OJI AKWU NYE NCHI NA NCHI ADE ALI ENU: He that has palm nuts should spare some for the grasscutter because it cannot climb. The deduction is that we should be kind to those that are disadvantaged.

EBE OGBA OSO GBADEBELU KA OJE IJE GA EJELU: He that runs and another that treks eventually reach the same destination. This is said to remind one who is successful and boastful about it that others considered 'trekkers' are likely to attain same or higher success. The expression calls for modesty.

ADE EJI ODIKA ETU ORI: You do not accuse a person of theft by mere suspicion. The addressee is advised to get his facts right. Here is a variant of, do not judge a book by its cover.

ONYE JEKATA IJE NYA TUA NWONWO OSO MAKA IFE OSO EME: One should sometimes run than walk, just in case the need for running arises. The expression stresses on timely preparedness that is essential in life.

MBELEDE KA EJI AMA DIKE: It is by sudden events that a hero is marked out. This feat is not accomplished by bravado. It serves as a caution to self-styled brave men.

OKWU OCHU ADAGBU GO OKWU ORI:A murder case supersedes that of theft. This is said of any event where a more serious case has to be giving more priority. In general, one is enjoined to prioritise his tasks.

ONWERO IFE OKELEKWU GA EME ITE ONA: There is nothing a rat can do to an iron pot. This is said to warn an opponent whose action is considered ineffective. It is often said boastfully and to square off.

OKE AMANA UMA TA AKPA DIBIA MA DIBIA AMANA UMA BU OKE ONU: Let the rat not rent holes on the herbalist man's bag and let the herbalist not curse the rat. This serves as a warning to spoilers to stave off their deliberate attack. The expression thus sues for peace that is, live and let live.

IFE NA ABO ANA EMEJI BU ISIE NA ITE MA OBU IRUYA NA OKU:A yam is either cooked or roasted. This is said in fury when one is at the top of his bent and could therefore not care a hoot on the outcome of the case at point. By the expression the speaker dares his challengers.

IFE NA ABO OFU ME: Out of two things, let one happen. The phrase is similar to one above. The speaker could not care less on what happens – good or bad – especially when he has been frustrated.

OJE NKILIKA AKWA, JE NKILIKA OKWU: He that wears rag is believed to wear/speak-ragged words. A person that is frustrated and in disarray is not expected to have kind words. This serves as a reminder to the addressee on what to expect.

NLISIA NNE NKWU OBULU SIA UKETE: Having climbed on tall palm tree, a short one would not pose any problem. This is said by someone boastfully to maintain his relevance.

EBE EGBE ADANA NYA DA NA IRU OGU: Regardless of where a gun is shot, let it land in the war front. Were the shots to land outside the war front it would miss the desired target. The implied meaning of the expression suggests that whatever yields result irrespective of one's approach/strategy is all that matters.

AKWA OKUKU TIPIA AKU, IFELE EME OKWUTE: Where an egg cracks a nut the stone should be ashamed. By implication, if a minor/disadvantaged person performs a feat the elder/advantaged person should be put to shame. The expression serves as an exhortation to those at vantage positions to meet the tasks demanded of them or be put to shame.

NWANYI GBEDEBE UKWU OLIE DIYA: If a woman stoops, she enjoys (eats) the husband. By extension, a humble and obedient person is often rewarded by his/her guardian. It serves as a counsel to people to be well mannered.

NWATA AMA JE OZI OJE NYA NJE NA ABO: When a child does not deliver a message right, he runs the errand twice. This is a counsel to children to pay attention to what ever is expected of them and hence expect early success or else fail or experience prolonged tutelage.

ONYE KWELU NA IFE OTU KWULU ONA GBO: If you agree to (what the market says) conditionalities of the market you go home early. This is a call to be in the wining party hence achieving early success. By the expression, the speaker tries to disabuse the minds of dissent group of people.

ONYE NUBA ONYE ASABA ONYABA UGBO UCHICHI: When one is betrothed to an Asaba woman, he learns how to paddle canoe at night. The inference points out that one is very likely to accommodate the habits of the wife initially and probably be in agreement with his wife's view most of the time. It is a reminder of the influence of women on men.

IFE ACHI MELU IKE: What the nut has done to the anus. Swallowing/eating of this nut does not pose any difficulties unlike when coming out from the other end. It is counsel that things often considered innocuous could have dismal after effect. The expression thus calls for circumspection and not to underestimate any person/thing.

ANA ESI NA UNO AMALU MMA WE PUA ILO: It is exigent to be beautiful right from the house before extending the beauty to outside. Being beautiful from home is here likened to harmony whereas extending the beauty outside is likened to having competitive edges. The expression serves as an exhortation that unity at home influences one's cheerful disposition outside and both stand to guarantee success.

UDENE SI NA NWUNYE YA DI IME MUA NWA OKENE CHUKWU, MANA OBULU NA NWA ONA AMU NWURU NSOGBU ERIRO NNE: The vulture says that if his wife in labour gives birth to a child he would thank God, but if the child dies there is not much trouble. The dead child would serve as a palatial meal to him. This sounds uncompassionate. The expression is said by someone that has been denied his dues. While total payment of these dues would be ideal, the speaker does mind another arrangement as long as it provides for his meal.

ONYE IKENGA YA NA ADIRO ILE AWAYA NKU: If a man's spirit of fortune represented in statuette – carved wood work is no longer relevant/effective, it would be hacked into firewood. Where one's hopes, back ups or master strategies fail, there is no need for recourse to them. By this expression, people are expected to do their damnedest best to be relevant or else be irrelevant i.e. being hacked into pieces of firewood.

OCHUPULU ONWE YA NA UGBO SI NA UGBO ELUTE ROYA: One who deliberately excludes himself from the boat laments that there is no place for him. This is a case of lame excuse to cover one's inadequacies. The upshot of the expression is that one should use all the opportunities available to him.

EWU IRA NWE AGU NA EGBU: The goat owned by all and yet starves. This is a case of everybody's responsibility is nobody's responsibility. A situation where everybody blamed somebody when nobody did what anybody could have done. This serves as an exhortation for teamwork.

ADAMU ETI MUO ANA AKWA AKA:I do not associate with a masquerade that is being pushed. A masquerade so pushed or aided is no longer agile or effective. The speaker boastfully asserts that he does not associate with failures.

ANU MUO ZUE OKE MA NYA EJUNA AFO: Let the meat for the ancestral spirits be complete even though it may not be enough to satisfy the people present during the sacrifice. During Inyedo Muo: a ceremony to validate the Onitsha ancestry of the householder, some pieces of roasted hen and fish are offered to the ancestral spirits and after that, all attendees have a share no matter how small of the remaining fish and chicken. The same ritual is applicable when a shrine is propitiated. In today's parlance, the expression calls for contentedness.

ONYE NA AZO AKA ANU NA ABO BU KA OWELU NWETA OFU: One who contends for two hands of an animal (goat) intends eventually to secure one. This is applicable to one who aspires for a higher position, believing that at worst he would get a second best. The pith of this aphorism is that if you think big as against lower ambition, you stand a better chance in life.

IJIJI NA ESO EFI: The is a case of houseflies trailing a cow. The chief reason could be adduced from the remnants of the dung at the cows rear end, the soft/sore membranes of the ears and perhaps the special attractive odour to the flies. The expression underscores the reasoning/logic for any action.

ALO KA EJI EGBU OKPA OWELU GBA MMEE: You need to employ special tactics in killing a cock for it to bleed. For a feat to be accomplished you require a carefully planned scheme. The expression calls for perception.

UZO ESI EGBU OKE ERIKA: There are many ways in killing a rat. This could be achieved by trap, bush burning, clubbing etc. By implication a mischievous child is warned that there are many ways to check his pranks.

ONYE UJO ADI ESO DIKE:A coward does not accompany (associate) with the brave. This is often said boastfully by a person who wants to establish his relevance. He likens his adversaries to cowards that are not fit to associate with him.

IYI OKWULU ADE EGBU ENE: Hardly does sexual vows/oaths kill an antelope. By extension, such vows by men carry no death sentence. This is said to embolden and justify the escapades of men.

EBE OKU NWUZU AWUSA OWA: Where the light quenches you rest the local lantern made of palm tree fibres. By implication when you have put in your best efforts and success is still far off, you rest. The speaker would like it to be known that he is committed to carrying his responsibilities to the extent his resources can take him.

AKA DI ONYE MMA KA OGA EJI FILI ISI: It is the hand which is suitable to a person that he uses to rest his head. The person is free to live the way he/she chooses. The expression however has negative deductions that one would equally be ready to face any problems that emanates from his choice of life style. It serves as a caution that as you make your bed so you will lie down on it.

ONYE AMU DI MMA AMARO IFE ONYE IBI NA AFU: A man blessed with good male organ does not realise what the man with hernia of the testicles goes through. There is a general human tendency for people in good position not to remember the miseries others go through. The upshot of the expression is a reminder that any body can face tribulations hence one is expected to be kind to the less privileged.

ONYE NA ABARO NA MUO ADE ATA OGA: A person that is not initiated into the world of spirits cannot play the whistle/flute of the spirits. In essence, one is supposed to know his limitations and not to go beyond bounds.

NCHICHI MALU OKE IMI: The leech that eats away human lobes is warned to know the demarcation of the nose. Going beyond the nose affects the eyes which is more dangerous. People especially upstarts are warned not to go beyond bounds, else they will face the wrath of the speaker, - likened to being dangerous.

OKUKU MMANYA NA EGBU AGA AFURO UVU ALA NA APU: The chicken that is drunk is yet to see the fly/pest that is mad. By inference mischief makers are warned on grave consequences their actions will attract from law enforcement agencies. This is yet another counsel that crime no matter the scale does not pay.

OJI DI MMA KA UTU NA AGBA: It is the good iroko tree that is often affected by pest infestation. The good iroko tree is likened to a good man while the pest infestation is likened to cause early death. In essence good people are visited by early deaths. The expression is an elegy.

AROBA AJADU MADU AGU: Where one insists on looking for virgins there will be no maidens to marry. Seeking/searching for perfection is an uphill task. By inference human nature is beset with flaws and as such moderation is called for.

BULU UZO CHUA UVU INATA NA UNO KA IBALU OKUKU MBA: Driving away the chicken pest comes first before scolding the chicken at home. The pest being a parasite; the foe must be extricated before reprimanding a relation that exposed himself to the infestation. The nub of the expression approves of admonition in privacy, away from others regarded as pest/enemies. The need to priortise one's task is also conveyed by this expression.

DIKE NA ATA NSI ARU ANA EGBE: The strength of a brave man dissipates as he bears his burden. The brave may not show emotion while accepting pains. However, such resistance is short lived. The phrase is a pointer to limited human endurance. The brave also pines away with troubles. There is however no substitute to perseverance.

NWOKE NA IFE: Man and his various things (encumbrances). This is said to show that man's burden is much but despite that the speaker affirms that he is doing his utmost best to sort his problems. Life goes on, he seems to say.

EJUNA NA AGBONYU ONWE YA SI NA ONA AGBONYU OKU: The snail thinks that his salivation would quench fire and whereas there is no fire, hence he salivates on his body. Such is the world of day dreamer/foolish person. The expression calls the attention of the character usually children on the futile exercise they are engaging.

EKOBE EKOBE NTI ECHIE DIKE, MA EKOTUE NYA NTI EYELU: At the height of argument the strong willed is deaf but when things go wrong in the course of the strong man's action, his ears become open as to hear the voice of wisdom. By the expression, stubborn children are reminded of the consequences of obstinacy.

EKWE ONYE OYA NA AKA ITIOBI AGUBAYA: When you offer a handshake to someone that is sick, he pines for a hug. This is a pointer that too much familiarity brings contempt. It also serves as an exhortation for upstarts to know their limitations.

EGWU ADE ABIA BE ONYE ONA ALU EGENEGE: You do not need to tiptoe to watch a musical group that is coming to you place. Why rush for something that eventually comes to you or is yours. The speaker affirms by the expression that he is cool and calculated. It also serves as an admonition to young ones worrying unnecessarily.

EBE SOLU NWAGBO KA OGA AKPUNYE ALA YA: Where it pleases the woman is where she (inserts) her breast. The woman as an adult is thus free to live as she chooses. The adult that is bestowed with such freedom should also bear the problems arising from her choice of life.

EWU NUKA MPI EJIE NYA: No matter how much fight that is put up by a goat with its horns, it can be restrained. The goat in the expression refers to man. The expression is a pointer that prolonged rancor/fight has dangerous implications. To avert such dangers moderate approach is considered by the expression as a better alternative.

EBE ANA EJE ANA KA ANA EJE ATO: Where you go out and get back safely can also be a place you go and get stuck or run into trouble. By implication, we are reminded of the gains and losses, ups and downs, in life. It calls for preparedness, alertness and perseverance.

IMA EGBU NWOKE UTU, GBUE NYA AMU SI NA OGA AMU OFUOFU UNO EJU: You do not after destroying one's manhood wish him virility. By inference you cannot after making things difficult-spiking ones gun, thereafter pray for the person's success. The expression calls for reasonableness and fairness.

INA ACHU NKITA NA NSI IGA ELI: Are you driving away the dog from the human waste you will eat? Why deprive one from what you do not need or prevent other people from enjoying what you cannot enjoy. By inference people are required to be magnanimous.

ADE EJI AMU EYI AGADI NWANYI EGWU MAKA NA IMARO MA OBU IFE KALU YA NKA: You do not frighten an old woman with a male organ because you do not know if that is what made her old. Obviously the old woman is not bothered by the threat of what she is used to. Why then spoil for a fight you cannot endure. The expression is an exhortation not to push one's luck, which is not to take dumb risks.

IFE ADA AYA OKPO EME NA AFO: The belly (ache) is associated with worms. You cannot talk about belly ache without worms that lives in the belly. The corollary is that it is easy for someone close to you to hurt you. This serves as an exhortation to be careful of your friends.

NWATA TUTUA UKWA OTUTU NYE NA ONU YA: A child that picks seedling of breadfruit puts some in his/her mouth. The expression infers that reward goes together with hard work. This is similar to ogbu opi na eficha onuya.

NWA ADE EKWU NNEYA OKWU NA AFO: A child in the womb does not talk to the mother. The expression points to the fact that the child is not matured, as to hold his/her opinion and then to challenge his elders. This serves as an admonition to obstinate children to be respectful.

NWATA KA ARU USA OKA ARU UGBOLO: A young person that dares to pilfer must also dare to accept the (bodily) punishment when caught. The corollary is that crime does not pay.

NTI KA EJI AMA NWA ENYI: You identify a young elephant by its ear. The ear of the young elephant represents a feat. The corollary is that great people are known for their achievements. The speaker attests to the achievement of someone by this expression. It could also serve as counsel for the addressee to prove his ability.

ONYE ANA EKILI EKILI ADA ACHA NTU: Someone that is admired does not look pale (ashy). The person instead is bright, cheerful, lively, energetic, and has dignity. Where these features are absent, the man is dead. The speaker by the expression would like to maintain his relevance and keep his honor. It is also an exhortation for one to maintain his reputation.

OBURO MBOSI NWATA RUFULU MMANU KA ANA AJUYA, OBU MBOSI ORUFULU EGUSI: It is not the day a child spills the palm oil but the day he pushes down the melon seed that he is questioned. The expression is directed to miscreants who eventually graduate to hardened criminals. The upshot is that crime no matter how long it takes is not left unpunished. A counsel there from is for kids to be of good behavior.

UTU NA AGBA OJI, DI NA OJI: The pest infestation of the iroko tree derives from the iroko tree. By inference, someone who is close to you can easily betray you. The expression serves as counsels for people to be circumspect and watchful of friends and foes.

LIE EBUNU NA NNAI NA AKPA ATULU: One is asked to eat ram meat because his father breeds sheep. The person that is offered the ram meat by inference is pardoned/excused for the sake of his fathers honor and fame – sheep breeding.

EGBU DIKE NA IFE, EGBUE NYA NA NZIZO: If a brave man is not killed in the open, he is killed secretly or in the dark. An evil doer who considers himself as brave is warned that there is no hiding place and that nemesis would catch up with him no matter how long it takes in the day or at night.

MMILI AMA EFI ANYA: The rain has beaten the cow's eyes. The phrase connotes lamentation on something that is shocking and unthinkable. It is used as an interjection showing anguish on the failure of a person or project.

ANA ASI NA UMU OYA EZURO OKE ASI ODALU IBI NYA TO AFO: As if the ailments are not enough, the person with hernia of the testicles is asked to have bloated stomach. This is a case of having compounded problems. The speaker laments this situation. The expression is often used when life/things are getting tough.

AWO AMANYEGO NYABU IFE MPALA: The toad has leaped into the scheme. Leaping into a particular plan is an impediment to the plan. The speaker thus confirms the hitch in the scheme.

EGWU ADE ATU AFO OBULU UZO: The stomach is not ruffled hence it takes the lead. By inference the boldness and being in the forefront signifies clear conscience. A person with such principles fears no harm/evil. By the expression the speaker maintains his innocence.

EBUBO KA ONYA MMA ELO: An injury inflicted by knife is easily forgotten or well taken than an accusation. This is an admonition not to accuse people unfairly.

INA ACHU ODUDU KA OTA ONYE?:Who do you expect the sand flies you have driven away to bite? By inference one is expected to share not only the gains but the losses. The addressee is expected to be alive with his responsibilities.

OMELU AKA NA IKE SI ARURU PUA: He that fingers the anus induces fart. The finger obviously has gone beyond bounds. Whoever does not mind his business faces tribulations.

'NWATA ADI EBU ORIKA': A child dare not carry a heavy load; an expression showing disapproval when one is subjected to do something that is likened to a heavy burden.

ISI BUKA ORA OKPU: No matter how large a man's head is, a fitting cap can be found for it. There is always a remedy, an alternative.

ONITSHA JI AZU AWU: Onitsha man usually escapes through the back door: Onitha man leaves a troubled spot unruffled.

IRU DI NMA ADIRO NMA ITU MBO: A beautiful face is not good to be scratched. Do not mar a good relationship. Do not look for trouble where there is none.

UDENE FULU IBEYA AKPUONU: Vulture with goitre sneering at a fellow vulture with goitre. Before you criticise someone, take a good assessment of yourself The fault you find in others are most probably in you.

IFE ANA ACHO NA ISI JI BU AWAYA: The most important part of a yam head is where the stem sprouts. Have an eye for opportunities than trifles.

ADA AGHA ISI AKA AGBA ULIO: You cannot snap your finger without the thumb. You cannot avoid the principal character.

ITE WARI, ITE DI NA EKE: When a pot breaks there are others in the market. There is always an alternative.

ETUKOBA UGBO ANYA ENWE AWANYELIAJI: If one assesses a monkey by its eye sockets, one would boil yam for it. Do not judge someone by his/her looks.

ATUA OMIMI LIE OGEDE EMESIA MGUGBOYA ESELU ENU: A banana peels floats on the river even though the banana was eaten in the deep river. There is nothing that is secret. The truth will always prevail.

ODOGWU EBERO AKWA, MANA AKPO ZALUYA: The brave man did not cry but his chins are swollen. There are several ways of detecting signs of difficulties/burden.

ONYE NA ANORO EBE ENILU OZU NA ESI NA UKWU ABO: Someone who was not present when a corpse was buried exhumes the remains from the foot end. If you are not fully involved in any arrangement you lact details about it all. A call to get one's fact together or hear from both sides is pressed.
UKPA KAA ODA: When a chestnut ripes it falls. There is time for everything.

OKUKU EBEREBE ONYUA ORU AKPANA NA ILI: A young zealous fowl does not waste time in messing about with its drops. This is likened to an overzealous person who is bound to make many mistakes.

MANYA FU ONYE OMALU OBE UGWU: A man carrying palmwine favours his friend he meets on the road with a drink. The tendency to respect and acknowledge the presence of those you know is the nub of this expression.

UZO OGO BU UZO MMILI NA ABURO UZO NKU: Marriage relationship is like a road leading to a stream and not to a woodland. That is to say that the stream has a longer course compared to that of the wood that is obliterated.

AKALUSIA ABANA ASU NYA NNI: Inspite of unpopularity of 'abana yam', it is still pounded into foo foo. There is good in anything. Something good will always reveal itself in what appears to be a disaster/an unfavourable situation.

OBI UNO NYILI ENYI OWE TINYE ISI NA OFIA: The elephant could not cope with domestic life so it took to the forest. Persistent problems may make people to resign their fate.

ENENIA NWA ITE OGBONYUA OKU: If you neglect a small cooking pot its contents will quench the fire. Do not judge a person by his/her size

IBU ANYI DANDA: No load is heavy for a multitude of ants to carry. Unity is strength.

ADA ANO NA NDO AFU ONWA: You cannot see the moon from beneath a shade. That is to say that if you do not work hard and smart you cannot achieve success.

ANYA ADA AFU NTI: One's eyes cannot see one's ears. The topic referred to is impossible, unimaginable and preposterous.

AKPUKPO UNO AFU NKU: When a house is demolished, firewood becomes available. You cannot achieve success without risks.

ONE MBOSI BU ALA NWA AGBO: How long does it take for a girl's breast to fully develop? Girlhood does not last forever. Infact no stage in life is permanent. One is expected to make use of the opportunities before it is too late.

ORU BULU AWOLO ISI ABANYA OFIA: When a slave dons a masqurade he runs wild. When one does what he is not qualified for, he gets out of hand. This is equivalent to having one's head in the cloud.

OKUKU ADA ECHEZO ONYE KWOLUYA ODU NA UDU MMILI: A fowl does not forget the person who clipped its tail/feathers during rainy seson. Do not forget your benefactor.

ONWERO EBE ESI JEBE UDO ODI NSO: No matter what route you travel, Udo shrine is still far. Nothing is easy as it looks.

NYKOBA NWAMILI NA OFU EBE KA OGBO UFUFU: Urinate at a spot to enable it to foam. Concentration on one specific objective at a time yields results or pool your resources together to achieve significant effect. Unity is strength.This is another definition of the phrase

ACHOBA ISI OCHU UZU ERO: If you search for the source of murder the blacksmith that makes the deadly weapons will be hanged. Some issues need not be over flogged because of their not too good implications.

AGWO GA AMULILI IF DI OGONOGO": Snake offsprings must be long; a case of all tarred with the same brush and sharing same characters/faults etc.

OKUKU NO NA NGIGE, EGWU, NGIGE, EGWU: A fowl that perches on a rope dances as well as the rope. This byword portrays a catch 22 situation where one action begets another, that is similar and often more difficult.

AGBA CHALUSIA IDEI AMA ZONYEYA UKWU: No matter how much you try to avoid a flood, you end up stepping into it. This refers to something inevitable.

IFU ODENE: Casing a joint. This refers to someone taking a walk within the neighbourhood to ask after a friend most often a woman. 'Iju ase'.

IKPA NDU: This refers to seeing off somebody like 'ifu Odene' the mission is usually connected with females. 'Idu pu madu'.

AKA YALU OTUBO OKWUE IFE ONA ACHO: When a finger goes below the navel it has another mission. This is a warning for one not to go beyond bounds.

OZU ADA ANWU CHEBELU ULE: A corpse is immuned to smell, or not bothered about decaying. This refers to a situation one is hell bent on doing something not minding the consequences, which are referred to, as 'immuned to smell',

ONYEBUTE IBI OGOSI EBOYA: Whoever develops hernia of the scrotum does not hide it from his kinsmen. Try as you can, you cannot completely hide/cover your inadequacies/predicaments.

MMILI NA AMA OGWE NA AWU OGWE ARU: The rain that falls upon a prostrate tree trunk merely washes it. This refers to an action, which is deemed to have a dismal effect but turned out the other way round.

ADA AMA NGULO NA UGBO: You cannot identify a lame in a canoe. That is to say that if a lame can paddle a canoe effectively, you should not underrate or judge a person by his/her looks.

KA MILI AMANA OGAZI, AKIKAYA GADI: No matter how a guinea fowl may be beaten by rain her picturesque feather cannot be defaced. This refers to an action that is deemed to be dismal but has no effect.

OKPUZO ENWE ILO: A thoroughfare has no enemy. Those that invade/trespass other people's land usually have enemies. Those who do not are likeable and peaceful people.

KA ONYESI DEBE UGBAYA KA OGA ESI WELUYA KPO AFIFIA: How you keep your dust pan determines how others use it. Dustpan is extended to other personal belongings and if left unattended/unprotected they become misused. This is a counsel to be sensible, careful, diplomatic and sagacious.

NWANE NA NWANE ADE ELIBE NNI ASI MUTA OKU: Relations can have meals together in darkness without distrust and suspect. This implies a high degree of trust between them.

ONWU BULU ICHE AMAFU NYA: If death were missiles, they would be easy to cast away. An impossible wish is conveyed by this expression.

EJUNA KPULU OKPULU IKILIKEYA: A snail carries its shell while on the move. This refers to a man who does not forget his loved ones, family and other relations, come rain and come shine in good times and likewise at bad times.

AGADI NWANYI DA ADA NDA NA BO OKOGUA IFE OBU NA UKPA ONU: When a woman stumbles twice, the contents of her basket need to be counted/weighed so as to stop the third occurrence. Incessant errors make one look foolish. The phrase calls for pragmatism.

IFE LUE NA ITO, OTO: The pun is on (ito) third and (oto) stop. It implies that a recurring incident has to be re-assessed for better results. A caution for one to get his act together is made.

ONYE NA AMARO ENUWA NYA JEBE NA OGBO OKWE: He who does not understand the world should go to where the game of draught/chess is played. Vicissitudes of life is likened to the win/lose chess game. The lesson calls for perseverance.

IFE ONYE LULU OGOYA ABURO USA: What you are qualified for cannot be considered as a bad conduct. This is often used to support the excesses of adults.

UNO OBOGU: Uno obogu ada aru oku: A house devoid of hostility is never hot. The house as it were that is suppossed to 'uproot' any dissension, rancour, hostilty etc. By implication such house/home is deemed peaceful and the inhabitants are wished well.

AMALU ISI OYA, AMALU ISI OGWU: If you know the cause of an ailment you know the principal drug to prescribe. Identifying the cause of any problem provides a lead to the solution.

OBIALU BE ONYE ABIAGBUNIA, MA ONAKO KWA NKPU-NKPU APUNIA NA AZU: A guest should acknowledge the hospitality of the host and no ailment (like hunch back) should befall the guest else he thinks his problems emanated from his host. The expression means well for the host and the guest and calls for reciprocity.

EKENE BU UGWO: Salutation is debt to be paid on spot. This underscores the importance of reciprocity/acknowledgement for effective human relationship.

AKA NNI KWO AKA EKPE, AKA EKPE AKWO AKA NNI: In the process of washing one's hand both the right and left wash each other. This is another case where reciprocity is a foundation for effective human relationship.

ONYE ALA NA UCHE YA YI: A mad man has his own sense. The expression shows that regardless of any difficulty likened to madness, one knows his direction. The addressee is therefore warned not to take undue advantages.

ISI AKARO NWATA OBULU ODO: A case of a young boy (unaided), carrying a motar (bigger risks). It calls for preparedness for any adventure, expedtion and assignement. It also serves, as a warning not to spoil for a fight the person cannot win.

IFE OKENYE NO ANI FU, NWATA KWULU OTO OMA FU YA: What an elderly person sees while sitting down, a younger person cannot see it while standing up. This touches on the wisdom, and sensibility associated with maturity, besides it calls for caution to the young ones not to play pranks and also avoid other wrong doings.

ODIBO EZE BU EZE: A king's servant is a king. A reference is made to the importance of a servant who is privy to many State affairs/secrets. Such a person is treated well or else he divulges the king's secrets.

MEM MEKWULU ADI ESE OKWU: Revenge evens out the scores. The expression serves as a counsel for restraint and forgiveness.

IFE MELU EDE OJI BE NWII: Something is instrumental to the creaking of cocoyam. There is a cause for any action or there is no smoke without fire. This is a case of justifying one's action.

MUO ADA AYO OLU GA EKILI NYA: A dancing masquerafe does not solicit the presence of spectators. This implies that what is good requires little advertisement; a case of a good wine that needs no bush.

EGO ABOLU IJELE: Money given to Ijele masquerade. The masquerade hardly recognises those that shower him with money. Such gesture may not attract appreciation. The expression is applicable when one does good to an ingrate.

UWA NA ATUALI ATUALI: The world tumbles. This is an expression of the vicissitudes of life and hence a caution to upstarts.

ISI BU ARU, AKA BU ARU: Both head and hand belong to the body, such that if any of them is affected by any problem the body suffers. The byword calls for restraint and forgiveness as what affects your brethren is likely to affect you.

AKA NA AKA RALU, OYI EJIECHI: When hands (efforts) are equal, friendship last longer. Here is another expression for receprocity, a factor that builds up better human relationship.

NWATA NA AMARO AGHA NA AKPO YA ANYA: A child who does not know how to pronounce agha (war) calls it anya (eyes). This is a case of one not knowing the implications of certain things hence a call for caution and sensibility.

NWATA AKWO NA AZU AMARO NA IJE TELU AKA: A child on piggyback does not know that a journey is far. Such a person aided fails to appreciate the efforts. A counsel to young ones to appreciate any support given to them is advocated.

ADI EJI IFE ANA AGBA NA NTI AGBA NA ANYA: What is used for the ears is not suitable for the eyes. This serves as a caution for over zealous ones that are likely to make mistakes.

EGBUE MA IWE, ENIE MA ISI: When you kill out of anger, you must bury the victim to avoid decomposition. A call to have a spirit of forgiveness is conveyed by this byword.

CHI EJI ADA AKULU UBOSI: The day is not over until it is dark. By the expression one looks forward with hopes despite setbacks. In other words so far there is life there is hope.

ADA AGWA OCHI NTI NA AGHA ESU: You do not tell a deaf that a war has broken out. The expression indicates that to be forewaned is to be forearmed.

OGINI JI NKITA ONWU: What stops the dog from dying? The expression demands immediate action. What are we waiting for?

IBUNA NKITA UZO OSO: Do not start the race before the dog. Do not beat the gun. Do not jump to conclusion without hearing from both sides.

NKE AKA ONYE KWUDOLUYA UME: A man stands by his own strength as against the support of others. This byword underscores the importance of hard work needed to excel in life.

OCHU OKUKU NWE ADA: A person who chases a fowl often stumbles. A person planning against somebody often falls into such trap. By this expression perpetrators of evils are warned.

OBURO INYE ENWE MMILI BU ISI, MANA OBU INATAYA IKO: It appears simple to offer a monkey a drink but difficult to retrieve the cup. An expression of hesitation in doing something that may not be acknowledged and hence ends in regret is conveyed by the phrase.

IKWO AKA TIELU ENWE AKU: Putting much effort in breaking the nuts for the monkey. The monkey savours the nuts but there is hardly any way to know his appreciation sense. The expression implies thankless efforts.

IGWE NINE NAKO NA UZU: All metals must end up in the foundry. All mortals must die. This revelation calls for rectitude.

OJI ONYE NA ANI JI ONWE YA: A person who holds another on the ground holds himself, portraying a catch 22 situation; a case of one bad action begetting another bad action of which escape is difficult as depicted in the phrase.

OKE ILOLO BU UJO: Deep thoughts often result to fright. Prolonged planning/scheme kills initiative. This serves as a call for immediate and timely action.

ULA SO BA USO EKWOBIE EKWOBE: The beauty/joy of sleep is when it is deep. By implication deep commitment will guarantee more success.

OKU AGUNYELU NWATA NA AKA ADA ARUGBU YA: Fireballs put in a child's palm ought not to char the child's palm. Authority is likened to fireballs. Such authority to carry a difficult task should also cover the child/not to get hurt. The speaker by this byword shows his determination to carry out task expected of him irrespective of doubts expressed by adversaries.

NKITA SI ONYE DA ONYE DA, NA OFU ONYE DAKALIA OBULU UJO: The dog pleads that falling down at play should be reciprocal else it becomes cowardly if it is one sided. Reciprocity of goodwill enhances better human relationship.

KA ARAPU IFE TALU NA ANYASI KA OBULU ANWU: Consider all that bit you in the night as mosquitoes. Consider your obstacles/problems/contentions as past and look forward with optimism. The expression calls for spirit of forgiveness.

IJINA IWE ANUNU GBA NWA NZA AKU: Do not shoot a bird under an unchecked anger else you miss your target. This calls for restraint when in bad mood.

CHUKWU KELU AKO OYIBO GA NYEYA MMILI OGA ALA: God who created coconut will give it water to feed upon. This is an acknowledgement that God works in mysterious ways.

EFI NA ENWERO ODU, CHUKWU NA ACHULUYA IJIJI: A cow without tail depends on God to drive away flies for it. This is similar to the expression above that God provides for those in dire difficulties:

OFUONYE YILU, ODUDU ATAGBUE NYA: When a person travels alone he is severely bitten by tse-tse flies. By implication if one has no companion he/she is likely to face the problems alone. Unity is strength.

OBU AMA ATU KA OBU NA UBE ADIRO NKO: Is it that you cannot aim or that your arrow is not sharp enough. This is likened to any task where one's ability or his tools are in doubt. The expression is used to remind one to be alive with his responsibilities.

MBOSI NA ACHU NTA KA MGBADA NA ALI ENU: It is the day I chose to hunt that the hare learnt how to climb. Hares run and do not climb. This is an expression of what an ill luck.

ELILI MALU NGUGU MA NGUGU MALU ONYE KELU YA: The rope can be identified with the packet whereas the packet can identify the person that tied the rope. This expression signifies that it is not everything that one knows. The counsel there from is that one should not poke nose in what does not concern him.

EBUNU RIE AZU OSO MPI:A ram retreats before attacking. This refers to one picking his battle carefully. The need for general preparedness is stressed before tackling any task.

IGBA MBU OTUA NA OGWE, IGBA ABO OTUA NA OGWE, AGANA ATOLU OGWE: When your arrow misses the target and strikes a tree trunk twice it becomes a waste. In other words, review your strategies and possibly relocate/re-position to be able to meet your goals (targets) and hence avoid waste. This calls for pragmatism.

ANU GBA AJO OSO AGBA NYA AJO EGBE: When an animal runs faster it requires a faster bullet to cut it down. This implies that a serious venture/case requires serious strategy/solution. Miscreants are reminded that no matter how crafty they are, the punishment that awaits them would be devastating.

MGBADA NYUA KA ENYI IKE AWARIYA: If a hare attempts excreting like an elephant, the anus will tear. The expression is a counsel for one to know his limitations and abilities.

SI WELU AKWUKWO TUKPUDO NSI WELU UDALA LACHAA: Let us cover the excrement then pick and eat the apple. This calls for forgetting the past contentious scenes. And hence forge ahead.

MBUYALI MBUYALI KA IKUKU NA EBU ODU IGU: The tail of palm frond sways when blown by the wind and hardly breaks. This is likened to a person that is impervious to adversities; a likeable person; a man of the people.

NWANNE OZU NA AWU OZU ARU: The relation of the deceased that bathes the corpse. This expression refers to a person who painstakingly attends to the problem of his kindred.

OKPATALU NKU ARURU SI NGWELE BIALIA UNO ONWU: He that fetches ant infested firewood has summoned lizards to kill the ants or as the saying goes, to attend the funeral of the ants. If you cause problems for yourself you cannot run away from it.

ORU FUA OKU ONO ANWULU: A slave inhales smoke while stoking the fire. This is often said to commend women and assure them that their efforts will be compensated.

WELU ILEYI GUA EZEYI ONU: Count your teeth with our tongue. Be your own judge. It also calls for thoughtfulness.

ENYI NYE AKA MGADA NYE AKA: Both the elephant and the antelope should help out. The expression underscores the importance of teamwork.

ETOBE OGOLI OWORI ALA: If you praise a fool he becomes mad. Excessive praise often makes people to do wrong things. The expression is used when one praised earlier is now over stretching the relationship. This is similar to the expression: 'Too big for one's boots'. The person concerned is getting an inflated or swollen idea of his own importance and is likely to do wrong things.

EYI KARI NKA OMIBA ALA NWAYA: When a rat ages, the milk of the young one sustains him. This is a case of an older person relying on his resources – human and material – to sustain him.

MBIDO AKWA NA AFIA ARU MANA AKWAMITE YA EGOBIE EGOBE: The commencement of weeping may not be easy but no sooner the tears flow more would flow. This refers to the early difficulties in carrying our any task but with determination the benefits becomes overwhelming.

ATUALU OMALU, OMALU MA ATUALU OFEKE OFENYE ISI NA OFIA:A parable is better understood by a wise man. A fool on the other hand heads into the bush/limbo. The expression calls for perceptiveness.

ADAMU ATU EGWU ALA AGA MAKA NA AGA AMA ATU IME:I have no fright having a sexual affair with a barren. The speaker is not worried speaking his mind as the facts of the matter are commonly known; talking cold turkey.

ADAMU ALA NNE NA EFIGBU NWA: Having a sexual affair with a mother and aiding in abortion is not my style. The speaker is unequivocal about his reasonableness with his dealings with the people.

ODUDU TADOLU NA AMU ONU KA EJI AFUPUYA: A bee that stings one's private part is removed by blowing it. A case is made here for extra care in handling sensitive issues.

OMASILI NTI OMASILI NYAM NYAM: What is good for the cheek/mouth is palatable. What is good for the goose is also good for the gander. Both are of the same kindred. The success of a man is also extended to his family.

KA ONYE NA EME KA EKWE SI AKPOYA: The assessment of one's performance is linked proportionately with the way which the gong is playing for him. A person's worth is not hidden, as the level of commitment/success of the person determines one reward/praise.

OJI NWAYO ADI EMELU ARU: One who is careful and not in a hurry does not sustain injury. The expression is a cautionary counsel to overzealous persons.

OBULU NA AFURO EBE EBIDOLU AKA EBIDO NA IKPELE: Where you do not find where to rest your hands, the knee serves as an alternate. The phrase calls for contentment in any circumstance.

WELU EFIFIE CHUA EWU OJI MAKA CHI EJIRI: Take advantage of daytime and drive the black goat home before darkness sets. Make hay while the sun shines. The addressee is counseled to be sensible.

ISI MKPI ABAGO NA AKPA MKPI: The he goat's head has gotten into the goat's bag. When what you lose is gained by a member of your family and when your action is of benefit to your relation etc. the expression fits. Nothing is lost by this arrangement. The expression is said to mean that there is no cheating in the arrangement hence all is well.

OKENYE ADA ANO EWU AMUA NA OGBULI: An aged person cannot remain insensitive when a goat gives birth while on the tether. By implication an adult must not condone evils/wrong things.

ONYE MALU EBE MMILI SI BA NA OPI UGBOGULU?Who knows where and how water got into the stem of melon. This is an expression of doubt when things go wrong.

IBU RIKA NNE AGWOLIA IDIGILIDI AJU:A heavy load requires a large pad with which to carry it. By implication complicated problem or task requires well thought-out practical strategy.

OGINI MELU MANYA KA OCHABA NZU? What informed the choice of palm wine to have the same colour with the white chalk (Nzu). This is rhetorical question on an issue that is doubtful.

MMA ONYE TU NA UKWU KA OJI ANA AKA: One uses his holstered knife worn around the waist to (shake hands) exchange greetings. By implication what you have is what you use.

AGAM ENWESIA ORIMILI WELU AKPU ASO NA AKWO AKA? Having a pool of water (river) and using saliva to wash one's hands. One need not suffer in the midst of plenty.

AKPA AKPA ALARU NA UTE: With mutual consent you sleep on the mat/or you relate with a woman. An articulate arrangement is likely to beget success.

ATU EGBU NWA OKOLOAFO NWA OKOLOAFO EGBUE ATU: Where the deer does not kill one, the person kills the deer. The expression indicates a no going back stance. The speaker as it would appear has taking an irrevocable decision not minding the consequences. The variant of this phrase is 'Ife di ibua ofu me'. Let one thing out of the two happen.

OBURO KWA UBOSI KA ANA AKPO ONYE UKWA NNE ANYI: It is not every day that you call the breadfruit seller our mother. As a mother, the breadfruit seller ensures that the children are giving perks. The expression is used to show that you do not get gratification/bonus always; that every day is not Christmas, and more so the (breadfruit) the source of the perks may not be available or adequate all the time therefore to be thankful in any situation is conveyed by this aphorism.

AKU FESIA ODALU AWO: A winged insect on loosing the wings falls down and becomes a ready prey for the toad. A child who is to be punished and who runs away but had to come back homes at night is an example. Dodging some responsibilities, which you are later compelled to do, also is an example. This implies that there is no place for a miscreant to hide.

KEDU KA AGESI KWO ONYE UKWU WALU?How do you carry a person with a slip disc? This expression refers to any complex task/problem. How do you begin to solve such complicated problem? The poser calls for more commitment.

AWO ADA AGBA OSO EFIFE NA NKITI: A frog does not run at a day time without a cause. The expression affirms that something is in the offing, that something sinister is likely to occur. The variant is "There is no smoke without fire".

KA NWAMMILI NA BURO IFE OKUKU NYA NYA: If urinating is that easy let the fowl urinate. A recognition that nothing is as easy as it looks, the expression therefore calls for appreciation of any achievement.

ONYE PUA OSO OPUA MGBA: He that boasts must also be ready for a fight. An expression to practicalise your thoughts is conveyed by the phrase.

OKUKU ADA ALU ULU NA AKWA YA:A bird does not bring havoc on its nest/eggs; An expression that one does not destroy his household. A caution to keep away from mischief is therefore sounded to mischievous persons.

OKUKU ELILI OBOSA ABOSA: If a fowl does not feed on something it messes and scatters it. A case of one with selfish attitude; an equivalent of a dog in a manger is portrayed by this expression.

KA ATA ATU KA EJIDELU OLUKPULU OFO: Brush your teeth with chewing stick to avoid plaque on your gums. This expression calls for taking initial necessary precaution to avoid blame.

**ASI ONYEORI JIDE OKUKU OSI NA OGA ATAYA
ALU:**When a thief is asked to catch a fowl, he figures that it will bite him. The expression is used to address kids who feign innocence or ignorance of certain things and acts.

OGBOMA AFU IFE OMELU ONYE ONYEYA ONOKO NKU: Where a wizard does not kill his victim he gives him piece of (lit) firewood. The expression denotes that the victim is either killed or maimed; a variant of Egbu ogbue egbu, akpajinya aka. Where you don't kill one, ensure that his hands are broken. Either way the victim is not let off. This is a caution to evildoers to be upright or else face the punishment, which they cannot get away from, try as they can.

EWELU IFE EJI AGWO NZU WELU GWO NZU OCHA KE: If you use a thinner in mixing the white chalk, the colour brightens. Where you put in place the necessary plans/foot works/strategies success will follow.

AKPANYE NWA NKITA NA ARU OTAKA AKWA: If you endear your self to a dog it will shred your cloth. The expression implies that familarity often brings contempt.

AGA EJI NA OKO KOLU WELU KOKPO ANYA?You do not because you are itched in the face then scratch your eyes or blind yourself. The desire for any thing must be moderately pursued. The expression points to the fact that too much of everything is bad.

AKATAKPO ETINYE GO ISI NA MMANU: Akatakpo is an oil licking ant that often gets stuck while sucking the oil. The dare devil has dared the oil. The expression indicated that one has crossed the Rubicon, that is to say that one has taken a decisive step; a point of no return notwithstanding the consequences.

MMA NOKWO NA MMILI NCHA ABAMU NA ANYA:I will not be by a river and allow soapy water to enter my eyes. I cannot be in a vantage position and yet be deprived of the benefits of such position. The speaker by the expression is assertive on his status and rights.

AZU AMA IRU ONYE ONA ANYALU ANWU:A man's back that is exposed to sun rays does not know the face of the bearer. In other words the back shields the face with no strings attached. This is a thankless job expression.

DIBA NA AGWO OTOLO EDEBELU IKE YA NE EBE:A medicine man that cures diarrhea must not overlook his anus. He must therefore take care of himself first. This is an expression of doubt about one who has not taken good care of himself before prescribing a panacea for another.

OKE SOLU NGWELE MABA MMILI ARU NGWELE KO ARU OKE AMAKO: When a rodent takes after a lizard in jumping into a pool of water, the body of the lizard will dry, whereas that of the rat will not. A caution for young ones to keep out of trouble by not joining a bad gang or in attempting what they cannot accomplish is conveyed by this byword.

OKUKU ADE AKPANYE NA AFO EWU: The chicken does not source food for the goat. This is a reprimand expression that nobody is a fool as to do things for others without doing anything for himself. In essence everybody finds his own way/pocket.

UKPANA OKPOKO GBULU NTI CHILIYA:A grasshopper killed by woodpecker bird is deaf. The woodpecker bird is noisy hence attracts enough attention. The expression is a counsel to avoid disaster. To be forewarned is to be forearmed.

NGWELE NINE MAKPU AMAKPU AMARO NKE AFO NA ALU: All lizards lie on their stomachs hence nobody knows which of them that has belly ache. This is likened to not knowing all the problems of a person. The person having them therefore knows the problems.

OJE AKWA AWUARU MALU ONWIE: He that bathes with his clothes on knows himself. A guilty person knows himself.

MGBILIGBA AMARO NA UZO DI EGWU: The ringing bell does not bother if there is danger on the way. The bell is likened to a daredevil; a fearless person.

AMA EWE MGBABU WELU YALU OGU: You cannot because some people are killed and hence stop a war. A counsel there from is made that failures of others should not discourage one. It is also a pointer that risks are necessary in life.

OJEKO EJEKO KENE EZE ONAKO NYA KENE KWA NYA: If on your way you greet the Monarch, it would be nice to greet him on your way back. This implies that you must not forget your benefactor or mentor.

OLILI AMU EBUNU JI IBI UGWO: He that eats the ram's phallus is indebted to hernia. The expression has emphasis on rams large bollocks but implies that the subject that (eats) borrows or is given something must be committed to some kind of repayment.

AKWU ACHAGO NA IKILI: The palm kernel has ripen up to its base. The inference is that success is imminent; that one is about to be compensated for his efforts. An expression of euphoria that one has made it is the nub of this phrase.

GA ANULUM NWAMU NA IFE YI: To be betrothed to one's daughter goes with other things (dowry). If you accept for example a position in the society you are expected to meet other obligations. A case is made that there is hardly anything that is free.

IJIJI NA ENWERO NDUMODU NA ESO OZU ELU MUO:A fly that is impervious to advice follows the corpse to the grave; A person who refuses counsels often ends up a disaster; a failure.

ODI NTI NJO NA ERUFULU, MMILI ANU: It is not pleasant to the ears that beef sauce is thrown away. This action is considered. A counsel to check on wastage is conveyed by the phrase. The addressee is thus counseled to be pragmatic.

IFE LILU NNI LACHA OFE: Let he who eats the food lick the soup. Let the matter rest. Let bygone be bygone. By this expression forgiveness is sought and peace sued for.

ANU SOLU NWA ENWE OMAJILI AKA: An animal that imitates the monkey in jumping is bound to break his arm. This relates to a person who takes uncalculated risks. Such a person is likely to find him/herself in trouble. The counsel arising calls for sensibility.

EGEDE BUNNIE OTIE ONWEYA: The drum that beats itself. A liar or evildoer is likely to be affected negatively by his/her action. The expression is thus a counsel to miscreants, that evil begets evil.

ANU NAA TATA ECHI BU NTA: If a game/animal escapes today, tomorrow affords another hunting day. This is an expression of hope. A counsel not to be discouraged by early failure is made.

UDENE KALU ARU NA AMAPU OZU ARU:A powerful vulture rips open a corpse. This refers to a feat or any accomplishment performed by a brave and courageous person. The person is considered a daredevil.

NKEKE ENYI NA ACHU IGWE ENYI OSO:A short elephant that pursues a herd of elephants. This expression is about a person who though has smallish features but has clout. A variant of odi nfe anyi alo; light by looks but yet heavy by performance and worth.

OKE EJIRO ANYA OMA AMA NA MKPAKANA:A rat trapped is not by the rat's design. Literally hunger is instrumental to the rat foraging for grubs and getting trapped in the process is not a deliberate act. By implication a person in need often runs into unexpected problems. The expression connotes that things are not normal for the subject.

MKPAKANA GA AMA OZO MA OZO GA ANA: The trap can catch the monkey/chimp but the agility of the monkey would guarantee an escape for it. This refers to somebody who is street wise and smart enough to seek easy way out of any problem. This is often said boastfully.

OJI ISI WEE KOTE EBU, KA EBU GA AGBA: The person who provokes the hornet nest is likely to be stung by the bees. Any body that causes any uneasiness or problem for others cannot go free. If you look for trouble you will surely be affected. This serves as a counsel to be cautious.

ONYE NWANNEYA NO NA ENUIGWE ADA EJE OKUMUO:A person whose relation is in heaven cannot be condemned to hell. Where you have backers, success is guaranteed. The expression seeks to remind those that are in good position to come to the aid of their kindred.

OMETUTA IMI, OMETUTA ANYA: What affects the nose also affects the eyes. By inference, what affects your child/relation also affects you. It serves as a counsel to be careful.

ONYE NODEBE NTI OMATAYA ULA: The closer to the cheek, the more impact of slap. By implication where you have a hang of a particular happening, you appreciate it or take advantage of it.

MBOSI NTA KA ANYI CHUA NA OWELLE NCHI: On hunting day let us meet at the games habitat. This is an expression to pursue any undertaking vigorously at the scheduled period.

NKITA SI NA NDI NWELU IKE AMARO ANO ANI: The dog is quoted as saying that those with buttocks hardly know how to sit. By implication those who are opportune in life often neglect to utilize such chances/opportunities. The corollary is to harness your resources.

OKE DI NA UNO GWALU OKE DI NA OFFIA NA AZU DI NA NGIGA: This is a case of rat at home informing another in the bush that there is fish in the storage at home. A close relation often divulges one's secret. The corollary is to be circumspect.

ODI NTI NJO NA EWU TALU NSHIKO: It is unpleasant to the ears that a goat has eaten a crab. Goats are herbivorous and hence cannot eat crabs. This expression is a warning to deviants to desist from their unaccepted norms.

AGA EWELU MAKA IFI AGBONO WE LARU NA UKWU UGILI: You do not because of the taste of 'agbono' a soup ingredient and hence sleep near the tree that produces it. The expression calls for moderation in anything one does. It is often said to check lewdness.

MADU ADI EGBU OZU OGA KWA: One cannot kill a person that he will be compelled to bury. By implication people are cautioned to desist from taking any action that one cannot complete or stand by its consequences. Sensibility is called for.

OJI AKA MKPILITE EGWU ONU ABUZU NA ASUCHI YA ASUCHI: One who uses a blunt pestle instead of a sharp and pointed stick to dig up a cricket, blocks the route instead. By implication, the person is a failure. Success does not come easy. It comes with smartness. The counsel there from is to be pragmatic.

NKITA ADI ATA OKPUKPU ANYABALIA NA ONU: A dog cannot eat the bone hung on its neck. One does not steal or mess up with what is put in his care. A case of too close for comfort is conveyed by the expression. To keep one's honour and to be principled is the nub of this expression.

AMARO EBE ANA ANYALU AKPA AFU ANU: One is not sure where and when to carry a bag and kill a game. The allusion is on hunting but by implication one should be prepared at all times. This expression advocates that one should be on the look out all the time.

AMA EWELU NA AGU GBULU ENE WE SI NA ENE ABURO ONYE OSO: You do not conclude that because a lion killed an antelope and hence consider the antelope as not fleet-footed. One's performance is relative. The expression calls for appreciation of any person's performance.

ALA NASIA OGBUNIKU ADA ANA: Even after madness is treated, traces of it remain. When the wound heals, the scar remains. The upshot is that someone can be forgiven but the bad act cannot easily be forgotten. It serves as a warning for kids to be upright and avoid the stigma crime carries.

EBE ONYE WULU ARU KA OGA ACHILU OGODOYA: Where you bath is where you pick up your wears. Where you work is where you get your pay.

EJIRO UCHICHI ALO ANYA: You do not wink in the night-darkness. Some unfavourable circumstance likened to darkness in the expression can cause one to neglect another or get things wrong. An expression that things can go wrong sometimes especially in an unfavourable circumstance is highlighted. Sensibility is thus called for.

EGO BU MMA NKO: Money is likened to a sharp knife; and by implication; money is might, power and authority.

IFE SI IKUKU KUE KA AFU IKE OKUKU: The choice of the wind to blow is instrumental to exposing or baring the anus of a fowl. A case of providence in exposing one's bad intention is underscored.

IKWE BULU NNI OGBAKUTA ANI AZU:A case of the mortar with food turning its back on others. This is likened to one in a vantage position that does not care for others. The subject is uncaring.

OPULU IFE ITE PUA IFE OFE:A person that can provide cooking pot and soup ingredients. The phrase refers to a wealthy and outstanding personality. He is up to the task before him.

OKOLO ELURO ELU WALU OGODO, IKUKU BULUYA OBOLU NYA NA OGODO YA:A young man who is not matured to wear a short is swept away by the wind. This expression is a counsel to upstarts to be prepared and committed in their endeavours in life and hence avoids disasters.

ONWA TIBE IJE AGUBA NGULO: When the moon shines the lame is eager to walk. This is a case of if you have support; you spoil for a fight/action or a lazy man taking advantage of the abundance of bounties. Do not be over dependent on someone or something.

AGWO ANYI GBULU ODI MKPILIKPI ONE?How many pieces are there of the snake we killed. The expression seeks to find out how concerted our hatched plan is. Is it intact or broken down?

AGADI EWU NA ATA MGUGBO NKU: An old goat that eats the bark of firewood. Normally goats eat vegetables. It is strange for a goat to eat the bark of firewood. The expression considers any person that does an anomaly like that of the goat in the text as foolish.

AKIDI AMA OKE: The spiraling bean plant knows no boundary. By growing far beyond the place it is planted, the expression likens a person who goes beyond his domain, person who extends his hand of fellowship to others as not having enemies. The person is considered likeable.

AGWO NO NA AKILIKA: The snake is in the roof. Given this happenstance the snake has problem to crawl effectively. The speaker confirms that he is in dire trouble or that things are not easy.

Afuro iru nwanyi mulunwa iwelu na aju ya ife olitelu: You have not seen/understood the expression of the face of a woman that put to bed and you want to know the sex of the baby. Understanding the facial expression will let you into if she is happy, that is if the baby survived, if the baby is well and hearty or not. By implication it calls for hearing someone out first before taking any action or visiting someone with blames.

Anwunyenam odu abuzu na aka: Do not put the tail of a cricket into my palms. By doing so gives one away as having the cricket. By implication it makes the person a fall guy; a scapegoat. The speaker makes bold to refuse being made a scapegoat.

Aju na ewo muo isi: The head support pad of the masquerade has turned abrasive. The expression is likened to an unbearable encumbrance. The speaker admits by the expression that he is having difficulties.

Ana ekwu na oku gbalu fada inaju maka afo onuya: Why ask after the beard of a Reverend Father when you know that the Reverend has been burnt by fire. This is case of a hopeless and helpless situation.

Azotasia ani ewelu zoba ute: Acquire the land first before seeking/acquiring the mat. The expression seeks ordering one's priorities

Ada agba aka afu nwata eze: You do not see a child that is teething without a gift. A teething child is a welcome development stage of the child. By implication you cannot get something good for nothing.

Atulu mulu ebunu gba aka nwa: A sheep that begets a ram is considered as childless. That the ram mates the mother confirms the waywardness of the ram. By implication when ones child because of his stubbornness/waywardness turns a liability, the child is considered useless.

Amaka eme imi nkita onwero ka odi akolo: No matter what, the dog's nose will always be moist. This refers to an irredeemable and hopeless situation.

Obu ka asi akuna nsi, asi si efene aju? Just for the fact that making one permanently mad is frowned at, nothing stops you from making the person to be mildly or temporally mad. The upshot is that a moderate opinion is better than an extreme one.

Ofu onye ada agbabido mgbada: A person cannot chase and round up an antelope. The antelope being a fleet-footed animal requires more than one person to encircle it. By implication one needs the relationship of others to progress.

Onwero ife anya fulu gba mmee: There is nothing the eyes can see to make it bleed. This is a case of being impervious to problems, having gone through a good number of them in the past. The character is undaunted.

Onye bulu osuba nsu: When one is burdened, he stammers. By implication, the person becomes more confused.

Ukwu naga gbele gbele, anya naga gbele gbele na afu ya: One who stalks is caught by another with sharp eyes. By implication nothing is that secret. The expression is a counsel for children to be upright.

Ozu anu isi: A corpse that is immune to smell. The expression refers to a foolish and tactless person who does not study his ground before taking action. It could also refer to someone who is hell bent on taking an action regardless of the consequence.

Nte malu ife omelu oji welu aja gbachi onuya: The cricket knows what it has done hence by blocking his route with sand. By implication he that runs away from trial admits his guilty.

Oburo obele ife ka mmili melu agwa na ugbo: It is not a small thing that flood did to the bean plants in the farmland. The expression is used to show the extent of the devastation/failure of any particular action.

Oburo obele ife ka afu na ife Juachi: It is not a small thing that is sighted in a woman's bosom or closet. This is another off colour expression, which by implication means that what is earlier seen as easy/fun is after experience not as such. Other implications and obligations are now evident. The expression calls for restraint.

Ewu dina ani dina na akpukpo ya: A goat lying down is doing so on its hide. The expression portrays that one is acting within his domain; an assertion that all is in order and nobody is hurt. The subject is home and dry.

Onye rulu ewu mmili ka ifele ga eme maka na nna ewu adi awu aru: The person that pours water on the goat takes the shame because the goat family never bathes. This refers to action taken without considering the aftermath. This is usually applied when invoking a curse.

Obioma bu utu nkeni: Happiness arouses and enhances sexual desire. The expression though a bit off colour implies that one's relationship with others or attitude towards others to a large extent is dependent on the person's disposition.

Onye ogboya na echi eze ona enwo eze: Someone whose age group aspires for the crown but is still teething. Aspiration for the crown implies greater feat and achievement while a contemporary still at teething stage has no ambition. The subject teething is considered a dullard.

Nwulu obu na aka: Come along with a dove. The dove crows earlier than other birds. The crow by implication is expected to wake one up early enough. Getting up early is therefore a lead to being punctual or arriving early for an appointment.

Ka ogili fu ife ule fulu na ofe: Let the soup condiment (ogili) experience what the soup thickener (ule) has experienced. Both are introduced into the boiling pot of soup. By implication the experience is not pleasant. The expression is a counsel for people to be careful otherwise the consequences that had befallen others who strayed away will befall them.

Ifi isa na anya: The phrase advocates that one wipes his eyes with seven fingers. Application of extra two figures amounts to being extremely careful or cautious. It has also a negative connotation of doing something deliberately.

Usabu Uyabu: Usa is greed and Uya is agony. Those things acquired by greed or illegitimately usually are not well used and could bring further problems/pains. This is an admonishing phrase that what comes easy goes easy and portends ruination.

Ibiliachi enwe uche oto na olili: An adult that is not sensible remains fun seeking chap all his life. By implication the character is wasteful, improvident and is considered foolish.

Mkpu bu na aru: The bump manifests on the body. The phrase is said to check the excesses of one's life style or else face the (bumps) pains, or wear and tear.

Egwu kwusie olue uno: This literally means that at the end of musical performance outside the performer's domain, the associated paraphernalia are taken home. This is said of someone whose achievement outside his domain also manifested at home. The phrase is also a reminder to be committed; to bring home the bacon; to succeed with ones projects or to earn enough to support the family.

Elisiro anu usa agu: Having eaten so much meat does not stop one from savouring such desire later. It serves as an admonition to an ingrate or greedy person reminding him of another situation he would have to seek favour again.

Akalanya sa: Ka anya sa: Ensure that your eyes are clear at all times, so as to focus on what you want to do. The addressee is advised to be careful.

Onye bute ibi oto na olu: If you have hernia or any visible ailment as it were, you are quarantined in the farm. For any wrong doing/crime you commit, you are to face the consequences. This is tantamount to allowing someone suffer the natural unpleasant consequences of his own folly.

Obu amusia nwa obulu zia ikpa koba ukwu bu okwu: After childbirth and the accompanying travails, how could mere putting the legs together pose some problems? Having gone through an onerous task other little ones would not matter.

Igba abaka abaka: In a disorderly haste. The phrase refers to any confused state.

Iyoo: The word perhaps originates from Edo as it is widely used there. It means my bosom friend. It is also used on calling one's attention. Nwokem and Okwum are variants of Iyoo.

Oku na oku ka eji ala onye ala: You do not waste time while making love to a mad person. An off colour remark that refers to any mission that demands quick responses else your advantage would be reduced.

Adaru: The prefix **ada** means to stumble, to fall while the suffix **ru** means to stop. The phrase connotes any activity that changes course, or goes anti clock wise. When positive it is an advantage and when negative, it signifies losing grounds or being unstable.

Imalu sua, isua na odo, imaro, isua na ani: If you want to pound (food) well, the mortar is your best choice and where you do not pound well, it is likened to pounding on the ground. The expression serves as reproof to be upright.

Ana ebe nni, ona eri: The size of the food is reduced as one eats it. The phrase refers to a task or commitment that is handled by a systematic and gradual approach.

Ofu aruru ada ebi no onu: An ant does not live alone in the hole. By implication one is not expected to be alone. The phrase is often used to back extra marital affairs of men/women.

Anam aga no oke ada azogbu ome ji: One who does not trespass, who minds his own path does not trample on the yam seedlings. This is said of a person that is peaceful and does not meddle in other people's business.

Onye nwelu ogugwu iyi ozo ga egbue: Not minding that one has shrine he worships, another shrine may not protect him or spare him. This is often said to play down on sexual excesses of mankind.

Afuro onye lolu ogwugwu ka alolu Ojedi: Hardly can you have one who worships, offers sacrifices and appeases a shrine like that of Ojedi. Ojedi shrine demands extra attention. The person who meets these extra demands needs to be praised. This could be a eulogy or a flatter.

Olume epu na odu opue na isi: Yam seedling can sprout from either side i.e. from head or tail. When related to people, any member of the family regardless of his or her seniority position can be in a wealthy position than the others. This is often said in prayer for God to grant the family wealth through any member of the family.

Onye nnia obi ogbu ewu ime/obulu odogwu: If you have heart you can kill a pregnant goat and be valorous. This is a case of deliberately taking an irrevocable decision; burning one's boat as it were.

Okenye adi ebu ibu na abo: An adult does not carry double load. The first load is said to be the testicle and the second arises when one is pressed to urinate/defecate. By implication an adult prioritises his tasks and takes them one at a time.

Okenye na anuife nnu na abo: An adult hears something twice. A case of an adult calling for his recognition which entitles him to a second round of d rinks is likened to 'hearing something twice'.

Ana ebu ani ebu: Can the earth be carried? This refers to something impossible. Such impossible acts are questioned by the phrase; a rhetorical phrase that in most cases is said boastfully to show that the speaker is unmoved.

Nje ali nje ali ka eji ele nwa mkpi: Moving from one place to the other paves way to selling a young he-goat. This is said of one's reach-out, which makes it possible to sell any idea to the populace.

Agigo onye ibi bu nya kpo nnie akwa: A man who is bold to deny that he does not have hernia should not hesitate in raising his loincloth. A man accused of wrongdoing could be reminded of the phrase to make him honest. The suspect could equally come up with the phrase showing that he has nothing to hide.

Mgba ga adi okpoko na odunmodu mma: It would be thrilling to have a woodpecker, and a lion fight. Both are kings in their own domain but can hardly meet each other. The phrase is said of two people who are spoiling for a fight and are boastful. The phrase is sarcastically used on loud mouths.

Nene abum na aji adiroya: Take a look at my armpit and see that there are no hairs there. Kids that are yet to have pubic hairs are considered guiltless. A case of innocence and do not get me involved is established by the phrase.

Iko nku anya: Shaving ones lashes. The phrase refers to one who is shameless.

Okpoko si na mbosi nne ya ga anwu owelu onu gwue ini. Eluzie mbosi ome okeiso sonya na onu: The woodpecker said he would dig his mother's grave with his beak but unfortunately when the day came he had boils on his beak (mouth). This is said of a boastful person, a loud mouth and the counsel there from is to be realistic.

Oso na aburu oso ka nwanyi na agba kwudoaka na ala, Nke bu osu lue ala apiaba kpaka kpaka: When a woman runs a race that is not that important she holds her breast but when the main race comes her breasts flap as she runs. This is said to remind those not experienced in a particular task to be strong-hearted.

Ade ekpudo afo ime aka: You cannot cover pregnancy. Anything as obvious as pregnancy cannot be hidden; this is a warning that any misdeed would sooner than later be blown up and thus could not be hidden. This serves as counsel to kids to be upright.

Agamu ebu anya mmili na anya na agugu madu? Must I have tears in my eyes and yet be out to console someone else? The phrase by implication advocates that one should take care of himself before taking care of others. There is usually a vehemence expressed by the speaker that if you do not come to my aid I would not care a hoot when you need care.

Offia isa, Ozalla isa: Seven bushes and seven forests. Somebody who crosses seven bushes and seven forests must have come a long way. It is considered a feat. This is an expression denoting committed efforts of somebody.

Itam alu na isi ma izero ntutum, ntayi na ike nma ezelu nsi: If you bite me on the head without minding my hair, I will bite you on your buttocks without minding the faeces. Such deliberate and wicked act is reciprocated by a similar act with equal retaliation; tit for tat; a variant of 'mem mekwulu'.

Wepu aka enwe na ofe na onyilu aka madu: Remove the hand of a monkey from the soup because it does resemble the hand of a human being. By implication the hand should not be there. The person who is asked to remove the hand is meddling where he is not wanted. The person is also not sincere. It serves as chide to children to be upright.

Iwu aru na afo: Bathing the stomach. A child is likely to reach the tummy than the head while bathing. An adult who is said or who claims to be bathing from the stomach is innocent. This is a denial phrase that I know not of any allegation.

Ume ka eji afu oku: You need strength to blow/stoke the fire. You need to summon enough air in your lungs to keep the fire aglow. By implication any task must be addressed with vigour, and determination. The phrase is also advanced to play down on sexual exploits.

Anya fulu ugo nwulia maka na ada afu ugo kwada: Eagles are hardly seen hence the sight of one calls for euphoria. Eagle is associated with prowess and beauty. By implication any works/effort that is outstanding should be recognised.

Alam di be na ukwu amu: Sexual intercourse ends at the base end of the phallus. Another off colour remark suggesting that no matter the urge and desire, the joy is short-lived. The phrase serves as a caution for restraint and application of control is directed to kids that are wayward.

Obu ka ife nlacha si aso: Is it how a sweetener taste. This is said to one preoccupied with mundane desire and in the process loses his focus. The phase is a reproof to this character.

Kpam ogwu na ukwu: Remove the splinters from my foot. Such act is a favour. The phrase is widely used by masquerades demanding for perks.

KAM DI IME ASULU ORA NNI: When I was pregnant I was pounding food for the populace. Pregnancy here implies fullness and buoyancy. The speaker thus refers to the past when he was buoyant and generous to many people and was recognized as the man of the people. This is said with disappointment that the beneficiaries of the speaker's past benevolence no longer remember him now that he may not be too buoyant.

AKPAKWANNAM AKA NA OTU UGULU: Do not touch me on a sore spot. During harmattan the skin is usually dry. Otu is likened to a sore. It implies that the speaker does not have what it takes to soothe the 'sore spot' hence he does not expect anybody to ask him for such favour. This is a risqué phrase used in denying favour to people.

K ABIA KA ABIA KA AWO EJIRO ENWE ODU: So much delay denied the toad from developing a tail. Here is a caution to get the lead out of one's arise hence avoid procrastination.

MBA NA ASU NA ONU NA ONU: Communities speak in different tones. Recognizing that tradition differs from people to people, mutual respect of each other is preached.

NKE ONYE JI EKO AKONNIA: May whatever that boosts your ego not be lacking. A supplication for prosperity and progress is highlighted by this byword.

ONWU EGBU UTU OGA ELILILI IFE GBALU AFO ONU: So far as the penis is not dead it will savour the desire to mate. The bearded animal is euphemism for vagina. As long as there is life one can achieve his desires. The phrase heralds optimism and hope.

ANYA BU OKE ONYE: One's eye is his share. One's eyes confirm his presence. His presence during negotiation ensures he gets what is due to him as opposed to if he is not there. His presence guarantees his right.

ONYE NA AGBALU ONYE MUO OGU ARU YA ABU SO AJA: He who defends a coward, his body would be covered with sand. By implication the coward may turn around to castigate/antagonize his benefactor, who is likely to blame himself, or regret ever helping out.

OFU NKPULU AKWU ADA EFU NA OKU: One palm kernel nut cannot get lost in the fire. The only son in the family is likened to a lone kernel nut, who is expected and prayed for to live long, procreate and prosper hence does not get 'lost in the fire'.

ADA EBULU OZU ENYI NA ISI WELU UKWU NA EGWU ONU ABUZU: You not carry a dead elephant on your head while digging out a cricket with your toe. This implies that you cannot have a serious task at hand and be involved in other frivolous activities. This phrase serves as a caution to priotise one's tasks.

OMA UMA ACHU NGWELE KA AKA GA ETU UKPO: He that takes pleasure in pursing lizard would end up with blisters on his palm. In other words retribution awaits anyone that hurts an innocent person.

MGBADA AMU IBI BU ULU DI NTA: A hare that has hernia of the testicle is of benefit to the hunter. Such disability slows the hare and makes it an easy target for the hunter. A case of one's ill fortune being an advantage to another person is depicted by the phrase.

OBUSO IKO NA EJE BE UDU: Should the cup always visit the water pot? When the object i.e. cup and pot are related to people, the phrase means that one always visits another without reciprocity. People are often reminded about returning one's call through this phrase.

ULA GA ANYI ONWULU ANWU: The dead would get tired of sleeping in the sense that the dead will sleep forever. A miscreant is reminded that truancy does not pay and that he would sooner be tired because of the prolonged punishment his act carries.
ULA KWELU IZU ABULUGO ONWU: Sleep that has lasted four days has become death. An uncontrolled pleasure begets negative consequences. People involved in these excesses are thus cautioned else they face the consequences likened to death.

UTU AJU ORU: Refers to unrestrained sexual desires of mankind. A risqué phrase which by implication means that the character is covetous, insatiable; hence he has no preference – a variant of 'Onoko', one who eats anything; a greedy man.

JI GU NA OBA AGBALA AZABA OKU IKE: When the yam barn is depleted, a woman feigns deaf hence she does not answer at first call. This implies that when a man's fortune is depleted, hangers-on, which include women, have fewer regards for the man. It highlights ingratitude and a caution for one to save for the rainy day.

AGAM ANO NABEM NOPIA MKPULU AMU: Will I stay (sit) in my house and crush (sit on) my testicles? One is supposed to be in control and comfortable in his home. A rhetorical question warning intruders and at the same time an affirmation that the speaker is ready to challenge anyone that causes his discomfort.

EZI NA UNO: The house and its grounds. The expression refers to a man's family including his concubines.

OMALU MMA NA UGBENE: Beautiful feathers; that which is beautiful only on the outside. The expression connotes outward beauty while the inside is yucky. A case of 'window dressing', something fake, a charade, something that cannot stand the test of time is portrayed by the phrase.

ODI IME KULU NWA NA AKA: A case of a nursing mother who is also pregnant. This signifies a myriad of problem.

ONWELU NKAKWU PIA NYA ONU, ONWELU AWO WA NYA AFO: He that has skunk should clip its mouth and he that has toad should incise the stomach. Skunks have beaks whereas toads have bloated stomachs. By implication, parents are warned to caution their children/wards to avoid unpleasant consequences.

ANALU ONYE OLU AZU, ANALU OLU NINE: If you deprive a riverine man of his fish you have in turn deprived his kinsmen from such benefit – fish. It connotes extended family effect where the breadwinner is deprived or has no means of livelihood. It also connotes unity. For any negative effect on any member of a clan, other members would back him. Perpetrators of such deprivation are thus warned.

UGO OLU OYIBO ANA ETUYA NA OKPUNEKWE: The plume (pride) of civil service work is worn behind the back of the head. Whereas plume worn in front or by the side of the headgear can be noticed when it drops. That worn at the back on dropping cannot be noticed. People are by this aphorism reminded not to be overwhelmed by the splendor/perks from the office to such a stage that they should forget to plan for the rainy day. The upshot is such that people should invest in the future wisely/or have a long term plan for their lives.

ODU ADU NWATA NWENNE KA NWA NA ENWERO NNE JI AMUTA IFE: An advice given to the child by his/her mother is a source of learning to a child whose mother is dead. The expression has two major implications. The first is that those in vantage position should use the opportunities available to them wisely. The second and the nub of the expression is a reminder to those in despair that perseverance pays.

AZU AKA ADIRO NMA NKWUKOBA: The back of the palm is not good to be folded. As a matter of fact the back of the palm cannot be folded. This is an impossible task. Why ask for what is impossible? The speaker by this expression chides those that are demanding for impossible tasks and the futility of such suit.

ULA EMEBIRO ANYA: When one sleeps and wakes up, all is fine and normal. On the contrary, when one sleeps and fails to wake up, all is not well. Death occurs and invokes sadness. By this aphorism,-ula aka emebiro anya-the speaker confidently or boastfully asserts that whatever the problems/obstacles that might have exited, do not elude his success.

OFTEN FORGOTTEN WORDS/NAMES

Anumpama	Foolish person
Ofumagbe	Idleness
Isi Aja Aru	Unfortunate calamity
Gbalagugu	Swellling on groin when one Hurts his leg.
Chi	Guardian spirit
Ikenga	A statuette representing an individual spirit or fortune.
Ndi Muo	Ancestral spirits.
Oli na ofe	An opportunist
Uzabulu due and undue	Benefits of any kind i.e.
Iyaji	Compromise
Jape of hot drinks.	Small quantity, usually
Dandara	Even, draw game

Ile ebeletutu — Being inquisitive

Ili ami lie mpio mpio — Refers to a greedy person who besides his share takes that of others.

Ineline Na Ineline — This and that expression

Asumasu — The main subject/issue

Ile Mgbada — A talkative

Oloma — Old dialect of ofuma; something good.

Nseke — Confusion

Otanke — Spy

Apule — Scruffy and unkempt fellow

Ile Nfe Nfe — This is said of one who is garrulous.

Ayaka Na Iguoma — A group of disparate/diverse persons/groups

---

Gulu Guluo   Mind yourself and be
careful

Ile Nnu   This is said of someone who is a sweet talker, a glib tongue.

Itu Ukana   Grumbling and feeling
cheated

Ilu Olili   Committing havoc

Ime Akanabo   Stealing

Iko Ofusilima   Talking foolishly

Ita Agbono   Talking rubbish

Nni Inyima   Witches brew

Aramura   Exception

Nwa Okponu   An orphan

Omejilieke   A miscreant

Onu Nnunu   An insincere and
unreliable person

Omekatalu Ife Da Ujo   A retired criminal.
Somebody once steeped in crime.

Also refers to an active person that is withdrawn later in live.

Akwa Inyingiga
tears

Shedding crocodile

Akata Isi Ebue

A rogue

Abani Di Egwu
marauder

A thief/night

Ekelemu

An informant

Omali Omali
associated with faces

Familiar, often

Ina Ndena
withdrawn.

This is said of someone

Igba Abia Ukwu Nabo
who double deals.
Ichakiwa

This is said of someone

A rascal girl.

Mkpokija

A rascal boy

Itetemite Inanamina

Long long time ago. A phrase usually used in the begining of folklore.

Epulu Ka Epu Aburo   Germination is not
fruiting. This implies that what is
Amili Ka Mi: inborn cannot be
equated with what is learnt.

Okwukwu   Owl

Nwaobala   Pussy cat

Ike Nkwucha   To be on guard. To be
alert, circumspect

Ojogbulu Udene,   An extremely bad
situation.
Sigbue Nkakwu:

Tutuntu Ani   A fact finder

Si Onui Lulu   Hold back your
statement

Ukwubenka   A knowledgeable old
person. An anthill is
also called ukwubenka.

Nwa Mkpukpu Nmee   This is said of someone
who is not matured; a weakling.

Ofu Ogoli   Unserious person

Osaka
A prodigal

One who is wasteful?

Adina Nta Adi Nimo
who is lazy.

This is said of someone

Ekpenta

Leprosy.

Okitikpa

Small/pox

Otolo

Diarrhoea

Nkpolochichi

A smallish nocturnal insect that make shrill sound. A smallish person who talks too much is also called by same name.

Oji Onu

A boastful person

Itu Onu
boasts. A braggart.

This is said of one who

Inye Nzo

An act of betting

Omaka Gbulu Okwulu

All is fine expression

Oghom

Loss

Ulu	Profit
Aguba	Local razor
Mmili Ofia	Euphemism for excreta
Azu Uno	Euphemism for toilet. The back yard is also generally referred to as azu uno.
Mbekwu Ako Na Iro	A notorious person
Ngige household item (A rope)	A line for drying
Ngiga preserving dried fish/meat	A wired basket for
Ibeli used in swatting files	Bound leather strings
Ubelegede Ebe	Last caution
Mbelede	Surprise
Ogbolo made out of bamboo	An outdoor bench

Abana Odikwo Mma Oju Oku: An expression seeking if all is well.

Imalima   Known and unknown

Agbagalasa   A large tray made of
mat material or pan

Nkpodu   A basket which is hung
above the fire place
and is used to preserve
soup items

Ogbu Ebunu   A doctor

Ekpelima   A bandit

Mpeli   Nervousness or lack of
confidence. This is associated
with shaking of limbs.

Uma   Something that is appetizing
and palatable.

Onye Ufufu Na Asukporo   :An idiot

Ajelekpe   A weaved raffia tray

Owa Na Ikpo   One who is restless/active
hence always roving about.

Ntite	A sponge made out of banana/plantain trunk and used for painting floors and walls.
Mkpilite	Small mortar used in grinding soup ingredients.
Mbazu	A tool for digging up yams. Also said of part of someone's body that is seen as enormous.
Mbazu ukwu:	A large waist.
Onu Ulolo	A drainage hole, made on the wall surrounding the compound.
Usokwu	Kitchen
Ikpo Nchala	Something that is depleted/empty
Akpaife Ocha/Oji	Slightly fair or dark skinned
Ona akwu nakwo?	Is it all well expression?
Ute Agini	A mat made out of palm fronds
Ere	Groin

Ute Mkapala fibre	Mat made out of a bamboo
Ichekuliche	A type of soldier ant
Ido	Light brown soldier ants that habit on guava, mango, orange and pear trees.
Inye Ori	The initiation of kids into masquerade, during which the kids lie down and the mou ogonogo, a masquerade, steps over.
Ijagbo Madu	Scolding one loudly.
Oli Nni Aguta Oku	A lazy person
Akpulekwe	Cane
Akpuluke	A short person
Ogige compound	A fence and could also be a
Oba	A barn

Ogwe

A tree trunk used as footbridge over a stream or gutter. Ogwe is also an exclamation cautioning a masquerade that there is a gutter or similar obstacle across its way.

Ekelesu

Said of someone's position or something that is in order or sorted out.

Ekpo Ekpo

Havoc/Despoliation

Iruanwulinwu
Mild misunderstanding/dissension

Okwu Na Uka
Disagreement/disputes that generates much mistrust.

Ile Buza Buza

Being inquisitive

Akpata
Bamboo shelve usually in the kitchen

Onuilo

Village playing ground

Efulefu	A good for nothing. A lay about
Onye Uma	A nuisance
Uko	A kitchen shelf that is placed over the fire place. This is used for drying grains, vegetables and other food ingredients.
Igba Uko	Seeking consultation
Omekitolo	A notorious person
Bulo Bulo	Something done half way; half measure
Ekwulekwu	Irritating outburst/talkative
Okwule	A house chamber/room
Oda	Outdoor chamber from where masquerade like Ijele, Aku ne eche enyi take off and to which they retire.

Okeakpa	A long broom used for sweeping outdoor ground. It is made from branches of a shrub.
Itu Keni Keni	Spoiling for a fight
Onunu Ochu	A case whereby one is badly hurt, or dispossessed of his important belongings.
Orummili Atu Nnu	Sea that dissolves endless salt. 5Said of someone that is insatiable. When positive it refers to a well to do person. The wealth is considered as the sea that dissolves endless salt.
Ukpaka Njuwa	Someone who is carefree
Ukpolo pebbles/missile.	Older name for 'iche' stone
Mbekele Eju	A piece of earthenware
Otungbulu Muo	A compulsive lair
Itu Ngwe Ngwe	Spoiling for a fight
Okolobuba	Butterfly

Ugwulube	Locust
Kpalakwukwu	Pigeon
Nduli	Dove
Okwa	Bush fowl

Ubii — Said of a person that is indolent, lazy.

Abu Na Mme — Blood and pus: Said of a person that is wicked and vindictive.

Akaje — To mock, to taunt, contemptuous reproach

Ukubu	Shoulder
Mpala	Stride
Ugbogulu	Pumpkin
Ukpana	Grasshopper

Ikpo Efeleke — This is said of an unstable agenda/act

Ibobo — Aura, charisma, fame, prestige

Ubi	Cobra
Obu	Crow
Edi	African Deer
Iso Isi Ka Edi	Acting blindly
Onwunwu	Mockery
Ubosi Di Obuonye Obuonye:	About being dark
Igbarira	Unnecessarily being difficult
Ulili	Squirrel that eats grains
Osa	Squirrel that eats nuts
Uli	Chica indelible ink
Abuke	Fowl with scanty feathers
Ikwunye Okwu Na Ese	Complicating matters
Odudu	Sand fly
Ili Ami Lie Mpio Mpio	Greedy person

Ino na uju	In a state of mourning
Igba Ndu	An oath swearing by two or more people not to harm themselves or not to leave themselves in case of a man and woman in love.
Mbekwu Ako Na Iro	A notorious person
Olokoto	Abundance of wealth
Ama afia	Tooth Ache
Akuebelisi	Loner
Ofeke	Scallywag
Ebu	Wasp
Ozu Anuisi	Foolish person
Imilikiti	Multitude
Ndalagugu	Trough, Ditch
Obole	Itchiness in female organ caused by walking across cassava water or bitter leaf water.

Ajo Ukpa	Bad company
Ukpa	Wall nut
Ida Mba	Despair
Ntumade	Taken by surprise
Agwo Enwe Enyi	Wicked person
Ikpa Oke	Discrimination
Ikwu Igono	Hopping in a stream
Ilu Egenege	Standing on ones toes to gain a better view of something
Okili	Corn seedlings
Ugom	Prison
Otulukpokpo	Woodpecker
Iku Ngbanu	Excessive haste
Iyi Eli Oba	An evil doer
Utu Na Alu Obosi	Spoilsport
Nkonko	Whitlow

Ikuku Ama Nonya	Artful dodger
Otua Poo Nya Lima	If the worse comes to worst
Ije Ngugu Ogili Na Ikelike Nnu:	Dubious activity
Anasi	First wife
Mbanna	Older form of greetings
Ikwu Na Ibe	Entire community kinsmen and women.
Ogbo Na Uke	Militant and aggressive band of spirit adversaries.
Okwu Na Uka	Endless wrangling
Nta Na Imo	Odds and ends
Mmaoge	Machete
Obejili	Machete
Odum	Lion
Iyi uwa	Oath
Alu	Sacrilege [defiance of natural law]

Igba afa   Divination

Ezi ofia   Boar

Nkpu   Anthill

Ibubo iyi   Abrogation of oath

Okochi   Dry season

Iju uno   Activities to spiritually
                               cleanse a home where
                               sacrileges or other
                               abomination were
                               carried out.

Uga agba   Muzzle made from
bark of palm frond.

Ogbugba nkono   Esophagus

Ume julu   Liver

Ugbogulu   Pumpkin
Ife nru   Homage

Ugani   Famine

Ogwe   -A trunk across a stream, gutter,
ditch

---

designed for safe passage. It is also an alert to masquerades to avoid a ditch or similar obstacles.

Ukutazu   Offspring

EXPOSITION OF EGWU OTA AND UVIE

EGWU OTA

Egwu Ota is the royal dance of Onitsha people. It is also the name of the orchestra that supplies the rhythms for the dance. It is perhaps a unique aspect of Onitsha cultural heritage for it has neither rubbed off on their neighbours on the East Bank of the Niger nor been adopted by them.The Egwu Ota orchestra is made up of ozi, the bass drum, kpikpili, the alto drum, nwoke, the tenor drum, njanja, the cymbals and uba or ida, the baritone drum. The cavities of the drums, except the uba, have no opening at the bottom, like other drums. This peculiar shape derives from Benin.There are only seven egwu ota orchestras throughout Onitsha; one resides permanently in the imeobi while the rest reside in the abode of the six Ndichie Ume.Egwu ota, like okpu ododo or red cap, is one of the paraphernalia bestowed by the Obi on the Ndichie Ume, Onitsha first class Chiefs at their conferment. These paraphernalia, though financed by the individual Chiefs, come under the jurusdication of the Obi.Egwu ota is performed by the Obi during Ofala festival, Umatu festivals and the ceremony of Iselu Aka Anu all presided over by the Obi. The is performed by ndichie ume on the occasion of igbunye ewu, inata okpu, ite umato and igba ogbalido. It is also features at the second burial obsequies of an Onitsha householder, a woman whose son is an Ozo title holder or one who is initiated into Otu Odu or the mmuo cult.When the egwu ota orchestra performs, ndichie take their turn, in ascending order seniority, to dance to its rhythms. Others including non-titled men may dance when the ndichie are not doing so. It is the preserve of an ndichie ume to end his dance performance by stopping the orchestra. The rhythms these instruments produce blend so well that they become such easy flowing music that move men and women to want to get up and dance or at least to nod and sway in ther seats.

UFIE

Ufie is the pair of wooden gongs with which royalty at Onitsha announces the dawn of a new day. The gongs are dedicated to an Obi's service during his consecration rituals at the Udo shrine. Kola nut is broken and libation poured amidst prayers to make gongs and the two playing sticks worthy of the service into which they are being commissioned. Thereafter, they are played to announce the installation of a new Obi.Every morning at about 5.00 a.m. the drummers hammers out a salute to each Obi starting with Chima. The salute wakes up the Obi. He takes his bath, ritually breaks a kolanut and performs his other early morning rituals. These he must conclude before the second playing of the ufie, which signals the opening of the palace to the public. Throughout ofala day, praises of the Obis are hammered out intermittently on the ufie. The sound is unmistakable.A long time ago, so recounts Onitsha tradition, before the succession dispute that brought Oba Esigie on the throne of Idu royalty at

Idu played the Ufie to announce the dawn of each new day. During the dispute Chima, the contestant to the throne, seized the ufie, the only emblem of royalty he could capture. No ufie ever played again in Idu. Instead, the palace made its female slaves to crow like cocks to announce each new dawn.Following the death of Eze Chima at Obior, the final march eastwards, away from the long reach of the arm of the Oba, was temporarily halted. When it resumed, the princes and elders agreed that whoever was able to produce and play an ufie, an act royalty alone could perform, would become Obi. Everyone had assumed that the original ufie was in Ukpali's custody in Obior. But Oreze had brought it secretly with him and lashed it to his raft. Thus while other aspirants to Obiship went to the forest to cut trees for the ufie, Oreze simply scrubbed his ufie clean, played it and won the Obiship for himself and his heirs.

FESTIVALS

INTRODUCTION

Prior to the advent of money economy, Onitsha was basically an agricultural community. Its economy was therefore agrarian. Its social order was governed according to the prevailing agricultural seasons. For instance, there are festivals celebrated during the cleaning and tilling of new farmland. Others are celebrated during planting, weeding and harvesting periods. On the day of rest (that is Eke) from farming engagement, the people employ themselves in domestic work. There are four days that make the Onitsha week, namely: Oye, Afor, Nkwo and Eke.

OFALA FESTIVAL

Various interpretations have been made of the precise nature of the Ofala Festival. Its importance has rarely been in doubt and every Obi of Onitsha, presides over the ceremony.It is the Onitsha Festival of the year, one of those fundamental observances that have stayed strong and healthy despite local enthusiasm for change. Most popular and simple explanation is that it is the climax of the New Yam Festival, the traditional, annual, thanksgiving celebration.In fact, each year, it serves to emphasize the complex nature of the Obi's duties: pure government and the appeasing of the desired (perhaps outmoded) of his subjects.

The tremendous rate of change in the social attitudes of the Onitsha people makes it difficult to pinpoint the root purpose of Ofala. Efforts to do this have resulted in tradition and folklore blending two entirely different stories into a drama which people plunge with great if vague sincerity of purpose.The first story relates to the four days immediately preceding Ofala. They are spent in "retreat" (Inye-Ukwu-Na nlo) in his templum by the Obi. In keeping with his role as a "divine" king and as the sacred repository of his people's prosperity the Obi devotes those days to communicating with the earth and fertility god. He spends them trying to bring the forces of nature under control so as to ensure his people's welfare. The "retreat" is preceded by a divination service conducted by the chief priest of Umuikem, the Levites of Onitsha. Throughout this period the Obi, painted all over with white chalk, wears only a white loin cloth and a white cap. He neither shaves nor bathes. He receives no visitors no matter how distinguished, abstains from all pleasures and suspends all state matters. He meditates, performs acts of purification on behalf of his subjects and himself and some say, he mourns the loss of those of his subjects who died in the preceding year. The successful completion of his period is as of vital importance to the people as it is to the Obi himself. To the people because it guarantees for a better future and to the Obi because the non-completion of the "retreat" would cost him a royal funeral and a fitting place in the life hereafter.

The other story on the origin of Ofala concerns the dramatic association of the Onitsha people with yam, Discorea spp. Forced by famine to explore every possible avenue for food, the people decided to eat yam, until then regarded with suspicion. Precautions were taken to avert its supposed harmful effects. The smallest kindred were commissioned to eat yam first. Following a set course-roasted yam treated with nn'edi leaves followed by yam pounded into foo-foo and served with nsala soup (all accomplished by prayers, incantations and offerings to the gods and ancestral spirits to make them allies) – kindred after kindred with no fatal results. Yam thus became a solution to their problems and a cherished source of foods.Because he was successful in negotiating with the earth god for the prosperity of his people, because he did not die while mourning the dead and because of his joy at the discovery of yam as a valuable source of food supply, the Obi, "a virtual prisoner in the palace compound" was released by tradition to rejoice and give thanks to the Great Unknown.Might not ofala have descended from or been modeled on the Igue festival at Benin? When it is remembered that for many years "the Onitsha people were living in the realm of the Oba of Benin," the possibility is not far-fetched.

Ofala Festival runs for two days. The evening preceding the first day,the "retreat" ends and the Obi leaves the templum. His relations, singing and dancing, keep vigil. In their homes the Ndichie Ume busy themselves with preparations against the morrow; their trumpeters, working on bush cow horns, herald the coming show. Everywhere there is noise which decreases as the night advances.As the new day emerges, daily life in town runs its normal course except for three cannon shots fired from the palace at intervals. Each shot carries with it a message to the people. The first at about nine, tells the people that the big day has come at last. The second at noon warns them to cook and eat their lunch get ready to report to the palace. The third at three invites them to throng the palace square.Spectators begin to throng the square. In the past men and women entered it by different gates and took their positions on opposite sides of the ground. People wearing dresses of different patterns and hue take their seats in palm-leaf booths or stand in the shade of overhanging leafy boughs. It is for this occasion, tradition tells, that the Otumoye lake (to which is attributed a mysterious origin) supplied dresses to the people on the understanding that the clothes or their rags must be returned. Some climb trees in order to have a better view.The square is full of activity. Drums beat, men dance women sing. Female relations of the Obi parade the square. They are looking their best, their necks and wrists ringed round with coral beads. Waving the horse's tails they carry in their hands, they sing and dance traditional pieces in honour of the Obi, their voices rising high above the din, which pervades the atmosphere.From one corner of the compound a pencil of smoke twists lazily into the air, revealing to the observer the presence of the rainmaker and his efforts to scatter the gathering clouds.Away in the distance and closing in on all sides, orchestras perform. Each heralds a member of the Ndichie Ume arriving to pay homage to the Obi. Closely attended by his retinue as he enters the palace grounds, each Ndichie Ume first dances round the square to the rhythm of his own orchestra and then to that of the royal drums before taking his seat. He is wearing a robe or a skirt and jumper of damask or velvet, a necklace of dull red, egg size coral beads, writ lets to match and a plume-studded, wide-brimmed hat. The other member of Ndichie wears ceremonial robes less dignifying.Drumming, singing and dancing continue until at a sign, the Onowu (Prime Minister) leads the Ndichie to the Obi and present him to the public. They move to the entrance of Ime-Obi palace through which the Obi is to enter the square. Gradually the noise subsides.   Conversation, drumming, singing and dancing cease and a hush settles on the square. All eyes become fixed to the gate around which stand the Ndichie. Then the Obi enters. His entrance is greeted with full-throated cheer from his people. The Ndichie make way for him and another wild cheer runs through the crowd as he comes into full view. Standing there, his tall and balanced frame is full of majesty. He is dressed in a sleeveless jumper of brown velvet with dark spots, fringed at the wrist with strips of the same material hanging down to his ankles. His trousers are of blue and white striped velvet. Round his ankles are tied strings of little brass bells, which jingle as he walks. His arms are circled with brass armlets. In his right hand he carries a state sword of brass, in his left a horsetail said to protect him from evil machinations. The most striking aspect of his dress is two-foot high headwear, crested with many coloured ostrich plumes. In it he towers high above his attendant chiefs, attractive and dignified. Beneath its wide brim, his fiery eyes are alert and watchful for Ofala, though a joyful occasion, affords some the opportunity to test his vitality. Tradition tells of the days when the Obi celebrated Ofala in a loincloth, his body bare. It adds that the first Ofala suit was procured from Idah for Obi Omozele by his grandson Idoko, whose mother was Igala.

As quickly as it rose, the noise greeting subsides into a din. A bass soloist burst into a chant:

The king! The King!
The king is benevolent

The chant attracts the full-throated chorus of ''Ewo! Ewo!'' as the Obi moves forward flanked on either side by two boys wearing embroidered signal red gowns and caps and carrying shinning brass swords. Attended by a train of Ndichie, Ozo titled men and his relations; he goes in an anti-clockwise direction. He stops once or twice in his course and salutes shrines which line the sides of the ground and which were once regarded as indispensable to a prosperous reign and good government. After covering about one-third of the ground, he dances to the rhythm of the traditional royal drums and retires to rest in the templum. There is a report that in dancing, the Obi ''carries a great weight, generally a sack of earth, on his back to prove that he is still able to support the burden and cares of state. Were he unable to discharge this duty, he would be immediately deposed and perhaps stoned''. The Onitsha people who argue that no one ever remembers them happening and that they are neither reflected in their tradition and folklore nor traceable in present-day celebrations have denied these statements.In the interval, within the templum, the Obi takes the official salute of the Ndichie in their order of seniority. Outside, the square is alive with drumming and dancing which ceases immediately the Obi comes out.

Twice more he parades the square, saluting the shrines as he goes. Each time he adds another third of the ground to that previously covered and each time he does the royal dance before retiring to rest. Tradition has it that at one time it was the practice for the Obi to sit "in state surrounded by his subjects and foretell the events of the ensuring year". After that he retires escorted by the Ndichie and acknowledges the respects paid him by his subjects. These respects include entertaining him with a display of dances from the neighbouring towns and with wrestling bouts. Today these forms of entertainers are no longer in vogue. Age grade societies have taken over. Wearing its uniform and carrying its banner, each society now dances from the enjoyment of the Obi and his Ndichie.

Reproduced from Ofala Festival by:
J. O. Nzekwu
Published in Nigeria Magazine No. 61 of 1959

AJACHI

Ajachi, which comes first, marks the beginning of the Onitsha traditional year. Ajachi is made up of two words, Aja and Chi. Aja is sacrifice. Ichu Aja is sacrifice that is offered to malevolent spirits only. Chi is one's chief guardian spirit, commonly spoken of as god. It must not be confused with Chi-Ukwu contracted to Chukwu, the great God, Chin'eke God the Creator or Olisa ebuluwa, God that fashions the world. Everyone has a Chi, the guardian deity that deputizes for Chi-Ukwu. Chi is physically represented by Mkpulu chi, consecrated pieces of egbo stem about four inches long, which have been stripped of their bark. A child shares his father's Chi until he is old enough to obtain one himself.Ajachi literally means sacrifice to one's chief guardian spirit. It is however not a sacrifice as such. Rather it is a service of penance for sin. The people show their contrition by wearing ordinary or more customary old clothes. They do not dress in their best like in other festivals like Ofala. Additionally, they celebrate the feast annually around June when food is scarce than any other time of the year. At this period, the new crops like yam are not yet matured while old ones are running out of stock.At Ajachi the Head of the family brings out the Chi and other ndi mmuo, like ikenga into the open compound. He takes his seat facing them and explains to them that the

feast about to take place marks the beginning of Onitsha traditional year. He thanks them for the good things of life given to him and his family in the outgoing year and prays for an abundant harvest and other goods things of life in the year ahead. Then a little water is sprinkled on them so they can wash their hands before partaking of the food provided. The next item is the presentation of kolanuts as a token of friendship. Then follows a gift of pounded yam previously dipped in the palm oil soup, a small portion being placed on the head. Each wife contributes her portion to the food cooked; that of Anasi the head wife being accepted first. This ceremonial offering of the food having been completed, it is assumed that the spirits are satisfied, that they have absorbed the spiritual essence of the food. A child is then invited to collect the food from the ndi mmuo. He carries the food away and shares it with other children.

Pouring a little palm-wine and gin over the Chi and the ndi mmuo then makes the drinks offering.

Finally, more water is sprinkled on them in order that the spirits may comply with the custom of washing the hands after food. After this principal performance by the head of the family, merrymaking continues in various homes while the youths male and female disperse; some others go to the village square (Onu ilo) to watch the activities of masquerades like Ulaga and Otuiche. The festival lasts one week.

By Obiora Obiogbol

IFEJIOKU

Ifejioku, some say is a composite word derived from

"Ife" to worship, "Ji" yam and "Oku bu Oku" riches.

Thus Ifejioku means worshipping the yam crop that is

generally accepted as wealth. I am however inclined to

subscribe to the view of those who say Ifejioku is a abbreviation of "Ife Ugbo Ji Wetalu Oku" that is because Ife Ji Oku is a harvest festival that is connected with the yam.There is no gainsaying that yam is the favourite food of the inhabitants east of the Niger. It is to him what the potato is to the typical Irish man. A shortage of yam supply is a cause of genuine distress for no substitute gives the same sense of satisfaction.In years gone by, it might be legitimately affirmed that the life of the people was bound up with yam supply, hence wealth is measured by the size and number of yam barns one has. These enumerated factors suggest the motive behind the feast of Ife Ji Oku that might be described as an offering to the spirits of the field, with special reference to the presiding deity of the yam crop. The fowls offered must be carried to the farm and slain there, the blood being sprinkled on a few choice yams. When the ceremony is completed, everything is taking home. The yams are laid before the ancestral altar together with the farming implements. The fowls are eaten at the subsequent feast. The whole community shares in this harvest thanksgiving.In some cases, the feast is celebrated once a year and is observed at a scared spot. It is held when the first new yams are available (i.e) Yams, the seed of which were planted in the first month of the year in order to be ready in time for the feast of "Ife Ji Oku" whereas the main crop is planted in the second month.In the ceremony, which is service of "Ilo Mmuo". The sacrificial offerings consist of Kolanuts, Fowls, Egbo leaves and yams (the latter being boiled). Kola nuts are produced and standing in front of the ancestral altar the petitioner says, eat this kola nut and help the yams in the small farms grow. If the rain be too much may they not drown and if the sun be too strong may they not cause them to wither? If I plant yam as small as this when I dig up may it be as long as this (indicating with his hands and arms the size he has in mind). He prays that fever may not trouble him or his people and that all things may prosper in his hand. Thereafter, the petitioner handles the fowl and repeats same then the throat of the fowl is slit across and the blood sprinkled. The carcass is given to the children to make soup. After the ceremony, feasts and merry making continues. A month later the people begin to dig up new yams.Also, it is essential in native laws and customs to distinguish between" Igo-mmuo" a propitiatory sacrifice and Ilo mmuo a festival to placate the spirits. The motive behind the services to " Igo mmuo" – (strange spirits) corresponds somewhat with the burnt offerings of the Israelites. The underlining principle is derived from the word "Igo Agugo" meaning to deny. The offerings are presented with an element of protestation. The petitioner asserts that he has done no wrong; he has not trespassed against the law of the land or against the community then asks why this evil has befallen on him? If however by any chance he has sinned inadvertently, he now makes this sacrifice as atonement for these unknown misdeeds.

As it is all so uncertain, the food brought before the Igo mmuo is left untouched. It is holy "NSO". The reason is that there can be no sharing in a feast where there are no happy mutual associations. Almost in despair, because he does not know why he is troubled with sorrow, ill health or whatever form the visitation takes, he leaves the sacrifice at the altar. He cannot partake of it. A man who knows perfectly well that he is guilty of wrong doing will on no account venture to make sacrifice of Igo Mmuo. He would be in mortal dread lest the spirit should take summary vengeance on his hypocrisy.

ILO MMUO

The services to the Ilo mmuo (Familiar spirits) have somewhat similarity to the "peace offering" of the Israelites. There are propitiatory services, which having proved acceptable brings about a sense of reconciliation hence the act of sacrifice, which has established peace between god, and man is followed by rejoicing and feasting.

By Obiora Obiogbolu

UMATU

The Umatu festival takes place during the harvesting of maize, vegetables and fruits. The principal feature of the festival is nni-oka (pap or corn food); goats and fowls are killed on the occasion for the preparation of Ogbono or Okwulu soup. First of all the goats and fowls are offered to God and the ancestors on the shrine. Prayers are then said for good health and prosperity of individuals and the community.Nni-oka is placed on top of the list of local menu. After the festival this type of food is eaten on special days, especially on Sunday in modern times. It is generally taken in the morning but can sometimes be taken at mid-day or at night.During the festival people are found moving around from place to place making merry. New dances sometimes make their debut in the village square for the entertainment of eager spectators. The festival lasts for sixteen days beginning with the exclusive celebration by the Obi of Onitsha for a period of four days after which the celebration by the populace takes place in the following order for four days respectively:

Eze-idi

Ikpala Isi

Umueze Chima

The last day of the celebration is known as Ikpoko Akwukwo Ogili, that is the clearing of the vegetable containers and packages.

Nnanyelugo S. I. Bosah.

OWUWAJI

After twenty-four days the Owuwaji festival begins. It is the premier annual festival because it marks the eating of new yams in the year. Harvesting of new yams is at its peak. The celebration lasts for twenty-four days and is performed in turn by different sections of the community, before the Obi of Onitsha. The reason is that in days gone by when yam first became known for human consumption it was feared to be poisonous. Subsequently, it was decided that before the Obi ate the new yam various parts of the community should first eat and its reaction watched.This is how it became the custom that the Awada village, which is the smallest clan in Onitsha, opens the new yam festival for two days after which the Eke na Ubene clan for another two days.On the fifth day, the Ubulu na Ikem kindred – the Obi's diviners, celebrate the new yam. On the following day thay remain in retreat till the next day in preparation for the Obi's retreat, which takes place on the seventh day. For five days the Obi remains in-communicado during which he undergoes purification and maintains spiritual contact with his ancestors.In the interim, the

Ikolobia Ekwensu and the Ikpala Ugwu na Obamkpa perform their ceremonies for one day respectively. Ikolobia Ekwensu are men who have achieved great heroic deeds like killing a person during war time or killing fierce animals such as tiger, leopard, buffalo, hippopotamus, etc, during hunting expedition. Their new yam celebration has therefore an additional purpose of observing an anniversary of their past act of heroism and also of propitiating the gods to protect them from any fatal accident. This is known as Ogbalido.Three days after the Ogbalido comes the end of the first phase of the new yam festival. On the following day the Obi emerges from his retreat and prepares for his Ofala festival, which takes place the next day.With the passing of the Ofala, the owuwaji festival is resumed. On the day following the azu ofala is the new yam celebration of Ikpala eze who are the diokpala or heads of various families of Eze Chima. The next day is the observation of Ito Ukpukpa, which signifies general washing of utensils and abstinence from further eating of new yam preparatory to the Obi's owuwaji celebration.The Obi's new yam celebration known as Ikelebeji takes place the next morning and lasts for a whole day. As a mark of respect for the monarchy, nobody else should prepare a pounded yam food for that day, expect the Obi.

Nnanyelugo S. I. Bosah.

OSISITE

Osisite literally means cooking. One may be tempted to ask the motive behind the name given to this feast. The reason or answer is not farfetched because the festival entails superfluous cooking of many dishes as a thanksgiving to God Almighty for sparing the lives for the populace in witnessing the New Year festival. It is also a jubilation commemorating the survival of the king after eaten the New Yam. Yam no doubt is a major staple food that is prepared in different ways. With other foodstuffs, the community is hardly in want of food and can weather through famine.Osisite comes up nine days after Ikelebeji, which is the king's celebration of new yam. The Ugwu na Obamkpa clan celebrates on the first day, while the Ezechima celebrates on the second day. Every family prepares various foods. Visits are exchanged and guests are lavishly entertained with food and drinks. On their departure, the new farm products are given to them to take home. The idea behind this gesture is two fold. The first is a proof that the season's harvest is rich and plentiful and the second derives from the saying – Oji lue uno okwue onye chelu ya; implying that when a gift reaches home, it explains how it came about.

The festival is celebrated around mid-November when the rains have stopped and during which inter-village wrestling matches, marriages, marriage engagements, and debut of new musical outfits take place. The female folks are not left out as the bethroted also perform the 'Ije Uri' custom during the period of the festival.Osisite in all intents and purposes is a period of galore celebration. The memories of this festival are remembered for a long time. This explains the saying 'Na Osisite ka ona ebe; implying that all the preparations of the new musical outing and other engagements earlier highlighted would showcase them during the festival.

By Obiora Obiogbolu.

AFTERWORD

As I said in the beginning, this project of unraveling Onitsha names, perhaps the first of its kind cannot be all conclusive. One thing about Onitsha names and likewise the town is that the people are proud to be associated with them. With delight we introduce ourselves to non-indigenous associates while not forgetting to mention that we are from Onitsha; a fathomless amour-propre which others sometimes consider as arrogance and uppity. This association is not unconnected with the past glories that propelled Onitsha to a front line town.

This is traceable to the efforts of our progenitor Chima and his kindred. The final crossing to the East of the Niger was planned to afford them a peaceful place to carry on their farming and trade. By 1840, Onitsha had become a great trading post attracting people from Igala, Lokoja, Nupe, Idah, Illah, Aguleri, Anam, Nzam, Ossamari, Oguta, Warri, Aboh, Atani, Odekpe, Ndoni and others. It is a glaring oversight that we have not put in place edifices to immortalize our progenitors- Chima, the successive Obis, Okomanya, Ogbodogo, Idoko and other personalities. I reflected elsewhere on the need for an Onitsha museum. Back to the town's glory, from early 20th century to shortly after the Nigerian civil war there was hardly and field of endeavour that Onitsha was not adequately represented – Judiciary, Medicine, Engineering, Clergy, Politics, Bureaucracy, Sports, Civil Service, and Army etc. The list of individuals that made marks in these various fields is rather too long to mention. Some few numero uno will suffice. On politics and government Dr. Nnamdi Azikwe, the Owelle of Onitsha was the first Nigerian Governor-General and First President of Nigeria amongst other first positions he held. In field of Judiciary, Sir Louis Mbanefo was the first Justice of Eastern Nigeria and the first Nigerian to serve on the bench of the World Court at The Hague. Onitsha has produced over thirty Justices since independence. Doctor Uwaechia was the first Ibo Doctor to establish private practice in Eastern Nigeria. John Cross Anyogu was the first Ibo Catholic Priest to be consecrated Bishop and Reverend Anyaegbunam was also the first Ibo man ever to become a Reverend Pastor in the Anglican Protestant Church. He was ordained in 1898. Bishop Onyeabo was a precursor Anglican Bishop in Eastern Nigeria. Professor Chike Obi is a pioneer Professor in Mathematics and late Ben Enwonwu was also a pioneer artist and sculptor. Late Colonel Emmanuel Ifeajuna won the first medal in high jump for the country in Vancouver Canada Commonwealth Games of 1958. Late Colonel Sokei and Major Nzegwu occupied high positions in the Army and Air force respectively before the Nigerian Civil War. Ukpabi Asika, Ajie of Onitsha was the

Administrator of East Central State. On both the federal and Regional levels, our people held various ministerial positions.In Foreign Service, Mr. B. C. Obanye, Mr. Akunwafo A. Osakwe, late L. O. V. Anionwu, Mr. Ugokwe Chike Chukwura were pioneer ambassadors that represented the country. You cannot talk of Onitsha without the Onitsha main market, which was once the largest of such markets in West Africa. The first modernization of the market was the initiative of enterprising Onitsha men, Mr. P. H. Okolo, Mr Ogo Ibeziako, Onoli of Onitsha, Mr. Peter Achukwu, Mr. J.C. Oranye, Chief Isaac Mbanefo – Odu of Onitsha and others all blessed memories. A loan of 500,000 (Pounds Sterling) was raised by Onitsha Town Council from Eastern Nigeria Development Board to build the market. Another field of endeavour was the establishment of colleges. Apart from (CKC) Christ the King College and (DMGS) Dennis Memorial Grammar School and (QRC) Queen Rosary of College, that were set up by Missionaries, a good number of others were founded by Onitsha indigenes, namely; Etukokwu Commercial College by Chief J. U. Etukokwu, Oduah of Onitsha, Metropolitan College by Mr. P. O. Chude and Associates. Modebe Grammar School by Akunnia Victor Modebe, Ziks Commercial School by Mrs. Lily Arinze, Washington Memorial Grammar School by Chief Emengo – Onya of Onitsha and Associates. It is also on record that Dr. Namdi Azikiwe – the late Owelle of Onitsha founded Lagos City College, University of Nigeria Nsukka and Premier College, Onitsha. In Sapele, Mr. Chude also founded Chude College.

It is sad that these competitive edges of the town are now dulled. It is rather worrisome that those we taught how to run now reach the finishing line without us in sight. Those that lived in our back houses and found succour there are now buying us out even at Inland town that was for a long time the preserve of indigenes. The blames are not far from our doorsteps. The ills are multifarious – decline in school enrolment, burgeoning crime wave, laid back attitude, lack of communal commitments etc. The late sage, Dr. Nnamdi Azikiwe, the Owelle once cautioned that a town always in a festive mood cannot progress. So much of our resources are wasted on non-wealth creating ventures.There are cleavages on business front and as well as on political front where we are yet to make a mark even on Local Government level. For Onitsha to survive and prosper it requires utilizing the full latent abilities and connections of our people. Dare I say we have not used our connections very well compared to the manner other comparably famed towns do. The rate we are losing grounds is frightening.

For a better tomorrow, we need to put in place committed efforts to address these ills. We need a united front in tackling the development tasks. In fact we shall have to run extra miles to be competitive as others are not likely to stay aloof. Of great importance is the need for the Igwe to be sensitive to these ills hence begin to mobilize our people. As the saying goes, when the king steps out to dance to the beat of the drums, he should look back occasionally to see if the crowd is following. All other ruling arms of the town must live up to expectation demanded of them. The same clarion call goes to all Onitsha men and women of diverse professions.

Let me seize the opportunity to call for fence mending amongst the members of Obi-In-Council. Apparently a good number of the Ume .i.e. the first class Chiefs are not resident in town while I do not suppose that it is mandatory for them to reside permanently in Onitsha, there is the need not only for them to visit home regularly but also to meet their various roles and besides and most importantly to influence positively on the development of the people and town.

This cannot materialize with the prevalent schism, which is gradually becoming internecine amongst the various ruling arms and the town in general. A worrisome angle is the endless suspension of the Traditional Prime Minister, Onowu Iyasele. I asked a Third Class Chief, if the town can afford not to have a Prime Minister. His answer – yes and no – was unhelpful. Further he quipped that he has come to find out that there is hardly any difference between First Class Chiefs and others. With an atmosphere of insincerity that is pervading the ruling class, what is not in order is bound to crumble. When the head is no good, the body does not have a dog chance. The ethos of the people can be shaped by the quality of their leaders who are pivots around whom the people revolve. The saying 'Ana esi na uno amalu mma welu puta ilo' means that one's goodness ought to start from home before going outside. We must be united to be able to check on our common foes and hence be in position to progress.

Let me return to the name exposition and also make a case for fence mending between the Church and Onitsha people. There is hardly any Onitsha name that does not invoke God's mercy, assistance, protection, intercession or call for his praise. Our antecedents hinged their faith on Chineke; God the Creator, Amama Amasi Amasi; A Super Being whose make up is beyond our comprehension; an unfathomable mystery. The Christian faith is also wrapped up in our belief in one God, the Omnipotent, Omniscience and Omnipresence. Likewise the Muslims hold Allah as the Exalted Super Being. Though the mode of worship differs, every theological position derives from God, The Creator, and Our invisible and All-Important Observer in heaven.

For a long while, the Church/Onitsha people relationship has remained sour. Most of the people's mode of worship and other social activities are considered fetish. The case here is that the Church has married their doctrines with that of our neighbouring towns. This pattern was the case in ancient Israel, Greece Rome, Russia and England etc. I would agree that what we call culture/tradition could be modified. They have actually been so over the centuries and the Church has had her own changes too. Giving this trend, the Church in Onitsha should try to accommodate some of the traditional rites of the people. Come to think of it, these rituals have been in existence before the advent of Christianity. The people at the time were cajoled, brainwashed, brow beaten and inveigled in giving up their traditional practices that were considered ungodly.

The situation today requires better understanding from both quarters. It is amazing that some people would consider prayer offered during the breaking of kolanuts as fetish. Some cultural die hard on the other hand would not entertain the mention of Christ while breaking the kolanut. This is going beyond the pale. The Church, which is supposed to invite the populace into her fold, is now distancing herself from the populace. The major issue at stake concerns initiation into 'Ozo' and second burial rites. Sensitive as they may be, I believe that consensus can be reached. One can recall that Late Obi Okosi II had a special seat at St. Mary's Church in the fifties. The history of Immanuel Church cannot be complete without the role of Late Odu Mbanefo II. That the Church welcomed the participation of our Late Monarch and First Class Chief who also administered the rites of the town reflected a good understanding then. Why this understanding has not worked out now in Onitsha is traceable to the squealing and caviling nature of our people in both quarters. It is high time we joined the constructive crew hence quit the demolition team. Else if the inveterate rift is allowed to continue we will be denying ourselves the common front required in addressing the various development ills of the town. Some people will cite urbanization as a reason for the rot and ills we are experiencing. A good number of others would trace the multifarious problems to our spiritual/moral deficiency. Both perspectives lend credence to the matter but the latter is something we must address urgently.

The final settlement of our forebears after an exodus from Benin that lasted for over fifty years must be seen as a spiritual victory. The question is, have we thanked God enough or have we renewed our commitments to God for guiding our progenitors to the Promise Land – Onitsha. It is rather unfortunate that this important cradle of the town is not immortalized in any art form.Most of the covenants are now broken. The ark bequeathed to us by our ancestors is now despoiled. All the sacrosanct grounds are befallen by same pillage. Our faith has dithered. Our attitude is laden by insincerity, hatred and divisionary tendencies. We hurt ourselves and deny ourselves the opportunity to maintain the past glories and be on the cutting edge of development. I would subscribe that we have gone astray. Time to propitiate is now such that God will reduce our scourge. We need to follow up every spiritual triumph with a commitment to God Almighty who made it possible.

Finally, my hope is that we should be made aware of these multifarious problems that have dulled our competitiveness and the development of the town. We should also begin to produce solutions to these problems. I sincerely hope that the issues raised will strike responsive chords.

OKEY MADUEGBUNAM AGUNYEGO
Ifediba Retreat
Ogbeoza, Onitsha, 1999.

APPENDIX I
ANCIENT FAMILY NAMES

Adele	Ogagwu
Affah	Ogbada
Agadagba	Ogbo
Ajeh	Ojedi
Akah	Ogbodogo
Akazua	Ojiabu
Aguziani	Ojidoko
Ajagba	Okakwu
Alabo	Okoligbo
Alamuzo	Okomanya

Alibo
Okwulinye
Alumona
Anwula
Anyo
Anyaso
Awuma
Azibu
Bachi
Chimedie
Chimezi
Chimukwa
Daike
Enema
Ezumezu
Ibeneweka
Idoko
Ihama
Igwo
Ijelekpe
Inosi
Inwagwe
Isagba
Isolo
Mekem
Navia
ZoliNdugbe

Olisololi
Okwuona
Omo
Omozele
Onaje
Onira
Onogbo
Oreze
Orezeabo
Orezobi
Orowa
Osodi
Osuma
Otankpologugu
Owowo
Ozoma
Oza
Seli
Semia
Tasia
Udogwu
Ugbelede
Ulutu

APENDIX II
OZO TITLE NAMES

1. Akajiaku

    aka

2. Akubueziokwu

    Oku

3. Akubuko

    33.Mnilillienyi

31. Kwocha

32. Kwasie

4.   Akukalia

   34.Nnabuenyi

5.   Akunne

   35.Nnabunie

6.   Akunnia

   36.Nnyelugo

7.   Akunwafo   37.Nwa

   Amulnama

8.   Akunwata   38.

   Nwbunie

9.   Akunwanne

   39.Nwachinamelu

10. Akupueome

   40.Nwaezeoku

11. Akurienne   41.Nwakbie

12. Amalunwaeze   42.Nwalie

13. Belugo

   43.Nwanonaku

14. Chibundo   44.Nwolili

15. Chinweozo

   45.Nwawulu

16. Chinyelugo

   46.Odinigwe

17. Chukwuebuka

18. Dakwasienyi

19. Egonwanne

    49.Okudilinwa

20. Enyikwoku

21. Eselu Enuego

    51Ononnaenyi

22. Eze Afulukwe

23. Ezennia

24. Ezenwata

25. Ezenyeluaku

26. Ibaku

    56.Ozodinaobi

27. Idei

    57.Ugocukwu

28. Ifedioramma

29. Ifechukwukwulu

30. Kpajie

    60.Ugonwanne

47.Ogbu

48.Ojinnaka

50.Okutalukkwe

52.Onnaku

53.Onwa

54.Orimili

55.Ozdioramma

58.Ugochukwu

59.Ugonabo

APENDIX III
ODU TITLE NAMES

1. Akurienne
2. Amalunwaze
    25.Nwmulunmma
3. Anuenyi
4. AzumdialoChinedu
5. ChinyelugoDibueze
6. Dibugwu
7. Dibu ndo
odu
8. Enyikwesilu
Enyi
9. Ezenwachidebelu
10. Ezenwanyi
11. Eziogolidi
12. Ifechukwukwulu
    35.Olimalunwanne
13. Maduaburo chukwu
14. Melunwa
15. Nnabuenyi
16. Nwabunie
17. Nwachinemelu

24. Nwanonaku

26.Nwawulu
27.Obidie
28.Odoziaku
29.Ogolikalia
30.Nwaogalanyatijie

31.Ogbatulu

32.Ogollikalia
33.Ojinnaka
34.Olmadi

36.Olimanwa
37.Omennwata
38.Omeorafu
39.Omenyi
40.Ononenyi

18. Nwaezebuona	41. Onyenwanne
Bulueze	
19. Nwakwonazu	42. Osoenyi
20. Nwalie	43. Uduakomili
21. Nwannebuenyi	44. Ugodie
22. Nwa nne bulu eze	45. Ugonwanne
23. Nwanyikaibie	46. Ugobueze

APPENDIX IV
ONITSHA SOVEREIGNS

Obi Eze Chima	16th Century
Obi Oreze	16th /17th Century
Obi Chimaevi	17th Century
Obi Chimukwu	17th Century
Obi Chimaezi	17th Century
Obi Nafia	17th Century
Obi Tasia	17th Century
Obi Eze Aroli	17th/18th Century
Obi Eze Olisa	18th Century
Obi Chimedie	18th Century
Obi Omozele	18th Century

Obi Ijelekpe   18th Century
Obi Udogwu   1820
Obi Akazue   1840-73
Obi Diali   1873-74
Obi Anazonwu   1874-99
Obi Samuel Okosi   1901-33
Obi James Okosi   1935-61
Obi Joseph Okwudili Onyekwe 1962-1970
Obi Okechukwu Ofala Okagbu1970-2001
Obi Alfred Ugochukwu Achebe 2002-

HOW TO GREET OBI OF ONITSHA

Igwe, Agu, Agbogidi, Eze
Ogbuonye mbosi ndu na guya
Ogbu Agadagidi, okwue obe
Onye Okwunine dino onuya

EZE IDI (King with circumscribed authority)

The title of Eze Idi is assumed by the Okpalas of the
following clans:

1. Obior

2. Obamkpa
3. Eke
4. Ubulu na Ikem
5. Ubene

APPENDIX V

ONITHA AGE GRADE

1.	Ejiji Akpa	1852/54
2.	Uchichi	1855/57
3.	Iwenofu	1858/60
4.	Akilika	1861/63
5.	Ochokwu	1864/66
6.	Edommani	1867/69
7.	Akali	1870/72
8.	Ikusi	1873/75
9.	Omekome	1876/78
10.	Akaka nma	1879/90
11.	Achoba Efuru	1881/82
12.	Iru Ugo	1883/84
13.	Ekwueme	1885/86
14.	Akagba	1886/88
15.	Anidimma	1888/92
16.	Ganiru	1893/95
17.	Nnokoka	1895/97
18.	Adobisi	1895/97
19.	Ositadima	1898/1900
20.	Otundiofo	1901/03
21.	Otuago	1901/03
22.	Odinani	1901/03
23.	Ndokwaka	1904/06

24. Isiogbo   1904/06
25. Omeka Okwu   1904/06
26. Ifechukwu   1905/07
27. Douglas   1907/08
28. Odoziaku   1909/11
29. Nwayobuije   1910/11
30. Kpajie   1910/11
31. Anwuli   1912/13
32. Kaizer   1912/14
33. Nsopulu   1912/14
34. Onitsha Wenite   1914/16
35. Ugobueze   1815/17
36. Osilike   1917/19
37. Ifunanya   1918/20
38. Nkiruka   1919/21
39. Anyayaligwe   1919/21
40.   Ifedimma   1920/22
41. Ifedichie   1923/25
42. Onyeoma diuko   1923/25
43. Igwebuike   1925/27
44. O'connor   1925/27
45. Nchoca   1926/28
46. Ifeatu   1929/31
47. Ife kandu   1929/31
48. Ngozika   1930/32
49. Oyileze   1933/35
50. Aghaeze   1933/35
51. Obianeze   1935/37
52. Odinuche   1935/37
53. Ezudimkpa   1937/39
54. Ejemili   1937/39

55. Ezinwanne	1937/39
56 Ifeoma	1938/40
57. Aghadiegwu	1938/40
58. Egbenugo	1938/40
59. Ifedioramma	1940/42
60. Usobunandu	1941/43
61. Ifenkili	1941/43
62. Ugochalacha	1942/44
63. Anyafulugo	1942/44
64. Odiatu	1943/45
65. Nkolika	1944/46
66. Officer	1946/48
67. Adoamaka	1948/50
68. Udoka	1948/50
69. Ifeadigo	1948/50
70. Onyeoma Ejeogu	1950/52
71. Ugochalacha	1950/52
72. Ozoemezina	1950/52
73. Nwannebuife	1952/54
74. Anyibofu	1954/56
75. Adobuisi	1954/56
76. Ngozika	1954/56
77. Nnebuife	1956/58
79. Anioma	1956/58
80. Independence I	1958/60
81. Independence II	1958/60
82. Malunwanne	1960/62
83. Onitsha Amaka	1962/64
84. Akaekpuchi Onwa	1963/65
85. Udogadi	1966/68
86. Ayaedo	1969/71

87. Aniamaka   1972/74
88. Umu awele   1975/77
89. Ugudibeze   1978/80

APPENDIX VI

HOW TO GREET ONITSHA WOMEN

Onitsha daughters are greeted according to their village or family origin as follows:

Okposieke and Igwo (Obior) daughters

-       Igwe

Ogbolieke and Ogbendugbe daughters-

        Abii

Umudei, Ogbeodogwu and Ogboli Olosi daughters -

        Odua

Ogbeabu, Ogbembubu excluding Umu Osodi

    Igwe

Umu Osodi daughters of Ogbeabu

-       Osodi

Ogbotu daughters

-       Oyowu

Mgbeleke daughters

-       Ojie

Umu Onogbo daughters

-       Ayiuwa

Umuikem, Odoje, Isiokwe excluding Umu Odimegwu

Gbuagu daughters

-       Ajie

Umu Odimegwu Gbuagu daughters

-       Odu

Umu Ase dauthers

-       Onowu

Obikporo daughters (Oreze Section)

-       Oreze

Obikporo daughters excluding Oreze

-       Onyeagba

Iyiawu daughters

-       Owelle

Umu Aroli, Ogbeoza and Ogbendida daughter   -

kpari

Ogbe Ozoma daughters   -

Akpe

APPENDIX VII

NINE VILLAGE GROUPINGS – EBOITEANI

1. Umueze Chima -
      Isiokwe,Umuezearoli,

      Olosi,Okeb
      unabo,
      Awada,Obi
      kporo,
      Ogbe Otu.

2. Ugwu na Obamkpa -
    and Iyiawu

      Umuasele

      and   Umu
      Odimegwu
      Gbuagu of
      Odoje
      Ndugbe.

3. Ubulu na Ikem

4. Ulutu -
    Mgbelekeke

5. Obior

6.   Isele na Awada   -   Ogbe Ozoma

7.   Eke na Ubene   -   (Umu Okwulinye)

                                            Odoje

Ufesi Ilo

                                            Ogboli

Eke.

8.   Agbornute

9.   Achala Igwogidi

SIX ADMINISTRATIVE DIVISION OF ONITSHA
OBA ISI

1.   Isiokwe and Ogboli Olosi

2.   Umuezearoli and Awada

3.   Okebunabo

4.   Ugwu na Obamkpa

5.   Eke na Ubene

6.   Ogbeolu – Umuikem, Ogotu, Obikporo

APPENDIX IX

CALENDAR OF ANNUAL FESTIVALS

1.	Ajachi	June	(a)
	Ika Ajachi		
			(b)
			Ilo Ajachi
2.	Umatu	Aug.	(a)
	Ika Umatu		
			(b)
	Umatu Eze Chima		
			(c)
	Umatu Eze Idi		
			(d)
	Umatu Ikpala Isi		
			(e)
	Umatu Onitsha		
			(f)
	Umatu Ogidigbo Ikpobo		
			(g)
	Akwukwo Ogili		
3	Owuwaji	Sept.	(a)
	Owuwaji Ikolo Awada		
			(b)
	Owuwaji Ikpala Awada		
			(c)
	Owuwaji Ikolo Eke		
			(d)
	Owuwaji Ikpala Eke		
			(e)
	Owuwaji Ikolo Ubulu na		

Ikem/Ubene.

(f)

Owuwaji Ikpala Ubulu

Na Ikem/Ubene

(g)

Inye ukwu na nlo Ubulu

Na Ikem.

(h)

Igo urai Ubulu na Ikem

(i)

Inyepu ukwu na nlo

Ubulu na Ikem

(j)

Awame Ubulu na Ikem

(k)

Owuwaji

Ekwensu/Ikpala Ugwu

Na Obamkpa

(l)

Ogbalido

(m)
Inye
pu Ukwu
na nlo Eze

4   Ofala   Oct.   (a)
     Ofala

Azu Ofala

(b)

Owuwaji Ikpala Eze

(c)

Ito Ukpukpa

(d)

Ikelebeji

(e)

5   Osisite   Oct-Dec.   (a)
        Osiste Ugwu na
Obamkpa

        Osis Umueze Chima

(b)

        Oruru Ani

(c)

        Oso Ekwulo

(d)

        Igo Onitsha

(e)

6   **Ifejioku**   Jan
        Emume Ifejioku.

NDICHIE UME – FIRST CLASS

TITLE	NAME	VILLAGE
Onowu-Iyasele, Onuiyi	Chief Okey Ononye	OdojeUbene
Ajie- Ukadiugwu, Isagba	Chief Osita Adibuah	Umuaroli
Odu-Osodi, Nkataukwu	Chief Onyeachonam Okolonji	Odoje
Onya-Ozoma,	Chief Dr. A.A. Obiora	Ogboli Olosi

Ukanagbaoji Nyaka Nyaka		
Ogene-Onira Ukpaka	Chief Prof. Ngozi Okafo	Umuikem
Owelle-Osowa, Anya		

NDICHIE OKWA – SECOND CLASS

Osuma-Afa, Akankposi	Chief Okey Chude	Umuaroli
Adazie-Ogulani, Alibo	Chief Dr. C.S. Agbakoba	Umuase
Ozi-Adamagwe	Chief Mike Maduegbuna	Umudei
Omodi-Daike, Alamuzo	Chief Okey Ibekwe	Odoje
Odua-Ngu, Alamuzo	Chief Emma Egbunike	Ogbendida

MGBADO UKWU

Akpe-Olodi, Jebeogwu	Chief Chulo Asika	Ogbeoza
Ede-Gbogbogaga	Chief Dr. Mike O. Areh	Ogbembubu
Ojudo-Enema	Chief M. Obiora Erokwu	Isiokwe
Ike-Mkpume, Akatakwuani		
Ojiba-Inwagwe	Chief Col. Dr. O. Emodi	Ogbeodogwu

OTHERS

Ojiziani Obi	Chief Comrade C.O Nwora	Ogbeodogwu
Oboli Boja	Chief Emeka Osemenam	Umuaroli
Gbosa-Obi	Chief Ikechukwu Areh	Obikporo
Ojiabu-Ugala, Ungbalobi		
Ogbuoba-Anya lagbom		

Ojiede-Eze		
Omodi-Obele		
Ojiede		
Unwolu		
Obioba		
Ojogwu		
Okwuagwe		
Okwugba		

OKWARAEZE- THIRD CLASS

Onoli-Oguda Iyele	Chief chuka Ife Jika	Umuase
Akwue-Isama	Chief Nathan Nzekwu	Odoje
Agba-Oriogu, Dike		
Eseagba-Igbala Udobi	Chief Ikem A Abadom	Ogbeodogwu
Igwuoba- Akalam		
Ijagwo-Obi	Chief Isaac A.Uyanne	Ogbendidi
Asagwali-Omeikpo	Chief Anthony Iwnjiora	Ogbeotu
Ajaka-Obi	Chief Achike Obi (late)	Umudei
Ubon-Negbasele	Chief Surveyor Chuka Oboli	
Asagba-Obi, Ojiuga		
Isama-Osuji		
Osuma-Ogwa		
Oziziani		
Ojiba		
Ozah		
Igedu		
Onika		
Ogbaike		

NOTE: Titles without names are vacant at the printing of this book

President Agbalanze
Nnabuenyi Uchenna Mbanefo
President Otu Odu Onitsha
Ugobueze Florence Osoka

President General Onitsha Improvemnet Union
Chinyelugo Osita Anionwu

President General
Ogbo na a chi ani
Ezenwanne Timothy Agusioba

HRM ALFRED NNAEMEKA ACHEBE OBI ONISTSHA

**LATE OBI JAMES OKOSI
OBI OF ONITSHA
1935-1961**

**LATE CHIEF ONYA
ADIBUAH**

**LATE CHIEF. E.C. OG.
NWOKEDI**

**LATE CHIEF ONYAS. O
EGBUNIKE**

**LATE CHIEF PHILP
MBANEFO
ANATOGU ONOWO**

LATE CHIEF ISAAC

ODU 11

**LATE HRM OFALA O
OKWUDILI
OBI OF ONITSHA**

1970-2002

LATE HRM

OBI OF ONTSHA

1962-1990

LATE CHIEF OFODILE   **CHIEF T. A.**
OMEKAN
ONOWU IYASELE   **OJIBA**
SAN

OJIBA EDIBOSS
OKOLOJI AT 64 YEARS

CHIEF N. ARAKA OJIUDO
AT 81 YEARS

MEMBERS OF NDICHIE UME. FROM LEFT, ONOWU
CHIEF P.O. ANATOGU, AJIE CHIEF J.A. UKPABI, ODU
CHIEF I.A. MBANEFO, OGENE CHIEF E.N. NWOKEDI,
OWELLE NNAMDI AZIKIWE

MEMBER OF THE NDICHIE OKWA AND NDICHIE OKWAREAZE. FROM RIGHT TO LEFT: THE ADAZIA (CHIEF L.O.V. ENWEONWU); THE OMORDI CHIEF F.N. IWENOFU); THE ODUAH (CHIEF J.U. ETUKOKWU): THE (CHIEF T.O. BOSAH); THE OJIDUDO (CHIEF N.N. ARAKA): THE OJIBA (CHIEF C.E. OKOLONJI) POSING BEHIND THE ADAZIA; AND THE AGBA (CHIEF I.A. OMEKAM)

LATE J.O. MBAMALI   LATE CHIEF
NNAMDI
    AJIE   AZIKIWE OWELLE

CHIEF E.N. NWOKEDI
OGENE AT 85 YEAR

CHIEF J.A.UKPABI AJIE AT 71 YEARS.

CHIEF ISAAC MBANEFO ODU II AT 78 YEARS

CHIEF NNAMDI AZIKIWE
OWELLE AT 71 YEARS

CHIEF J.U. ETUKOKWU
ODUA AT 68 YEARS

**CHIEF L.O.V. ANIONWU
ADAZIA AT 68 YEARS**

PATHWAYS THROUGH THE PARADOXES

PROLOGUE

The topic of the paper attached is on how to contain the paradoxes in the polity. I believe that a good many of us are aware of some lingering problems that includes uncompetitive attitudes that we have not been able to curb. Could our inaction be caused by lack of will? This is a critical poser.However I envisage that putting some of these dilemmas in print may likely strike a responsive chord, that is to say that the enthusiasm in working out solutions could be engendered.Talking about print, Barbara W. Tuchman an American Educator is credited with the following quote "Books are carriers of civilization, without books history is silent, literature dumb, desires crippled and thought and expectation at standstill"

Paradox is a global phenomenon. I highlighted few foreign cases, that of the country and that of our homeland with counsels on how to contain the problems

PATHWAYS THROUGH THE PARADOXES

Is it not worrisome that those we taught how to run

are now ahead of us and likewise those that found succor in our back houses are now buying us out? My previous work contains a short chapter on – Regeneration of our moral and spiritual strength and values. In it, I noted that no community is insulated from moral turpitude. However today's situation calls for the understanding of what is happening and our preparedness to cause a difference; a positive change. We need an arsenal of measures to deal with these problems. Our readiness to make things happen makes the difference between success and failure. Many communities now consider such reforms in their development agenda.

Paradox can be defined as contradictions, absurdity, anomalies, difficulties, inconsistence chaos etc. The word describes the dilemmas the world faces. The industrialized countries produce more food than they need but cannot feed the starving. This may be unimaginable but it is a fact thirty tons of surplus food was destroyed in United Kingdom in the first half of 2013. The gap between the rich and the poor is ever widening. Despite India's major thrust in technology their inner cities are scenes of pathos.

Nigeria has a large share of these contradictions. Agriculture which in the 60's was the mainstay of the economy is now abandoned. The cash crops, groundnuts, cotton, cocoa, rubber palm oil are now silhouette of what they were before. Subsistence farming is abandoned to the old people as the youths cannot accept the arduous tasks with low pay. As a result there has been a tremendous drift of youths to the urban cities in search of easy money. The food insecurity in the country and low income per capita portray high poverty level in the country. Statisticians estimate that about 65% of Nigerians live below poverty line. Also considered is another estimate that 1% of the population appropriates 90% of our national wealth. It smacks of injustice. In 2009 a Nigerian Senator earned $1.7 million and the member of the House of Representative earned $1.45 million per annum. By contrast an American Senator in same period earned $174.000.00 and the United Kingdom parliamentarian earned $64,000.00 per annum. The awesome paradox of the situation tells its own tale. The income per capita of USA in 2009 stood at $46,350.00 that of UK at $35.488.00 while that of Nigeria was at $2,249.00-Punch report18/8/2010. This juxtaposition will make one's flesh creep. The spokesperson of National Assembly recently boasted while addressing protesters that there is no wastage in the 3% of the 4.9 trillion naira budget which they receive rather they should search for waste in the remaining 97% spent by other arms of governance. With such arrogant and insensitive posturing every government institution protects themselves. The President on a recent media chat defended his numerous aides. According to him they are useful for efficient governance. As expected it is the Civil Service that bears the brunt of downsizing. The leadership of both Houses and their deputies are now pensionable after four to eight years service whereas the pensions of civil servants that put in twenty five to thirty years are hardly met. Little is cared about the people and that is a huge paradox as it is the same people that make things work. Such insouciance can easily arouse the people to further violence in addition to the menace of kidnapping, oil theft, cult brutality and Boko Haram gruesome massacre of people that the country is grappling with. Privatization in the country is nothing but criminal auctioning of Nigeria (ModiboKawu in Vanguard 18/8/11) Most of the assets of these companies/parastatals are stripped. I remember a cartoon in the eighties that had a General in an armored car saying that he could not see armed robbery. How could he? There is yet a tale about the first Republic Government helping themselves from interests generated by the National wealth but what we witness now is like scrambling for both the interests and the principals, thereby strangling the goose that lays the golden eggs and creating further burden for the populace. We are reminded that the giver of bribe and the receiver are guilty by law. The case of the oil magnate and a senator is still pending. It is in this country that we witnessed people stealing billions and after plea bargaining where a pittance less than one percent of the loot is surrendered are set free. A guy that stole a Governor's watch on the other hand got a three years jail sentence. What a wacky world? Nobody hears of Halliburton, Siemens etc. again. Corruption now attains a monstrous scale. Extra judicial killings abound while the police would often remind us that they are our friends.With each passing year the world is becoming more dangerous. The economic and security situation in the country is worsening. Is the situation beyond control? These paradoxes may not be wiped out completely but they can be reduced. The best approach as indicated in the opening page is to study and understand these inconsistencies and backed by strong ideology and rallying cry the way forward can be worked out. Every town is said to stamp her value upon herself. The town becomes great or little according to the will of the town. Similarly the strength and will of the people are measured by how they confront them.

LESSONS FROM ANAMBRA GOVERNORSHIP ELECTION

One can discern from the opening salvo that this piece is intended to discuss how the contradictions in our homeland can be contained. We have a great lot to learn and understand from the November 2013 Governorship Election in Anambra. Many hold the opinions that election is a game of numbers. In other words the town has no chance even to win a Local Government election.   In contrast the satellite towns in Lagos-Isolo, Ajao Estate, Festac and even Surulere have more non indigenes, yet most of the seats of the Local Government are won by the Yoruba people. In Benin and some of the towns up north, the Monarchs have some influence on those that contest elections. There is yet another opinion concerning the aversion other communities hold to our people such that they will not vote for any Onitsha indigene. One also wonders if the rally by Action People Congress on the same day Igwe Achebe, the Obi of Onitsha celebrated his Annual Ofala is not out of disdain?It is paradoxical that a frontline town east of the Niger is treated thus whereas such brazen action cannot take place in their towns. Whether the opinions are true or not the encumbrances are worrisome. What do we do knowing them of which some of them may be self inflicted? It behooves us to act urgently. We have men and women in Ivory Towers, various professions, trades and those with local wisdom that can chart the way forward.

General Moshe Dayan, Ex-Israeli Defense Minister observed that if you want to make peace/accord you talk to your enemy. Quite a good number of people from other communities were born in Onitsha, schooled in Onitsha and have businesses in Onitsha hence have benefitted from the town. I am sure we can talk with a good number of them. It should not be seen as weakness. A popular axiom says that when you rub elbows with others you will soon find out what they have up sleeves. How much have we fraternized with Ohaneze, Pan Igbo Congress, Association of Anambra State Development Unions and Aka Ikenga? Surely belonging to these groups would beyond fraternizing give us the advantages to be part of policy making of the State.We may not have the numeric strength but by lobbying and marshaling fund when it matters we can achieve a foothold. We must not forget that when things improve that tact is the knack of winning a point without making an enemy. We must be prepared to build bridges too.

ONITSHA IMPROVEMENT UNION

Onitsha Improvement Union will be 90 years in 2014.The objectives and aims of the Union may not have changed much but the commitments are nowhere near what the founders articulated.

Other communities Unions that are not as old as that of Onitsha Improvement Union now consider the Union as a platform for the development of their towns and people. In these climes, those who do not belong to the union where they reside are denied from participating in the town's activities. They are not allowed to take any chieftaincy and upon death of such people, their funeral will be boycotted by these towns except where the dues and fines are paid. This strategy works for them. Numerous town halls built by these communities are springing up in every town.While we appreciate the understanding of the Ruling Council not wanting to impinge on individual rights, the non participation of many of our people in the Union is inimical to the development of the town. As an alternative, a sustained sensitization by the Ruling Council, as a planned strategy may likely persuade and arouse our people to join the unions wherever they reside. Recently the planned attendance in Lagos is by village and satellite union representation. Others can take such step.

Another related worrying issue is the low financial commitments. Some few years ago, most monthly dues attracted twenty naira a month and today the bracket is between fifty naira and two hundred naira. What gets remitted to the Union Headquarters in Onitsha is thirty naira monthly by every member. Here again the low commitment tells its own tale. This is retrograde "Aka utu aka Okpo"; controversies arise anytime increase in dues are recommended. This unfortunately is becoming our hallmark. It is negative. There is another negative insinuation revealing the result of a study by a psychologist on Onitsha People, which states that we are not giving to self-help. It is not only negative but a conjecture because those that formed Onitsha Improvement Union in 1924 had self-help as their major objective. It is contradictory that those that oppose increase in dues host stupendous parties on their volition.

In Onitsha North and South, the combined strength that pay this dues is less than sixty whereas we have eligible people in thousands. In Lagos the members has dwindled from one thousand to fewer than three hundred. An appeal for the support of the Ruling Council and NEC in sensitizing our people and strengthening the Union is therefore sought. The color of the cat white or black does not matter as long as it catches rats. Any other strategy to get the Unions attuned to meeting the development objectives of the union and town would be appreciated

LAND MATTERS

Let methank AgbogidiIgwe Achebe on his efforts towards clawing back our farm lands in Trans Nkisi. It is by no means an easy task but would request that the efforts be sustained until all the deeds are perfected. The anomaly arose from Government acquisition of the land for industrial purposes and then their volte-face in allotting the same land to other people for personal use. It is a challenge worth pursuing using our contact wisely, lobbying and not daunted when marshaling of fund is required. The latter will be addressed later in this presentation. Quite recently the Ekwerekwu Family commenced the sales of their lands in Government Reserved Area. It is a purely family affair but for the interest of the town I envisage a grand plan backed by the Ruling Council in soliciting the land owners to earmark some of the plots at perhaps a slightly reduced rate to indigenes as a strategy for our people to move into GRA. In other sales of land by families and villages, same suggestion is made for the indigenes to get the first offer. This will benefit the town at the time when over 85% of the land in Onitsha has been sold to non-indigenes; our heart land. These measures will not only renew our confidence but will also boost our article of faith about Onitsha. Otherwise, the inconsistence that less than fifty of Onitsha people own homes in G.R.A will persist. Before I leave this topic, let me state that the errors made in Owelle-Ebo must be avoided where few individuals appropriated the family land and defied the family decision not to sell the land to non-indigene as the said portion of land is in Inland town.

FESTIVITIES/PEGEANTRY

Our dairy appears crammed with festivities and pageantry.
This is another case of our indulgence that is becoming our hall mark.It is the excesses that are worrisome. According to Late OwelleNnamdiAzikwe, a town whose past time is immersed in festivities without creating wealth and managing it is bound to stagnate. Here again, paradox rears its ugly head. We can fund festivities and pageantry but find it difficult to muster fund for self-help programmes

To curb these excesses, we would require not only

sustained sensitization but also good examples by various leaders. Another related drawback is that most of the items for the festivities are purchased from other people. It amounts to serious financial hemorrhaging which is our undoing. I noted in previous work that no community has a preserve for trading. We must do away with such prejudices about trading. We should also do away with vacuous slangs like "Nwa Onitsha adaagba boy" " Nwannukwu" and as well as inordinate ambition to take tittles. A friend told me that his main joy for taking up a title is for the praise name. He is pleased that nobody calls him by his first name anymore.

SELF-HELP

How best to contain these multifarious paradoxes are to boost adequate self-help to augment whatever government offers. When our decided advantages were at its peak the town was a cynosure, a focus of attention and had respect, charms and was eulogized. Expectedly, the wanes and ebbs would herald trouble, difficulties and sometimes aversion. It is all about competition where when you slack others, take over. People now overlook the counsel that says don't drown a man who taught you how to swim and if you learned your trade or profession from a man, do not set up in opposition to him. Our option is to heighten our competitiveness and excellence. To a great extent, the vehicle to engender this transformation is through self-help. Onitshaness my earlier work is about the elements that need to be reinforced in order to be relevant, to regain our pre-eminence and sustain it.

The follow-up book-In Search of Excellence is a minimalist approach to self-help. Self-help involves money, time, ideas and participation of individuals, Association, Age Grades, Agbalanze, OtuOdu, individuals, village meetings, Clubs and Ruling Council as a group and as individuals. From my previous analysis we can generate two hundred million naira if every adult Onitsha person of about forty thousand estimate pays five thousand naira a year which on monthly basis is less than four hundred and twenty naira. I believe too that we can reach two hundred Onitsha people that can donate five hundred thousand naira each or one hundred persons who can donate one million each. Both applications will give us ten million naira a piece.

You will expect many people to doubt this permutation because of accountability. As we are projecting a new dawn and Onitshanising various actions that will contain many paradoxes we must also strive to address with urgency, the issue of transparency and other selfish attitudes that are ruinous to the community. I would like to commend G36 and Ado Integrity Initiative for their bold steps in community development. We surely need more of their likes.

Do you know that Port-Harcourt celebrated one hundred years on 7th November 2013? Sokoto, you will recall celebrated their two hundred years of existence in 2004. Our dear town is yet to celebrate any of the over five hundred and fifty years of her existence. The fund which this celebration will attract when linked to a launch appeal is huge and besides it stands to create other unexpected openings.

I am informed that both Sokoto and Port-Harcourt celebrations were sponsored by the State Government. It may be defeatist to rule out pretty early such sponsorship from our State Government. We should be prepared to augment whatever we receive towards the planning of the celebration.

Let me therefore use this opportunity to call for advance scouts to champion this course and also exploit the extensive field of possibilities.

I leave you with the following axioms.

If your roof is leaking, you mend it. If the leaking becomes widespread, you change the entire roof else you will be drenched by rain water. If the structure of the house is failing you must urgently examine the foundation.

To look is one thing. To see what you are looking at is another thing. To understand what you are looking at is also another thing. To learn from what you understand is a different game. To act on what you have seen, understood and learned from is all that matters. Anon.

As we venture forth, let us turn swords into ploughshares and hammering spears into pruning knives. Let us actively engage in reaching solutions rather than complaining or sabre-rattling

Let us build bridges than stone walls. Let us close ranks than pull ranks. Let us dampen dissensions than put a damper on them. Let us keep faith than break faith. Let us be quick on the uptake than slow on the uptake. Let us forge alliances than creating frictions. Let us review our ethos, societal values and attitudes such that those that no longer provide relevancy and competitive advantages may be possibly dropped."Okwu Onitsha gaadika esikwue" Let us put a formidable front in the transformation of self-help projects for the benefits of the town and children unborn.

May the Good Lord grant us all it takes to keep the light lit over 550 years ago blazing.

Thank you for your attention and May God bless you all

OKEY AGUNYEGO
08023182092
His Grace Lodge
Isolo Lagos, November 2013
Title of the book comes from the text - The Empty Raincoat by Charles Handy.

AN OPEN LETTER TO IGWE THROUGH PRESIDENT GENERAL ONITSHA IMPROVEMENT UNION

7th July, 2014.

H.R.M Agbogidi
Igwe Alfred Achebe

**Through President General
OIU HQS
Onitsha**

Your Royal Majesty,

**Militating Issues against the town and request to confer
with His Royal Majesty
Agbogidi: We salute you.**

We write to express our views on some burning issues which if not challenged will leave our people at a disadvantage. This resolution was taken on 1st June meeting of OIU, Lagos.

The first issue concerns Trans Nkisi layout. We are aware of your efforts to claw back this layout. We had high hopes which did not last long before the gloom following your tenth Ofala address. You appeared pained to note that the former Governor Obi was not cooperating in this land matter. Quite recently, many houses have started springing up in this layout and we would like to know if you have any privileged information and other plans that you have contemplated. The Union considers it important at this stage for the town to take a stand via legal suit. The advice from our Senior Advocates of Nigeria and other eminent lawyers on land matters will be appreciated.

We are informed that the State Government (former Anambra comprising of new Anambra and Enugu) acquired the land for industrial projects and later made a volte-face to allot the same layout to mainly non-indigenes. This obviously makes our case crucial. We have also heard from another quarter that the layout was never acquired for industrial projects and that the allocation was open for non-indigenes and indigenes. Whatever the case may be, we figure that the allocation was not fair to the landowners. Along the line, we will suggest that Civil Rights Activists, Lawyers, Estate Surveyor etc amongst us should mount a serious campaign against this palpable deceptive scheme to deprive us of our land as well as a nursed aim to whittle down our fame. We must not give any room for others to think that we are tactless.

It may be important to know if the land owners were compensated at any time. Smarting from the total loss of shares in Onitsha main market in the early 70s, and following hard on the heels of it came the incursion of Obosi into Isi Afo. The people were audacious to mark Obosi on street signpost at Iweka Road. They also marked Obosi at Awka Road from Boromeo hospital. One of us recently wrote an open article to Governor Obiano requesting his compassionate attention and bringing to his attention also that in other parts of South East such issue would have precipitated unrest; murder, arson and other brutal acts. Our non-violence is now taking for granted. We do not suggest that we become vicious but to be fully committed to take a stand.

Another issue, is on how to strengthen OIU world-wide to be a formidable front in the development of our homeland. Despite the rejuvenation exercise in Lagos, the membership is far from desired. This is applicable to other OIU stations in other towns. The membership of Onitsha North and South are dismal. Some of us see the Union as local and non-event. Some have the cause of the town on their tongues but hardly support the cause. How do we expect to be competitive?. The attention and support of the Ruling Council are needful in sensitizing our people to participate in the Unions.In other climes especially other towns in South East the penalty for not joining the Unions is high, to the extent that such people are debarred from taking titles, other social functions and upon death, their funerals are boycotted except where the penalty and dues are paid. This measure is planned to engender better development and oneness. Some of us may consider this approach as draconian and an infringement on people's rights. While we do not subscribe to taking the situation by the scruff of the neck, we have rules and regulations governing our social activities. Our thinking is to appeal, solicit, canvass, counsel, sensitize and come to think about it, unity is the mainspring to success.

Therefore, we figure that if the sensitization is spearheaded by the Ruling Council,a reasonable success could be achieved.There are other issues for the town to be competitive; issues concerning quality education, unemployment, social infrastructure, sports, a bit of physical planning and how to muster fund for noble projects etc. A strong and focused Town Union will be an advantage. Some instances where our people compromised are worrisome and the need to generally slough off some of our bad habits are also part of the agenda. Another very important issue concerns our spiritual deficiency and the need for spiritual rejuvenation. **Onyemalu ebemmili sibana opiugbogulu?** An anonymous writer noted that: **Only God knows how soon our little life may close and as every passing moment flows, we need to redeem the time.** (Deuteronomy chapter six throws more light on warning against disobedience and on atonement.

We would appreciate a session whereby the above issues and others will be presented and discussed.

There is no doubt that this groundwork and other contributions will engender the way forward for the betterment of our home and our people.

Long live the Monarch
HRM Igwe Alfred Achebe
Long live Onitsha Ado N'Idu
Long live Onitsha Improvement Unions.

**For: ONITSHA IMPROV
EMENT UNION, LAGOS.**

M. C. ORANYE,
       OKEYAGUNYEGO,
President   Vice President

CC. PRESIDENT GENERAL,
OIU, Ime-Obi, Onitsha.

RED CAP CHEIFS 1960
Onowu Anataogu, Ajie Mbamali, Odu M banefo,
Ogene Nwoked, Owelle Orefo
BACK ROW
Eseagba Anwa, Akwue Chugbo, Akpe Okollonji
Ojiudo Araka,Adazie Chukwudebe.

AN OPEN LETTER TO GOVERNOR OBIANO OF ANAMBRA STATE

ONITSHA: BURSTING BUT BROKEN. A WAY FORWARD AND MODEL FOR OTHER TOWNS IN ANAMBRA.

The title of this article is drawn from the editorial by This Day Newspaper of Friday 20 August 2010. It concerns United Nations approach towards the development of Onitsha. The subtitle is mine. To a great extent the information provided by this piece serves as the thrust of this write-up. According to the report, since the end of Nigeria-Biafra war, 0nitsha; a huge commercial city that used to be haven of business and pleasure, has become a nightmare not only to residents but those that pass through the town to other parts of South East and South - South States.

The catalogue of the challenges facing the commercial city includes absence of systematic town planning, worsened by overcrowding, high crime rates, grossly inadequate security of lives and property, dearth of social amenities and ineffective refuse collection and disposal.

Other concerned writers raised some of these observations in the past. Obi Nwakama writing on Vanguard Newspaper of 25 April 1999 noted that – "Today's Onitsha is an anomic city. Onitsha is dead and the worms are feeding on it. It is the activity of the worms, which palpitates the corpse that the people see and think life still trembles in the city. Onitsha's case is the result of civil war which destroyed the city and from its ruin nothing came other than brutality.... There is a quiet predatory mood that pervades the dirtiest, the most dysfunctional and broken city".

Olamilekan Lartey writing in Punch Newspaper of Tuesday 18 May 2006 noted that-"Onitsha, the commercial nerve centre of Anambra State may succumb to the over bearing weight of refuse unless urgent attention is taken. This is compounded by the breakdown of basic social infrastructures, poor funding, and no will to muster a self-help programme by the residents.

Obi Nwakama in yet another article in Vanguard Newspaper of 30 March 2008 lamented the decay in Onitsha. According to this write-up, the sludge of human and industrial waste that runs on public and private spaces, the sense of the brokenness of everything, the disorder in city planning, in code enforcement, in street planning, in general ordering and layout of the city makes Onitsha the most polluted city. The city thus exhibits the marks of dystopia" he Traced the distortion to the barbarous rage of a most philistine generation for whom beauty and civility are alien values. He was however quick to note "that encrusted in the pod of waste is a gem ....a city of possibilities".

May I take another observation before returning to This Day Newspaper editorial of 2010?   Professor

Charles Soludo writing on Punch Newspaper of 26 May 2006 observed that- " Onitsha metropolis, inspite of being the largest city in the South East State is now a failed city with mass of building lying in dormant and dead capital and I will not be surprised if the town does not have one of the lowest life expectancy in Nigeria ".

These observations appear gloomy nevertheless they portray the lapses that have confronted the city. Besides, they lend credence to the byword that reads: Amalu Isi Oya Amalu Isi Ogwu; diagnosing the ailment paves way to the right prescription. The town has since then moved on with some palliatives and some concrete remedies.

The aforementioned This Day Newspaper's editorial of 2010 revealed United Nations demographic publication confirming what was already known about brokenness of Onitsha. Onitsha was rated the world fastest growing city. The report confirmed that five cities in Morocco, China, Malaysia, Brazil and Nigeria (Onitsha) will be on display in United Nation sponsored exhibition in October 2010 in Shanghai to mark the World Habitat Day. The UN explained that the choice of Onitsha for the project was because of its peculiar significance and unique attributes. The project will provide Anambra Government the needed partnership with UN for proper development of Onitsha.

Did this partnership take place? And if no, what went wrong? If yes how much of it was achieved? These are the questions many may be eager to know and the government owes the populace the duty to address this issue

.

The days of congratulatory messages, I believe are over and one looks forward to our Governor, His Excellency, Willie Obiano in tackling the various challenges outlined by the commentators, from where the former Governor Peter Obi (Okwute) stopped. It is encouraging that His Excellency, Governor Obiano has mapped out security as his first priority. Onitsha has many trouble spots, notorious Upper Iweka Road, Bridge Head, Ozoma Ogala and quite a good number at Inland Town. The task force should note that some organized crimes are often sponsored by some desperate politicians, traders and other individuals and therefore should extend their operations beyond the boys that smoke marijuana/weeds. The level of insecurity in the city has not only been a major disincentive to investors but also traders, fun lovers and other members of the town. It may be only in Onitsha that the main market closes by four pm and thereby limiting the turnover-total sales of many businesses. The town shuts down by 7pm except for beer parlors that operate in many places, no cinema houses, few standard hotels, clubs, recreational centers etc. The recent bombing in Nyanya, a suburb in Abuja is an eye opener. His Excellency is urged to beef up security around the markets, motor parks, and schools while the populace will be regularly sensitized to the security problem in the country.

One would hope that by now adequate Think Tanks would be in place to proffer solutions to our multifarious inadequacies. Close to that is the importance of Town Hall meetings where His Excellency will discuss State issues with the people, sell relevant government ideas and as well as seek the peoples understanding and support. Let me at this stage enumerate and enunciate later a list of projects which when put in place will bring back the old glory. The list is not priotised. Some are long term while others are short and medium term projects. These projects stand to benefit the State.

Education, Unemployment, Pipe Borne Water, Improved Tax Exploitation, Health Centers, Environmental Issues, Perfecting And Maximizing The States Oil Well And Refinery, Cargo Airport, Self-Help etc.

Former Governor Peter Obi made appreciable efforts towards improvement in education. There remains however the need for vigorous campaign for quality education to reposition the State in twenty five years time, if not more. A related issue concerns Rated Artisans. They include plumbers, welders, carpenters, draughts men, builders etc. The foremen and overseers of most foreign construction companies that operate in Nigeria come from this background. Lagos has an Association of Professional Carpenters and their members have various contracts from government, industries and individuals. What is obvious is that there is a huge employment for artisans. So much has been written on this and a year ago, Federal Government built two centers, one in Onitsha North and the other in Onitsha South Local Government. Unfortunately no machinery has been installed in these buildings. His Excellency may like to ask questions and put in good words where necessary. The Ibo race is industrious and such opportunities will give our people competitive advantages. Besides the Federal Government efforts, I suggest that the State Government sets up such centres in other strategic towns.

There are few Federal presence in Onitsha and the same are applicable in other towns in Anambra. Democracy allows for lobbying, of which our various Law Makers and State Government cannot afford dithering. Beyond that, I am looking forward to the construction of cargo airport which can accommodate passenger charter services only as we have Asaba and Enugu nearby providing general passenger services. This project may be long term but if made a priority it can be accomplished in few years.

The project will bring in Central Government presence, Immigration, Customs and other ancillary organizations while the business community will no longer have to head to Lagos to clear their containers. Other neighbouring States are likely to ship and clear their consignments from the airport and thereby boosting the economy of the State. Other projects that will attract Federal Government presence will be welcome.

Onitsha had pipe-borne water way back in 1927 but what is in vogue today is bore holes. Experts of Water Resources world-wide have warned on the dangers of uncontrolled bore holes. There was a World Bank sponsored reservoir and water treatment in Onitsha in the late 90s. Two giant tanks were cited at Owelle ebo. Pipes were laid and water meters were installed in many residences but alas the project failed to see the light of the day. The Governor may like to revisit this project and give it new life.

Trees are mowed down with abandon and people care little about the advantages of trees that include; wind breaker, erosion check, shade provision, aesthetic values etc. This is not a big task yet it is neglected.

In Lagos, trees and shrubs planted few years ago are now blossoming and beautiful. Where the Governor leads this campaign, and urges various Monarchs or Government Officials to do same in their towns, I believe the towns would sooner be lush and beautiful.

In Revenue Allocation, the States are classified under four groups. Each group has two streams, the higher and the lower. Anambra is in the first stream of group three. The margin between group three and four is marginal. What Anambra gets is about 1/8 of what the State with highest allocation in group A gets. Two things come to mind. The first is exploiting the taxable capacity of the State to generate extra funds for the development of the State. The second concerns the consolidating the State Oil Company and the refinery. This will possibly place us in the second group and enhance the State's revenue.

Health is wealth. It will not be out of place for each Local government to have minimum of two health centres. This is another talking point for the Town Hall meetings.

No doubt, urbanization is a double edge sword with benefits and ills. Most times the growth of the city is not matched with commensurate social amenities. The effects of urbanization on Onitsha indigenes are unwholesome. Take the land case for an instance. Most of the land acquired by Missionaries and Government for noble projects as schools, hospitals etc failed to provide the indigenes with full compensations. This is applicable to other towns but the case of Trans Nkisi is more of expropriation. The land was acquired for industrial purpose but only to have same land allotted to other people for personal use. The previous Government made promises to readdress this anomaly but failed to accomplish it. We urge His Excellency Governor Obiano to look at the case dispassionately. Elsewhere such case would have caused unrest.

Self help simply means what the community can do

for them selves or what individuals can contribute to the community. There are many such self-help projects that attract Federal Government assistance. Here again I will suggest to the Governor to stir the people to contribute meaningfully to the development of their communities during his town hall meetings.

This articulation does not preclude other ideas from Government and Individuals. Our prayer is for Government efforts and with commitments from the communities and individuals to restore the past glory of Onitsha and the entire Anambra State

Yours Faithfully,
OKEY AGUNYEGO
His Grace Lodge
Isolo, Lagos 18 April 19, 2014
08023182092
oagunyego@yahoo.co.uk
For the attention of His Excellency Governor Willie Obiano

OPEN LETTER TO THE OBI OF ONITSHA
THAT ONITSHA MAY BLOOM AGAIN (ABRIDGED)

2002

October 10th and 11th 2002 marked the first Ofala of Obi, Nnameka Alfred Ugochukwu Achebe; the 21st Monarch of Onitsha. This historic festival follows in the wake of (inye ukwu na nlo) activities of prayers and praises by Igwe to God for his benevolence to the people; a period of atonement for our misgivings and a period of appeasement for another fruitful and healthy year for the people.

Reconciliation

In the quest for better tomorrow, one cannot avoid to discuss things that divide us and reduce our competitive edges. In comparison, the schism and polarization resulting from obiship contest is minimal compared to that of 1962. However less this may be, my humble counsels that many people would consent would include setting up a committee for reconciliation. I would also seize the opportunity to call for fence mending that would pave way for the return of suspended and dissenting First Class Chiefs, such that would guarantee a formidable Obi-In-Council. The suspended Chiefs should also embrace this olive branch and work towards the development of the town. 'Igwe bu ike"

Balkanization

Some people may consider tenable the advancement for Balkanization of Villages and Age Grades. Even 'Ozo' is not spared, hence in some villages you have four factions 'Itiwa Ozi' – and yet all initiates are supposed to seek spiritual strength from same 'Ani', the village shrine. My concern here is that the manner these divisions are done is fraught with mistrust, hatred, enmity and unnecessary rivalry. In many cases, you have family members belonging to different groups with each boycotting the other's functions/activities. Following the rapprochement reached by warring parties in Obikporo Village in the '80s, one would have hoped that such rancour would be a thing of the past. It is sad that these divisions have continued to rob our competitive edges.

"Ana esi na, uno amalu mma we puta ilo" – Internal

peace is a prelude to achieving external peace. It is essential for the Obi-In-Council, the Political Head of each village and Ruling Age Grade to seek ways and means to reducing the fallouts of Balkanization and as well as suing for peace in the families and villages

Wealth Management

Economic waste is another issue, which is considered inimical to wealth creation. We have the tendencies as it were to deplete our wealth, which is equivalent to starving the goose that lays the golden eggs. These are exemplified during burials and other social functions. Quite often family lands are sold or huge sums are borrowed to meet these rites. Although there existed regulations on marriage and funeral rites, but at a stage people preferred to pay the fines it attracted than conform to the regulation. While advancing for further downward review of the regulations, I guess it would also require moral persuasion and sensitization of the people to stem such flagrant extravagancy and hence be able to provide for other needs of the town. According to the late sage, Owelle Nnamdi Azikiwe, a town which is always in festive mood and which does not create and manage her wealth is bound to stagnate.

Communal Development

One would posit that our nonchalant inclination to communal development might have arisen because we grew up with tap water, electricity and good roads in place. The installation of pipe borne water for example was commissioned far back in 1929 and within few years all the villages had central taps in their village squares.

Today, water and electricity are epileptic. While looking towards the commitment of both Local and State Governments, the community has an important role in reactivating the stagnated utilities and in general development of the town. Onitsha has influential and well-meaning people that can source funds and contribute generously. Those for example that are willing to sink water bore-holes in their villages would have their names written in gold. Other ventures to be considered include cottage industries, farms, cooperative shops, etc. We may have been barking the wrong tree in supporting pageantry while other communities are consolidating industrial
bases in their communities.

Family Values: Male Dropouts In Schools

The prevalent degeneracy in the community is gradually destroying the good old virtues that made

Onitsha proud. The community now holds people whose income is questionable high. As earlier cited our unrestrained desires to take titles often push people to sell family land or get involved in various illegal activities. With crime wave on the increase, education in the doldrums, respect and truth cheapened, sensitization of the populace starting from our various homes is very necessary. "Na Nwam Akaliam Bu Awewo"- For one to openly admit that he is unable to control his child is a defeatist attitude. Let us therefore make the activities of our bad sons and daughters known to the law enforcers whose cooperation is needed to check this wild drift.

We must also begin to readdress the rate of male dropouts in schools. If the trend continues, we would be nowhere in the scheme of things both at the State and Federal levels. "Ochupulu Onweya Na Ugbo Si Na Ugbo Eluteroya"- Unless and until we are prepared to identify and admit our past errors or weaknesses and then effect corrections, we must not shift the blame on anyone else.

Non-Representation In Local Government Administration
The lag on the business front is also replicated in the political front where we are yet to make our mark in recent times on the Local Government Administration, not to talk about State or Federal level. The question of representation for non-Onitsha Ibos dates back to the 50s. It was in 1956, following Government reforms in

electoral votes and after which Onitsha became the only town in the Federation where non-indigenes hold sway in the leadership of Local Government. It is a paradox that all the competitive edges we had in the 60s are no more. Total mobilization of our people is exigent for our survival.

Environmental Issues

With nostalgia we can remember the majestic trees including economic trees that doted around in the villages. All those have been mowed down. Litters and waste materials have now taken over. It would be rewarding if the Igwe can flag off tree planting every year for about five years. The result in less than ten years would be lush environment. Obi's place and Okwueze are bereft of majestic trees. Okwueze is rather barren. I made cases in different papers for the need of museum and cenotaphs as means to immortalizing our progenitors, our sovereigns and those that have contributed to the growth of the town. I guess it is still not too late.

Onitsha/Church Matters

The sour relationship between the Church and the people is yet another great divide. It is far from being healthy. The situation requires a better understanding and tolerance from both quarters. So much of the church dogmas have changed to meet the demands of people. Celebrating masses in local languages, playing drums and clapping are part of the metamorphosis in the church. The reading of Bible at a stage was restricted and instead Missal was widely used. The same can be said of the ethos of the people like cessation of killing of twins, practice of killing slaves that are buried during the burial of a monarch, etc. Our Ume now resides outside the town. The Monarch at a stage was not expected to travel or go about in the daytime. It is now very common for many Ozo titled men to seek for Jesus Christ intercession while breaking kola nuts. These are all possible because we live in a dynamic world. The bone of contention may include second burial rites and Ozo title. I believe that some understandings can be reached as it has happened in other communities.

We can recall that late Igwe Okosi has a special seat in the front row at St. Mary's Church. The history of Immanuel Church cannot also be completed without the mention of late Chief Isaac Mbanefo Odu II of Onitsha. Also, in the first Ofala of Obi Okosi II, His Grace Archbishop Charles Heerey and other expatriate guests graced the occasion and had photographs with Obi and the other chiefs.

If we allow the inveterate rift to linger endlessly, we shall be denying ourselves the common front required in addressing the various developmental ills of the town in as much as the church faithful are also indigenes.

Spiritual Deficiency

Urbanization no doubt has wrought-up some ills, but spiritual deficiency to my thinking have created more ills. I would like to further cite the books of Deuteronomy. In it, God reminded Moses and his people of the great things he did for them during their exodus from Egypt. They were therefore required to love God with all their heart, soul and strength. Besides, they were charged to teach the commandments to their children. "Repeat them when you are at home, when you are away, while resting and while working. Tie them on your arms and wear them on your foreheads as a reminder. Write them on the doorsteps of your houses and gates". The consequences they were reminded of doing something contrary would evoke God's wrath. My concern here is that all our sacrosanct grounds have been despoiled and this calls for spiritual rejuvenation.

Counsels

"Ka eze nwe ira ka ira nwe eze"- Just as his subjects belong to the King so the King belongs to his subjects. This saying calls for sensitivity of the Monarch on the yearning of the people and the need to mobilize and

carry the subjects along. What we saw in the last ten years of late Obi Ofala Okagbue widened the existing cracks. It can also be said that dishonesty and selfish counsels of some of our people did not help matters. My humble advice derives from another saying that when the king steps out to dance he should occasionally if not constantly look back to see if the crowd is following or as Proverbs 14:28 puts it; *"A king's greatness depends on how many people he rules, without them he is nothing"*.

The same clarion call goes to all the ruling arms of the town and to all Onitsha indigenes.

Long live the Monarch
Agbogidi Igwe, Obi Nnameka Achebe
Long live Onitsha Ado Na Idu
OKEY AGUNYEGO
October 15, 2002
Isolo, Lagos.

AN OPEN LETTER TO THE RULING COUNCIL STRENGTHENING ONITSHA IMPROVEMENT UNION AND RELATED MATTERS

So much has been written on the need to undergird Onitsha Improvement Union.Barely four months ago, Onitsha Improvement Union, Lagos branch dispatched a mail to His Royal Majesty, **Igwe Achebe**, through President General Onitsha Improvement Union, cataloging militating issues against our people. The poor attitude of our people towards the union is one of the issues raised.

Two major reasons prompted this write up. The first concerns a letter from **Chief Ngozi Okafo, Ogene Onira** who is also head of Ofala Steering Committee appealing for fund from Onitsha Improvement Union. The second relates to my observations in the Anambra State Town Union meeting, Lagos branch on **14/9/14.**

Before delving into the promptings, let me sketch briefly the founding of Onitsha Improvement Union. We must give credits to late **P.H.Okolo** and **his team** that were instrumental in establishing the Union in **1924**. Their immense contributions towards the development of the town are well known and they deserve our tributes.

Prior to this organization, Friendly Society was established in Lagos by **Mr. J.A Agusiobo- Alias Penniless** in **1920**. It is a British scheme that encourages people to pay small amounts of money when they retire or when they are ill. It was this formation that metamorphosed into Onitsha Improvement Union.

The aptitude of our people in **1920**in Onitsha parlance – *amani ezi dina ola* – to embrace such scheme and the development focus the union provided, paved way to the growth, fame and leading edge above other communities.

We are informed in the letter from **Ogene Onira that Glo's sponsorship for Ofala** is not a total package, hence the need for fund to meet other expenses. Yet, there is another disclosure that we are living on past glories; a truism that is detrimental to our survival and a lesson to buck up. How?

Let me bring up the details of the second reason to write this article and along the line treat the how question. The assemblage of quality representatives, comprising of Lawyers, Accountants, Engineers, Doctors, and Sociologists etc in the Anambra Town meeting in Lagos is captivating. Yet the Board of Trustees that addressed the meeting called for further quality representations in towns where they are lacking. The essence, we are made to understand is to have people who can analyze the constitution and contribute effectively. It may interest you that this array of representative attends their own Town Union

Meetings.

Unfortunately, it is not so with us. A good number of our professionals claim not to have the time and others consider the Town Union as local. Some of the young ones see it as past time for retirees.Intending members may like to know that Onitsha Improvement Union Lagos branch, has affiliates that include Ado n' Isolo, Ikpaja, Ikorodu and Ojo through which they can register and join the Union. The Village meeting is yet another media. Strange, there are others who hold negative views for associating with Anambra Town Union. To those that do not know, this Association is a power house where issues concerning the governance of Anambra State are articulated. If you are not part of this larger body, how do you expect to benefit therefrom. Hence the saying– *Anya bu oke onye-Ochupulu onweya na ugbo sina ugbo eluteroya-*

I have heard some people argue that Agbalanze meeting is superior to that of Onitsha Improvement Union thus, insinuating that titled men need not attend Onitsha Improvement Union meeting. This comparison is unnecessary and unhealthy for the growth of the town and our people. Those that advocate such forget that a **Red Cap Chief** was once President General of the Union. There are many titled and non-titled men that have presided over the affairs of the Union in Lagos.

Kajie Adibuah, now Ajie of Onitsha was the

President of the Union and under his able leadership in **2002**, Ado House was purchased. There are not less than six other titled men that have piloted the affairs of Onitsha Improvement Union Lagos. We have Also few committed Ozo titled men that attend **O.I.U meeting** regularly.My take is that the Association is the Umbrella Union for all Onitsha men.

There are those who believe that the town is doing pretty well, contrary to living on the past glories. One is reminded that Onitsha has more University students, more lawyers etc than any town in Anambra State. Statistics can sometimes be wooly. My take on this is that the competition/race is not between Onitsha and another town but between Onitsha and the rest of other towns in Anambra State. It is a race between twenty point six local government areas and Onitsha indigenes. Currently Anambra State has twenty one local government areas.Everybody wants to beat the champion and the champion that lowers his guard is knocked out mercilessly, hence the saying– *Ka onye si debe ugbaya ka aga si weluya kpo afifia-*.Loosing much ground sometimes begets loss of respect and mockery. I bought a ticket some years ago on a bus routing Onitsha to Lagos. I was required to indicate my town in the manifest and no sooner I obliged the information the sales clerk echoed Onitsha Ado.Minutes later he told me that Onitsha no longer reigns. In another case a dude from Utu was angry and sad that his townsman sold his property at Iweka Road. He likened it to how Onitsha people sell their land property with careless abandon. When he got to know that it was sold to a person from Osumenyi and not resold to Onitsha person, his faced beamed with smile. Both towns are in the same neighborhood and beside the guy's mother is from Osumenyi.

There is no guarantee that a town will always be on the lead position. What is important in present time is to phase in new strategies and development from time to time. As it affects us, we must learn from our past mistakes. We must begin to cultivate the ideals of communal efforts as against waiting for the government all the time. This is the area I figure that the Union and other Associations should spearhead.One of our sins is that we can marshal fund for pageantry for self more than for development of the community. We have this maxim; *Omasili nti omasili nyam nyam*. The implied meaning is that the success of a man is also extended to his family and community. From Biblical perspective, we learn that there is no failure more disastrous than success that keeps God away. It is so tempting when we are blessed by God to relax and think that we deserve it. Therefore, let us guard against turning back from the grace of God.One can also say that another great failure is the one that keeps the family and community away when one becomes rich.

In strengthening Onitsha Improvement Union, I believe that the Ruling Council has a pivotal role to play in sensitizing every Onitsha adult to be a card carrying member of the Union. The Monarch told me years back that he expects the Union, Associations, Age Grades to play a part in the governance and as well as in the wellbeing of the community. The aforementioned sensitization; the main plank of this piece, will help tremendously in reaching out to our people and enhancing the Union expected role and contributions to the town, hence the saying -*Igwe bu ike - Anyu koba nwammili onu ogboo ufufu.*

Other climes have favored the use of sanctions and penalties where their townsmen fail to be members of their town Unions. We cannot run away completely from such penalties. I earnestly request National Executive Council with approval from the Ruling Council to fine tune what is best for us to ensure that our people participate in the Union matters. As I mentioned earlier, a sustained sensitization as a planned strategy by the Ruling Council and at all the levels of governance including the Diokpas stand to bring in desirable results.

In my thinking, the Unions in Onitsha; Onitsha North and Onitsha South Unions ought to be the starting point of this reinforcing plan. I am not sure that both Unions can boast of combined thirty membership strength, whereas we have a pool of men over five thousand at home. It is a common saying that *Ana esi na unu amalu mma we pua ilo.* With such fostering, it would be plain sailing for other branches of the Union. This approach in no way forestalls the various efforts of branches in reaching out to potential members. And likewise, in meeting the aims and objectives of the Union which includes; promotion of our culture, promotion of development of the town and her people, providing brotherly support and welfare of members and also providing advisory role to National Executive Committee of the Union in Onitsha and by implication to the Ruling Council.

Beyond these, the Union is also one of the media whereby messages, directives and appeals are disseminated to Onitsha people in the country and abroad. I recognize other forward looking Associations, Societies, Clubs etc. and together we can go beyond Ofala and champion the cause of better development of our motherland.

May the light lit by our ancestors over five hundred years ago not dim?

May the focus on development of the town fostered by P.H Okolo and his team ninety years ago inspire us to greater heights?

Long live the King Igwe Achebe
Long live the various arms of governance in Onitsha
Long live Onitsha Improvement Union
Long live various Associations, Societies and Clubs.
May Onitsha bloom again?

OKEY MADUEGBUNAM AGUNYEGO
His Grace Lodge
Isolo, Lagos.
Date: 30th October, 2014.

CITATION FOR BRAVERY
MR. JIDE ONUORA

Startled by anguished wails, and billowing smoke, twenty five years old Mr. Jideofo Onuora of Ogboli Eke village sooner realized the red alert which must be dealt with; a baby trapped in a burning building.

He risked his life and limb as he braved the smoke, the conflagration and darted to the floor where six months old baby, Makua Chukwu Ofodile was lying. Imbued with passion and sense of urgency the mission was deftly accomplished within minutes. Alas the baby later gave up ghost. May her innocent soul rest in peace?. The valiant Jideofo Onuora was not spared as he sustained serious burns.

This ordeal happened on twelve November 2007 at Mr. Ofodile's residence in Ogboli Olosi village. It is a rare selfless feat which we have not witnessed for many years. We hope that in bringing up this gallantry to the public domain, no matter how late, the good old value, "Aju onye Onisha ama adanna rimu", the keenness to share the burden of any Onitsha person which we relished pre-war could be rekindled.

Spurred by Mr. Jideofo Onuora's daring deed, Ado Integrity Initiative presented him with a certificate of Bravery and the sum of One Hundred Thousand Naira.

OKEY AGUNYEGO.
Please touch someone's pains today and
Make this world a better place
FOR ADO INTEGRITY
Contact 08023182092, 08033071507
Date 2011

ACCOLADE: FAVOUR BARRISTER NWACHUKWU DOUGLAS EGBUNA, CHAIRMAN ONITSHA NORTH LOCAL GOVERNMENT

On a happy note, 1 would like to acknowledge the drive of the Chairman, Onitsha North Local Government, Barrister Nwachukwu Douglas Egbuna - Osite for renovating Ogbe Oye market, near completion of Health centre and maintenance of road works.

In my previous works on Onitsha matters spanning over fifteen years, 1 made consistent appeal to our people to support Ogbe Oye project and other self-help projects. I appealed also to the village that owns the market to have a re-think after an offer by late Engineer Theophilus Nzegwu to renovate the market as a contribution to the town was rejected.There is no point raking up the divisive village politics that was prevailing at the time. The principal characters have passed on. May their souls rest in peace?.

The market before the renovation was disorderly. Trading was carried out up to the main road, endangering the lives of sellers, buyers, pedestrians, motorists and motor bike riders. The market itself was unsightly with rusted pans. According to an advert of a popular drink, the difference is clear.

Bravo Osite.We have much ground yet to cover as our earlier decided advantages have waned considerably.There are some progressive associations that include Ado Integrity Initiative, G36, Onitsha Improvement Union and individuals that you can confer with on how to win back some of the town's decided advantages. I am optimistic that a brainstorming session with these groups will create dramatic results.

Finally may I use this avenue to re-echo to all and sundry on the importance of self –help? It complements whatever development caused by Local and State Governments. It engenders immense benefits to the community. The reveille had long been sounded and time to wise up is now.

Osite. Well done. Your good deeds are worth drumming and dancing

OKEY AGUNYEGO.
Vice President O.l.U. Lagos.
His Grace Lodge
Lagos.
June 21 2015. Father's Day.

CRITERIA FOR ONITSHA ROLE OF HONOUR

"No person was ever honoured for what he received. Honour has been the reward for what he gave" Calvin Coolidge30[th] US President 1872- 1933.

I understand this topic to be the requisite a person should attain to deserve an honour. The requisite encompasses diverse examples.

- *Our ancestors who conceived and perfected the sojourn to Onitsha Ado n'Idu are in the front line for honouring and commemoration.*

- *Those who cause various developments for the town are qualified to be honoured.*

- *For those that excelled in their professions / trades, their fame rubs off on the town hence they qualify to be honoured.*

- *Our foot soldiers that fought Oze war, Biafra war and our people that died during these wars deserve to be honoured and commemorated.*

- *A fellow who picked up a hand bag containing a good sum of money at the airport and handed it to the authority that traced the owner deserves an honour.*

- *Those that provide good ideas and leaderships in various forms have the prospect to be honoured.*

CITATIONS

- *The next requirement would be citations for those to be honoured. By and Large citations portray the character and achievements of the nominees.*

- *Another important aspect concerns how the nominees are rewarded.*

Primarily the honours are reserved for our people alive or dead but it would not be out of place to honour non-indigenous folk. Distinction must be made here between ordinary honours and chieftaincy honours. I hope to devote few lines on it and generally put up some counsels.

What follows is various names in no ranking order, their professions and achievements and types of honour.

OUR ANCESTORS

For our antecedents that perfected our settlement in Onitsha, erecting of statues is desirable. Although there is a status of Chima at lme Obi, there are also other manners our antecedents can be honoured. It is great news that Agbogidi commissioned the construction of a private museum named after Chimedie. Chimedie is one of the five sons of EzeAroli and father of Orezeobi, Orowa, OlodiOwowo, Nwazago, Ijelekpe, Akazua, OzaNzediegwu and Ajagba. This commemoration is history revisited. It is however worrisome that the town has no museum despite our rich culture. Its absence denies the young ones of the history and inspirations that museum heralds. Let us remind ourselves that our anthropology cannot be completed without the preservation of our historic endowments. Apart from museum, Hall of Fame is also credible.

POLITICS

We ought to have a deepened gratitude when we remember those that paid the price in obtaining independence for the nation. The late Owelle Nnamdi Azikiwe comes to mind. In as much as he has been duly honoured in many ways, it is sad and worrisome that the mausoleum of the Great Zik is still not fully completed. Though it is a Federal Governmentaffair, the State and Town should bring to the attention of Central Government of such lapses. Like museum, mausoleum is a tourist attraction and a bundle of history.

UNIONIST

Late J. A. Agusiobo, Alias Penniless with Associates formed Friendly Society way back in 1920. The money contributions from members enabled the group to support the sick and those out of work. That was welfare service at work – amani ezi dina ola. In the heels of this development, late P.H Okolo and Associates formed Onitsha Improvement union in 1924. A good number of the members that won election into Onitsha Town Council in 1934 were instrumental to tarring the roads, erecting public buildings and championing the first modernization of Onitsha Main Market alongside hard- nosed personalities that included, Late Chief Odu Isaac Mbanefo, Late J.C. Oranye, Late Chief Onoli Ogo Ibeziako and late Peter Achukwu. We need adequate literature to ensure that these achievements by this group are not lost. A hall fame would be befitting for them. We can name Onistha Improvement Union Headquarters at Ime Obi after late P.H. Okolo. Naming this group after other edifices,streets etc. are credible.

PROPRIETORS OF SCHOOLS

Prewar there were no less than six colleges that were

owned by our people. They include, Etukokwu Commerical College owned by late Chief Odua J.U.Etokokwu, Metropolitan College owned by Late P.O.Chude and Associates, Modebe Memorial Grammar School owned by Modebe Family, Zik Commercial College owned by Mrs. Lilly Arinze and Washington Memorial College owned by late Chief Onya Emengo and Associates. These institutions and others owned by missionaries provided early opportunity for our people to be educated. In many ways Education contributed to our decided advantages and singularity of the town. I subscribe to adequate literature to remember these worthy men.I suggest too that their statues with plaques be erected in the various schools. Onitsha Improvement Union can take up this challenge and likewise old boys Associations and individuals.

WORK OPPORTUNITIES

There are those that offered work opportunities to many Onitsha Youths. They include late Commissioner Ben Chude in Civil Service, late Ajie Ukpabi Asika in his position as Administrator, East Central State, late P.O.Osili of Federal Ministry of Works, late Engr.Izikel Ejogu of Federal Ministry of works, late Sylvester Ogbuah of University Teaching Hospital Enugu, late Mr. Egbuna of Nigerian Railways and his successor late Engr. Theo Nzegwu. Late Stan Mozie of Posts and Telegraphs joins this list. We cannot forget that late Ajie tarred the roads in In-land town. 	Anything done to commemorate and immortalize these great men with hearts of gold and hearts in the right places is worthy.Definitely we need adequate literature to inspire the young and generations unborn.

FAME

There are those that brought fame to the town through their professions. This list includes late Col Emmanuel Arinze Ifeajuna who was the first African to win gold medal in high jump at Common Wealth Games in Vancouver, Canada 1954. Innocent Egbunike won several medals in sprints in the 80's. Njofo Okala kept the post for the National Football Team, Super Eagles for years. Earlier we had late Godwin Achebe, late Okechukwu, late Onyeanwuna and others. Okey Emodi made his mark as professional coach. We cannot forget the administrative skills of late Justice Ikpeazu. Not many will know that Carl Ikeme who manned the post for the National Football Team before he took ill is from Onitsha. I wish him speedy recovery. They deserve a place in Hall of fame / gallery.

PIONEER PROFESSIONALS

Beyond sports, late Professor Chike Obi was a pioneer in Mathematics, late Professor Ben Enwonwu a was pioneer Artist and Sculptor, Philip Emeagwali of computer fame, late Akunne Frank Mbanefo, third Architect in Eastern Nigeria, late Surveyor Chukwura Owusi, late Surveyor Obianwu and many others deserve a place in the gallery. Dr.Nnamdi Akupueome Ozobia held sway as the pioneer Managing Director of Niger Docks. One cannot forget that our own monarch Igwe Achebe reached a top echelon in Shell before his coronation. Another of our brother Chike Onyejekwe also attained a top position in Shell.

JUSTICE /LAWYERS

Late Sir Louis Mbanefo was the first Justice of Eastern Nigeria and the first Nigeria Judge to serve on the bench of World Court in Hague. Late Onowu Chike Ofodile was the Attorney General of the country in the 80's. Onitsha boasts of many Judges that include, late Justice Ikpeazu, Late Justice Araka, Late justice Nwokedi, Late Justice Moses Balonwu, Justice Emeka Nzegwu and others. The town has a galore of senior advocate of Nigeria - SAN - that include, Kpajie Nnamdi Ibegbu. Late P.O Balonwu, Akunne Emeka Ofodile, Mr. Agatha Mbamali, Mr. Chike Agbu and many others. We have reputable lawyers and Civil Right activists. Olisa Agbakoba is both S.A.N and Civil Right Activist. Anali Chude is the attorney General in Anambra State.Mention must be made of Barrister B.C. Obanye and L.O.V. Anionwu of blessed memories. Like other professionals they deserve places in the gallery.

DOCTORS

This field boasts of reputable doctors, late Doctor Onyeachonam, Late Doctor Ejoor Mbanefo and Late Doctor Uwachie that was the first Ibo Doctor to establish private practice in Eastern Nigeria. The role calls of Doctors like lawyers are in hundreds. Here again adequate literature is required and possibly compiled by the league promoting interest of their members. It stands to inspire the young ones. The Doctors like other professionals that performed feats ought to be honored.

ARTISANS

Late Mr. Achukwu, alias Achukwu Ochanja had passion for exotic cars. These were displayed in his garage in the 60's. He had also a mechanic work shop which I think was the biggest workshop owned by an Onitshaman. Some of my mates had a stint in the workshop. Efforts by the family to keep the workshop alive after the war failed. Onitsha had few mechanics, late Ejoor Ikeme was trained by Armels. The workshop closed after his demise. Eddie Edekobi opened a garage, which did not last as he opted for another trade. Jimmy Ifeajuna was trained by Leventis but veered off later from this trade. Mr Austin

Onwuma, who cut his teeth with Cocharis on Rover brand currently on his own, may be the big time Onitsha mechanic.It is worrisome that our people are not giving much attention to artisans; plumbing, carpentry, masonry, etc. In doing this we deny ourselves the huge employment created for artisans. Late Achukwu deserves a place in the gallery.

CLERGY

In clergy, Late John Cross Anyogu was the first Ibo Catholic Priest and was later consecrated a Bishop.

Late Anyaegbunam was the first Ibo man to be ordained as a Reverend Pastor in Anglican Church. He was ordained in 1896. Late Bishop Onyeabor was a precursor Anglican Bishop in Eastern Nigeria. The role of late Monsignor Etuka Obelagu, first to support our people that were refugees during the war with fair share of relief materials and secondly his assistance in building destroyed houses of widows after the war was worthy.

Other Onitsha Priests include, late Father Dennis Sokei, Late P. Boy Ndulue, Rev. Obrota, Rev. Martins Onukwuba, Rev. Phlip Egbuniwe,Rev. Collins Ogbogu, Venerable Enwonwu , Venerable Imagie, Venerable Ikemefuna and others.We have also Reverend Sisters that includes late Rev. Mother

Anyogu who was the first Rev. Mother in Eastern Nigeria, Rev. Mother Mary Magdalene Oranu, Rev Mother Dominica Odita and others. Their role in the service of the church and the community is commendable. Monsignor Obelagu for his deeds deserves an honour in line with other people that cause some assistance to our people.

FALLEN HEROES

"Any man who wants to be a cowardly slave can have no honour". Adolf Hilter 1899-1945.

We have not fully commemorated our people that died during Oze war and during Nigeria Crisis 1966/70.It was a good step that we organized mass funeral for people that died in the crisis of 1966/70. But had we erected immortalizing monument where wreaths can be laid every year, we would have made a bigger mark. It is not too late to erect a monument with brief history inscribed in a plaque fixed on the monument. It is a bundle of history for tourists, visitors and generation unborn. There are soldiers that died in action. They include late Col Chude Sokei, Late Major Theophillus Nzegwu, late Col Emma Ifeajuna, Capt. Okaka and others.There were also students turned soldiers that died during the war. They deserve adequate spaces in the gallery. A cenotaph could also be erected to honour them.

Late Col. Ifeajuna's case is sad. Following the 1966

coup, Federal Government removed his name from the website of Athletics Federation of Nigeria, thus rubbishing the gold medal award he won in long jump in Canada 1954. During the Biafra crisis, what I term ideological differences caused him his life. He was branded a saboteur and shot. Many of our people were treated as suspects following his accusation as a saboteur.

If Ojukwu Head of State Biafra that prosecuted the war was pardoned by the Federal Government, why not Col. Ifeajuna that wanted to save lives by early negotiation with Nigeria. Despite his travails his mark in Vancouver is indelible. There is a deluge of his achievement in the internet and in International Athletics Federation Website. There is a need to honour him at home perhaps featuring his picture in the gallery.

The same is applicable to Major Nzegwu, who was shot during the reprisal coup of 1966 at Ikeja cantonment. You may like to know that his bust still stands at Air Force Base in Kaduna.

Onitsha also produced fine officers that include Retd Brigadier Eche Chukwuma, late Brigadier General Johnny Mbanefo, Retd Col. Osii Agbogu and others.

Onitsha boasts of high ranking police officers. The list includes late Commissioner Ibekwe, late Bay Agbakoba, and in later days late Commissioner Chike

Adibuah , Commissioner Osita Adibuah (Ajie) Deputy Commissioner Okey Obanye, Deputy Commissioner Nwachukwu Enwonwu, Commissioner Ikechukwu Aduba, Deputy Commissioner Egbunike, and others.

LITERARY

In literary field we have late Odinigwe Onuora Nwekwu, late Nnanyeugo S.I.Bosahand late Jerry Orakwue. The trio researched on 'Onitshaology' which is the study of ancient Onitsha culture. Others include late Ojinnaka Ifeka, Akunne Amuta and my humble self. My first publication, Ancestral Voices – Onitsha Names and Phrases Teased out, is the first attempt in demystifying Onitsha names. Namad iOkagbue has also written couple of fictions. These writers deserve slots in the gallery and other commemorative honours.

Late Onowu Olisa Mortune built a Police Station at Awada. The sole aim was to secure the boundary of Onitsha with that of Obosi in the 80's. This was a case of valour and verve. Unfortunately this aim was not sustained.

Henry Onukwuba single handedly renovated the statue of late Owelle Nnamdi Azikiwe that was destroyed by mobs. He also wrote a book on Zik titled TESTIMONIES TO A GREAT AFRICA.

The former Chairman Onitsha North Local Government, Barrister O. Egbuna made some impact in renovating Ogbeoye market, construction of Health Center, road works and town transportation. Both Onukwuba and Egbuna deserve places in the gallery and other honours.

We must not forget the selfless devotion of teachers that includes late Head Master Edemanya, late Headmaster Chukwura, late Mr. Ibisi, late Mrs. Okagbue, late Mrs. Ikeme, late Mrs. Analo, late Miss Obanye and a host of others. Gone are the days their rewards were said to come from heaven. They need more honours. I'd suggest that schools where they taught and possibly those teaching will have their names in plaques and on bill boards. This can be sponsored by old boys associations or by individuals.

AMBASSADORS

We cannot fail to mention distinguished Ambassadors that include, late Amb. L. Osakwe -Zaire, late Amb. L.O.V. Anionwu – Italy and Amb. Chief Odu Arthur Mbanefo – United Nation. Akunwafo A. Osakwe and Ugokwe Chike Chukwura were pioneer ambassadors that represented the country. They deserve recognition and ought to have a place in Hall of fame and "who is who" in town.

AVIATION

In aviation, Late Captain Ojinnaka Osakwe was a Senior Captain on DCIO. If we recall, he performed a feat in flying General Ojukwu to Ivory Coast towards the end of the war. Late Phil – Ebosie was the youngest Captain on DCIO. Late Amechi Nwokedi and late Ibegbu were engineers on Airbus. Emma Nwadiogbu joins the list of top airline engineers. He plys his trade with Boeing in America.

I must admit that this account did not treat other numerous professions. Going by the opening quote by Calvin Cooligde 30th US President "No person was ever honoured for what he received. Honour has been the reward for what he gave".Those not mentioned that 'gave' deserve similar honours. As the saying goes to begin is half done. It paves way for other efforts. The benefit of honouring our people remains huge. They stand to inspire both the beneficiaries and the community especially the younger generation. There is this saying that you grow to the extent you give and by giving you create more room to grow on the inside

Proverbs 1.5 says "the liberal man shall be rich. By watering others, he waters himself" Let us encourage giving.

My next attempt is on conferment of honours to non-

Onitsha people. Note this is not chieftancy title. When the Second Republic Vice president Alex Ekwueme visited Igwe Ofala Okagbue, he was initiated into an age grade. You may like to know that he grew up in Onitsha. This honour was skillfully handled. My suggestion is that similar honours be extended to other non- Onitsha people. They have to meet the criteria earlier detailed in the opening page. There must be evidence of contributions towards the growth of the town. Late Ekenedili Chukwu bus proprietor Chief Ilodibe employed some of our people working in his transport business and one of them was manager.

Another Group will include Government Officials, Businessmen, Academicians and other high profile visitors that pay visit to Igwe. One may not lose sight of political /business advantages in honouring our august visitors.

For both groups I subscribe the use of Onitsha symbols in arts forms, pictures, wood works, metal works and paintings of various sizes with Royal Seals engraved on them.

Though Chieftaincy honours is a separate topic but permit my preamble since I am treating the place of honour. Benin and Onitsha do not confer chieftaincy to non – indigenes. It remains cul – de – sac, despite the fact that some of our people have been conferred chieftaincy by Monarchs from other towns. Given our peculiarity and experience we ought to be wary, noting the advantages and disadvantages. Some will argue that selected few that meet the criteria can be honoured with simple appellation like, Odozi Obodo, Oka Ome, Ezi Oyi etc. Perhaps with dynamics of growth, the iron curtain may be raised and relaxed in the future. All the same, a cautious approach is unavoidable.

In my previous work I wrote citations for late Col. Emmanuel Ifeajuna and Late Odinigwe Onuora Nzekwu. The citations are attached as an example.

Long live His Royal Majesty Igwe Alfred Achebe
Long live Onitsha Adon' Idu.
May the light lit by our antecedents over 500 years ago never dim.
May the New Year herald greater vision and success.
To God be the glory

OKEY MADUEGBUNAM AGUNYEGO
His Grace Lodge.
(From Umu-Ezearoli Welfare Association, Lagos)
18/10/2017

ABOUT LATE LT. COLONEL EMMANUEL ARINZE IFEAJUNA

Born in 1934, he attended Dennis Memorial Grammar School, Onitsha and Ilesh a Grammar School. During the preparation of Commonwealth Games in Vancouver, Canada, Ifeajuna was not in the list. The selectors had many names to select from.

However, his chances become real in the championship in April 1954, two months before the departure of the team to Canada. He cleared 6 feet 5 inches and that gave him a direct ticket to join the team. At the game he wore a shoe on the left leg and in second attempt, scaled 6th 7inches and in the final jump he recorded 6th8 inches to become the first African to win a gold medal at the International Sports event in 1954 Empire and Commonwealth Games in Vancouver Canada. He was barely twenty years old.He read zoology in University of Ibadan and on graduation has a stint in teaching. He joined the Army in 1960 and was trained in Aldershot, England.

He was one of the five Majors that carried out the first failed coup in 1966. In Nigeria coup d'état when successful is legal and when unsuccessful is treasonable. What a distinction? Come to think about it most of our Military Heads of State carried out coups and a few benefited from the coup becoming Heads of State.

Major Chukwuma Nzeogwu, a co – plotter of the coup was buried with full military honours and statue erected in his memory in his home town Okpanam. For Ifeajuna it is a different tale. His name was removed from the website of Athletics Federation of Nigeria and his name was reviled. The event in the Biafran side where he fought caused him his life. General Odimegwu Ojukwu accused Ifeajuna and Banjo of plotting against him and the Biafran Nation; a case of treason which they denied. According to Ifeajuna they were trying to save lives and the country by negotiating an early cease fire with the Federal Government and reuniting Nigeria. He was executed alongside Victor Banjo, Philip Alake and Sam Agbam on 25th September, 1967 by 1:30pm. Before he was shot, his last words were that his death would not stop what he feared most, that the Federal troops would enter Enugu and the way out was for those about to kill him to negotiate for a cease fire and save lives. Barely two and half hours Enugu was hit by Federal troops and in the following two and half years over a million Ibos died. Arguably if his advice was adhered to many lives would have been saved.

If Ojukwu, the Head of State of Biafra was pardoned, what stops Ifeajuna who had advised on uniting the country not to be pardoned even at death? President Obasanjo is said to have a manuscript written by Ifeajuna but not published stating that "it was unity we wanted and not rebellion". Similar plan was the case in Biafra when he sensed that uniting the country would save lives.

Despite all that, his mark in Vancouver Games of 1954 is indelible. It may not be in the website of Nigerian Athletics Federation's website but there is deluge of it in the internet and in International Athletics Federation's website. There is the need to honour him at home.

Extracts from Brian Oliver's article in Observer on Sunday 13th July, 2014.

ABOUT LATE ODINIGWE ONUORA NZEKWU

He was a veteran author, teacher, journalist and choir master. He started teaching in 1946 at Mount St. Mary's Elementary Teacher's College in Oturkpo. He moved to Saint Charles Onitsha in 1951 and to Saint Mary's Practicing School Onitsha in 1952. In 1955 he moved to City College, Yaba, Lagos where he taught English and Comparative Religion. By 1956, he took up appointment with Federal Ministry of Information. He researched on Nigeria traditions, arts and crafts. He presented a historical article on Onitsha in the magazine. The approval of this article by the Editor earned him a promotion to Sub – Assistant Editor 1958 / 60 and subsequently he rose to Assistant Editor 1960 / 62 and Editor in 1963.

During the war, he became a Senior Information Officer and later Deputy Director, in 1968. At the end of the war, he edited the first volume of General Gowon's speeches. In 1972, he rose to Assistant Director of Information. By 1979, he become the protem General Manager News Agency of Nigeria and in the same year he was confirmed Substantive General Manager. He retired in 1985. He had the following novels to his credit,

Wand of Noble wood 1961, Blade among the Boys 1962. He co – authored Eze Goes to School 1964 and its sequel, Eze goes to College 1965 with Michael Crowther, a renowned historian, University lecture, former Editor of British Historical Journal – History Today. Both books were supplementary school readers. Highlife for lizards was published in 1965 and Troubled Dust in 2012.

He published two non – fiction books, Chima Dynasty in Onitsha, 1998 and Faith of Our Fathers, a compendium of arts, beliefs, Social institutions and code of values that characterize the Onitsha Traditional community in 2003. He wrote and produced three Igbo musical plays; Ogeneme 1997, Okumefuna 1986 and Onye mebie ani 1987.

He had the following honours – maker of NAN on News Agency of Nigeria 30th Anniversary at Abuja in 2006. In 2008, he was conferred with Nigerian National Honour in the rank of officer of the Niger OON. In May 2011, the office complex and media centre in Lagos was named after him.

He was President of Onitsha Improvement Union in the 90's President Umueze Aroli Welfare Association 1971 / 76 and Patron 1998. He was also Editorial Adviser of Ado Circle's Magazine - Ado focus 1995 / 1998.

OKEY AGUNYEGO

22nd July, 2015
Lagos.
Paper presentation to Ado Integrity Initiative on planned honouring of Onitsha people.

LATE ODINIGWEONUORANZEKW

LATE COLONEL EMMANUEL

THINKING ALOUD
PRAISE FOR ONITSHA ADO WOMEN PROGRESSIVE ASSOCIATIONLAGOS, ON THEIR SECOND ANNUAL MERIT AWARD/EMPOWERMENT PROJECT. 27TH NOVEMBER, 2016.

My pet subject Onitshaness is about the elements that need to be reinforced in order to be relevant, to regain our pre-eminence and to sustain it. It is directed to stirring our community to achieve meaningful developments and zest for the town. This introduction becomes necessary as our decided advantages; our raison d'être that heralded our past glories namely - Citadel of education. A town blessed with several first professionals in judiciary, politics, medicine, architecture, engineering, sports, clergy etc. Epicenter of Igbo modernity.A cultural and commercial centre.A nursery of burgeoning capitalism. A standard for measuring civilization east of the Niger up till 1967, began to wane considerably.

While part of the derailment may be traced to urbanization, there are also glaring lapses on our side. We failed to heighten our competiveness and became earth bound for too long.

How do we retrieve the situation?
There is no guarantee that a town would be in the lead all the time. Naturally when a community is placed on a commanding role for a long period, it is visited by resentment by others. That is our situation and the contempt is rarely disguised. Our complacency did not help matters. It fueled a bad situation, turning to an advantage to many waiting (naturally) to usurp our position. As a result the competition is not between Onitsha and another town but a competition between

Onitsha and other towns in the State. This postulation demands that we buckle down to a host of tough measures to boost our competiveness and also restore some of the advantages that have come apart from the seams. We appreciate the efforts of the Ruling Council, but the gargantuan tasks demands commitment from all and sundry. Teamwork divides the effort and multiples the effect.

While slogans motivate and spur morale, we must note that they have limited span. Most of the slogans we use today are yesteryears rallying calls that are now vacuous, otiose and have lost their bites. It behooves on us to create new ones.

There is an increasing propensity to and penchant in disposing lands on free holds for burials, marriages and pageantry. Decisions reached by the kindred not to sell Owelle Ebo plots to non-indigenes fell on deaf ears. Today, close to half of the estate is owned by non-indigenes. We should not shy away from penalizing those that flout the community decisions.

The market crises that reared its head forty-two years whittled down our franchise. Our farm lands in Trans Nkisi are disingenuously appropriated. You may recall that early in the year the town mobilized legal luminaries to pursue this case only to find out that the case elapsed twelve years the suit was first filed. This experience ought to teach us a lesson. We must ensure that our strategies are back on the rails without further ado.

Our dairy appears crammed with festivities. This is gradually becoming our hallmark. We can marshal fund for festivities and pageantry easily than for development. We splurge on socials. A check on these excesses will surely provide for other contending issues. A check also on inordinate ambition for title taking is necessary as some people in the past appropriated family lands.
There was a known case of an intending initiate who sold a land belonging to a dead person. To me, letting such a person off the hook is compounding our problems.

Strangely we consider the place and role of artisans as menial hence denying ourselves huge employment opportunities the economy creates for tradesmen. As I write the two skilled acquisition centres in Onitsha North and South Local Government are yet to be equipped. Again we must not let grass grow under our feet. I would like O.I.U. Headquarters and Ruling Council to bring up this short falls to State and Federal Governments.

We would further require a sustained sensitization/reorientation programmes to disabuse the minds of our youths on the notion that the jobs of tradesmen are menial and also harp on its importance.

I have often counseled that in a pursuit of excellence

we cannot defer issues that divide us. They have to be thrashed for posterity sake. The issue that comes to mind is the Okpalaship of Onitsha that is contended by Oreze and Chimaevi quarters. Both are brothers and sons of Eze Chima. This historical contention requires thorough perception. We have also some disturbing and lingering trend associated with Diokpaship and family feuds.

There is a strong apathy when levies are sought but then how can you seek distinction without money. To a great extent the vehicle to engender genuine transformation is through self-help. Other climes have embraced this strategy without qualms. Why not us? Think of this, a mandatory contributions of yearly N1,000 by every Onitsha adult estimated at about Forty Thousand people will add up to N40 million while N2,000 yearly contribution yields N80 million. Where the mandatory contribution is stepped up to N5,000 it adds up to N200 million a year. This is a handsome amount to pursue various projects every year. It is a challenge and I look forward to approval and blessing from the Ruling Council. I expect Onitsha Improvement Union Headquarters and other think tanks to get down on brass tasks. It is of utmost important for all adult Onitsha men to be card carrying members of Onitsha Improvement Union. In other climes those that are not members of their town unions are precluded from taking chieftaincy title and at death their funerals are boycotted expect they meet all the financial requirement of the union. Without infringing on human rights we should devise our own penalties but more emphasis must be made on sensitization. Onitsha Improvement Union Headquarters and Ruling Age Grade should look into this and recommend appropriately.

The pursuit of Onitsha dream cannot bloom in isolation, it calls for committed participation of our people. There are many other tasks that stand to enhance our advantages but let me in conclusion touch a bit on honouring our people.

The benefits of honouring our people are huge. It does not only inspire the beneficiaries but also the community especially the younger generation. Barely two (2) years ago, Umueze Aroli (Lagos) honoured their patrons. In the wake of this feat, Onitsha Improvement Union (Lagos) honoured some of the past presidents. I am glad Onitsha Ado-Women Progressive Association; Lagos **(OAWPA)** is hosting their Second Annual Merit Awards/Empowerment Project.

I sincerely congratulate them on this occasion Bravo!!

Let us charge ourselves to think boldly and sell brave ideas that will create dramatic results – Onitshaness.

OKEY MADUEGBUNAN AGUNYEGO
His Grace Lodge
1st November, 2016

Praise for Onitsha Ado
Women Progressive Association
Lagos, on their Second Annual
Merit Award/Empowerment Project.
27th November, 2016

A CHAT WITH PRESIDENT AGBALANZE NNABUENYI

OK: You clinched the post of President Agbalanze in the recent election. Congratulations. May we know whatever challenges you encountered and your game plan that made you to win?

PA: Thank you for your compliments, I can tell you that the personalities that contested the Presidency of Agbalanze are men of substance. I believe that my approach in selling brave ideas intended to rejuvenate Agbalanze appealed to the members.
The young ones particularly endorsed my candidacy. I must not forget to thank the final umpire, God Almighty.

OK: News about town acclaim positive steps your executive has adopted. May we know some details of these changes?

PA: I see discipline as cardinal. Our first move was to urge our members to imbibe orderliness and decorum. Further, we agreed that members from eighty years will be exempted from participating in ceremonies while their benefits are guaranteed.

OK: Proverbs 29v18 says that where there is no vision, the people perish. The place of vision and strategy is imperative to the survival of any association. Can you let us know the vision and strategy your executive/Agbalanze has mapped out?

PA: Our vision is to enhance the position of Agbalanze for the betterment of the members and the town. Having discussed discipline, we have plans underway to set up a functional skill acquisition centre for our youths. We also have plans to examine the questionnaire initiates fill before they are initiated. It would no longer be mere formality. In as much as it is the duty of the family 'Umunna' to screen those that will be initiated, we on our own will cross check the questionnaire appropriately. We are also considering other strategies that will complement our vision.

OK: Considering the formidable strength of Agbalanze, are we expecting some development of the town in your regime?

PA: I think my previous answer covers this, but I can further inform you that plans are ahead to marshal adequate fund that can tackle our proposed projects.

OK: The word "society" was removed from Agbalanze in the eighties and according to Late President, Akume Fred Umurma, the name denoted secrecy but the dictionary definition is very positive; organized groups/association with common aim and interests. What is your take on this?

PA: I accept the positiveness of the word society. I believe too that the regime of Late President Fred Umunna must have envisaged some aspects of secrecy then. Where the need arises for restoring such name, we will consider it.

OK: As a third or is it fourth level of arms in governance, do you provide advisory role to the Ruling Council and may we also know the relationship of Agbalanze and the Ruling Council?

PA: Yes we do, Do not forget that the Red cap Chiefs at a time were members of Agbalanze. We meet from time to time to discuss Onitsha issues.

OK: There are scores for instances where Agbalanze initiates go through the rituals before their elder brothers. I see this act as widening the existing crack in the family. How can these unsettling acts be checked?

PA: Let me take the recent case of Onyejekwe family in Odoje. We intervened when the family could not reconcile both Brothers. We went as far as suggesting that the Brothers carry out 'Ibu Ego' together and later perform the 'Macha Ozo'. Unfortunately, the senior Brother could not be persuaded to accept the truce. A situation where the Elder Brother opts out because of disagreement or religious beliefs and when such decisions are written or oral, the junior can commence the initiation processes. Mind you, such cases are not common.

OK: It is sad that our people, especially youths, deem the profession of artisans/tradesmen as menial. In so doing, the town is denied the huge job opportunities that are provided for artisans. What role can Agbalanze play to disabuse the minds of our youths?

PA: I agree with you, I mentioned our intention to set up a functional skill center earlier. We would also implore the State, the Federal and well-meaning organizations and individuals to equip the two centres at Onitsha North and South Local Government. It is unfortunate that three years they were built, no equipment has been installed.

I believe that it is the duty of all arms of governance, associations etc. in Onitsha to sensitize the youths. We will use every opportunity to drum this message and would request the Diokpas to convey same to their youths. The next stage is to empower those who are successful. We appeal to associations and individuals to assist.

OK: The wastage that abounds in burials and pageantry is huge and burdensome. Any savings made in curtailing these expenses can be allotted to other demanding commitment of the families concerned. What can you advise on this issue?

PA: The fines for flouting burial regulations are no longer effective. Most of our people these days accept to pay these fines of ten to twenty thousand naira and then entertain their friends with drinks and food. I cannot envisage now a burial without alcoholic drinks served. Possibly the duration can be shortened and after that may be a stringent measure could be applied. In Asaba the fine is One hundred thousand naira.

The authority it appears are satisfied in collecting the fines and not mindful of the policy to stem burial costs. I would expect 'Ogbo na achi ani' and the executives of Onitsha improvement Union Headquarters to reshape this policy realistically.

Differently, they should also strategize on how to raise fund for developments and maintenance of 'Ime Obi'. They should be able to sell these ideas to the Ruling Council.

OK: Often times, we fail to take care of our health. May I ask if Agbalanze has a heath scheme and other investments?

PA: Health care and investments are very important and we have them on our agenda.

OK: I am an apostle of jettisoning and some of our norms, ethos and societal attitudes that no longer provide relevancies or meaningful advantages. Let me cite some few unsettling cases: The first concerns 'Inu manya nwunye outside Onitsha'. The second concerns Diokpa handing over his position to someone else to act on his behalf. Are there any guiding rules? There are cases where these deputies refuse to hand over when demanded by the bona fide Diokpa. The third concerns Agbalanze. Who is Ugonabo has not been documented in writing and people hold all kinds of opinion. The fourth concerns the unclear Okpalaship case between two brothers Oreze and Chimaevi descendants of Chima. It is openly said that Oreze family is extinct. To me, it is contentious but what is of uppermost importance is not to defer issues that divide us for posterity case. Is there a room for a workbook or perhaps a kind of white paper to guide people to diffuse dissensions that are unhealthy? Knowing what to do and not doing it to me is calamitous and unhelpful. May we know your take on these unsettling issues?

PA: On the unsettling issues you raised, let me put my views as follows. I believe that 'Inu manya Nwunye' should be conducted at home, Onitsha. The elaborate procedures of the event brings the two families together and where the groom is not from Onitsha, conducting the event in Onitsha will enable him to know his in-laws, appreciate the family values and that of the town. We live in fast changing word if the family heads, Diokpa and Ruling Council think otherwise, so be it. It is important that this issue is addressed.

I will like to harp on the difference between 'Uko' and 'Ozi'. The first signifies the authority to deputize for the Diokpa if he the Diopka is not and Ozo titled man. 'Ozi' on the other hand is an authority given by the Diokpa who may be out of town or indisposed, to any member of his large family to deputize for him. 'Ozi' is a short term lived exercise than 'Uko'

Behind all the hue and cry about Diokpa tussle are selfish heart and greed, period.

'Ugonabo' is someone who further to taking Ozo title initiates his son or brother. In that of the brother, the sponsor will perform some of the processes of the initiations like 'Igba ugwo ozo'. Those who finance their brothers initiations without performing some of the processes mentioned earlier are not Ugonabo.

The last case which concerns the Okpalaship of Onitsha requires urgent attention by the council.

OK: Thank you finding time to grant these interview.

PA: Thank you too for your effort in conducting the interview.

**Chat covered by
OKEY AGUNYEGO
2015.**

AKUNWATA IBISI   **NWAKIABE. ORAKWUE
EGUNIWE**

Chinyelugo chudi Oranye

RESTORATION OF ONITSHA MONUMENTS

Let me enlarge on the title above. There is little advantage in monuments as a record of their existence rather, there are many advantages when ideas required to put the monument to better use are made. Buildings, Statues, Cairns, Tombs, Recreation Parks, Bridges, Cenotaphs, Obelisks, Shrines Museums, Halls of Fame that are erected in commemoration of persons, events especially for their historical importance are catalogued as monuments.

There is a stark neglect of monuments in Nigeria. For example the National Stadium in Surulere is now a shadow of what it was in 70s and 80s, just because the country has a new National Stadium in Abuja. The case is same with Federal Secretariat at Ikoyi. If not for the efforts of artists the National Theatre in Iganmu would have faced same fate; neglect. At a stage former President Obasanjo tried to sell this historical endowment but failed. You wonder how the government and some of us behave with crass insensitivity.

This piece is however chiefly on Onitsha Monuments. One is staggered with the neglect and deterioration of the town's monuments. On another hand, it is worrisome that we fail to create new monuments. Take the case of Ani Onitsha; the First National shrine of the town that is dedicated as a guardian of entire Onitsha Community .The ground was the landing point of the immigrants. The sprouting of anthills a day after OREZE and team celebrated their arrival was a promising sign. I reckon therefore that the ground is a commemoration for the victories earned by our forebears in successful settling in Onitsha. Not long ago, on the anniversary of Black American History, the American Ambassador to Nigeria and his team were in Onitsha primarily to visits historical sites. The custodian of Ani Onitsha made frantic move to clear the litters at the ground. Blood smeared white cloth was hurriedly tied to the Stave. That was all that was there. The grove is no more and the ground is desolate. I am not sure of the impression the Ambassador had compared to what he previously read.

The village shrines also exhibit sheer neglect. The groves of Aze Urai, Ogwugwu(s) have vanished. Otumoye is now a built up area. What has happened to Udo-Coronation ground? How many of us can identity it. Can we claim the ground that is in another Local Government Area? How strong is our revanchist policy to address this misfortune and anomaly?

Okwueze; the King's grove is the second national shrine located at Ime Obi where the monarch stays. Three quarter of the ground in Okwueze UmuezeAroli is now a football pitch and the remaining quarter shelters the tomb of Obi Okwudili Onyejekwe which is yearning for attention. The intimidating ambience associated with Okwueze Igwe Okosi and the grove cannot be compared with what we have now. The neglect on these monuments could also be traced to loss of age long social values. People hardly care for others and neither do they care for the community. 'Ewu ira nwe agu na gu'.

What to do? I have no doubt that where the shrines are spruced up, beautified, signposted, have trees planted around them, harbour sculptures and have a brief history inscribed in a plaque, they will attract tourists, anthropologist and students on excursion. It is said that a society without ideas has no history.

Museum is another prominent monument we are yet to exploit. A museum of Onitsha history will attract same advantages with that of shrines. With a Hall of Fame encompassed, our people who have made their marks and broken records will be honoured. It is a bundle of history for young ones and generations unborn. There was a move to purchase the palace of Igwe Okosi and turn it into an Onitsha museum. The outcome of it is not known to all but we understand that Agbogidi has plans for a Museum. This is a good idea no matter how late.

When it comes to events our performance is abysmally low. I am referring to Oze war and Second World War which our people participated. As would be expected in war many of our people died. The Nigeria crisis of 1966/70 falls into this category. The pogrom of 1966 in the north of the country consumed the lives of Ibos. Onitsha lost many souls from this brutal and horrific planned massacre, Before Onitsha fell to Federal troops during the war most of our people became refugees in different towns. Those that did not experience this would not appreciate the agonies disdain and hatred our people went through in some of the towns. Following the alleged coup by Colonel Emma Ifeajuna, most of our people were labelled saboteurs and imprisoned.

We lost a crop of young officers. It is unfortunate and sad that we have not tangibly commemorated this event and the people by any means of monuments. To perfect grateful tributes to our fallen heroes I will subscribe the use of cenotaphs cairns and other artworks that will last. The monument should have a brief history inscribed in a plaque fixed on it. Such commemoration will attract the young and generations unborn. Tourists and visitors will have a field day absorbing our past. It did not dawn upon us to purchase and preserve one of the houses riddled with bullets. That would have been another befitting and mother of all monuments; a history for generations unborn.

I must acknowledge that a mass funeral was held for our people that died during the war. This took place in 1971. It was a bold step but it was not packaged for people to remember. Had we dedicated a place to lay wreaths every year and possibly erect a monument immortalising the fallen ones we would have made a mark. Recreational parks are other important monuments, but unfortunately we do not have them.

The statue of ZIK, Owelle Nnamdi Azikiwe at Denis Memorial Grammar School roundabout was destroyed during the war. It was renovated later but as I write this piece the block works around the monument have crumbled. There is no metal frame around the monument. The ground is unkempt. What a neglect! In as much as the State Government is responsible for the maintenance, the Local Government can step in to correct this anomaly. What has happened to our ideas? One wonders how this scenario did not catch the attention of our indefatigable Chairman. Still on ZIK, his mausoleum is far from being completed. For such an important historical monument, I would like to beseech the Ruling Council and our people to lobby and remind the State and Federal Governments to complete this monument. Do you know that in Europe the entrance to such mausoleum is free but the tea, coffee, snacks, other drinks and brochures about the mausoleum that visitors buy generate a handsome amount to maintain the mausoleum? I am not sure when Onitsha hanging bridge was erected but as a boy in the 50's I visited the bridge several times. This is a monument worth preserving. Where it is conserved it would be visitors' delights. I would like to recognize the efforts of the Ruling Council in erecting the statues of past Onitsha Monarchs at Ime Obi. We would welcome more statues in strategic parts, possibly in every village square. For example where Obikporo village deems it fit to erect the statue of Onoja Oboli or that of Idoko-Use from whom they trace their genealogy, it would be a welcome idea; giving life to history.

Major Theo Nzegwu who was shot in the 1966 reprisal coup has his bust erected at Nigerian Air Force Base Kaduna. He was the first commanding officer of the base. It is not out place to honour him posthumously at home. There are quite a large pool of our people to honour, Professor Chike Obi, the Master Sculpture and Artist Professor Ben Enwonwu, Sir Louis Mbanefo, Colonel Emma Ifeajuna, Colonel Sokei and many more in no special order. They can be featured in the Hall of fame or other artworks. Dignitaries and visitors who visit the Hall of fame will appreciate its grandeur and a good memory of the town will sink in. Whereas the tomb of Chima, our progenitor at Obior is beautified and signposted from the high road, those that claim that Monarchs' tombs are shrouded in secrecy are wide off the mark. In any case the tomb of Igwe Okwudili Onyejekwe is not secret. Tombs are other historical monuments which can attract tourists, writers, researchers, anthropologists and students on excursion. But first they have to be beautified. The attention of the Ruling Council, Chimedie and benevolent folks is paramount.

I cannot end this piece without citing books. Books are important in propagating our history. In the long past, our history was orally recounted. Much of it has been documented now in books. My campaign seeks also to encourage more historical books and reprints of those not in circulations. We are blessed with many historical authors; Jerry Orakwue, Odinigwe Onuora Nzekwu, Nnanyelugo S. I. Bosah Tom Onono, H.N. Ntephe, Akunne Amuta Ojinnaka Sam Ifeka, Nnanyelugo Ben Chukwudebe, Nwakibie Egbuniwe Orakwue Patrick. Mention will also be made of Eke Prince, P. O. Ekwerekwu who had a book - Know Onitsha Families and my humble self who made a bold attempt at demystifying Onitsha Names in my book titled – Onitsha Names and Phrases Teased Out.

In summary, it must be noted that our social anthropology cannot be complete without the preservation of these historical treasures. Quoting Barbara Touchman, an American Educator, 'Books are carriers of civilisation. Without books, history is silent, literature dumb, desire crippled, thought and speculation at a standstill. Books are also likened to embalmed mind, easily activated when opened. I believe that this treatise and issues arising from it can be handled by Villagers, Individuals, Associations, Unions, Local Government that are swayed by my campaign.

May God strengthen and bless you.
I hope too that this short piece will infuse the young ones with hopes and morale.

OKEY MADUEGBUNAM AGUNYEGO
His Grace Lodge
Isolo, Lagos.
10/6/2016.

AWARENESS MESSAGES FROM ONITSHA IMPROVEMENT UNION, LAGOS BRANCH.

Dear Esteemed Brother,

We intend by this short brief to bring up the aims and objectives of Onitsha Improvement Union, our efforts,

setbacks and other remedial that stand to strengthen not only the Lagos Union but all other Unions and further boost our competitiveness.
Basically, Onitsha Improvement Union is an Umbrella Union in every town the Union exists.

The Aims and Objectives include:

> *Promotion of development of the town;*
> *Promotion of our culture*
> *Providing advisory role to National Executives of the Union in Onitsha and by extension to the Ruling Council. It is also media to disseminate messages from Onitsha.*

A cursory examination of the Union's membership strength shows a steep decline. It is estimated that there are over twenty thousand adult males in Lagos, yet less than thirty people participate in the meeting The decline is also applicable to other Onitsha associations namely, Agbalanze, Age Grades, Village meetings, Youth wings and other Social groups. Some of the village meetings have ceased for a long time. Consequently the dues from less than thirty people can hardly improve our members not to talk about carrying out a major project in Onitsha. It is baffling that our people can fund pageantries easily but see it difficult to marshal fund for community development.These mortifying setbacks are not applicable to other Town's Unions. Those of us that have associated with these towns will testify not only the growing membership strength but also the quality representations from various professions.

To countervail these setbacks the Union organized a joint meeting on 4th August 2013 with village Associations, Age Grades, Agbalanze, Satelite stations, with the sole aim of mapping out the way forward. This was followed with another meeting on 6th October 2013 to harmonize the issues discussed earlier. The gain on membership drive was marginal. In December 2014 the Union introduced a life insurance for members. We have plans afoot to extend same to satellite associations. We are optimistic that we can attract over sixty people. The End of Year Get-together is a further strategy to sensitize our people. We hope too to crown it with ONITSHA DAY by November next year.The Union belongs to, and participates actively in Anambra State Town Union meetings in Lagos. If you are not part of this larger body, how would you expect to benefit therefrom.

The following Onitsha phraseologies are evident:

"Anya Onye, bu oke onye"
"Ochupulu Onwe-e n'ugboo, si na ugboo eluto-ro-ya".

While we are poised to moving the Union forward, our efforts will not be complete without your participation, support and contributions.Further in strengthening Onitsha Improvement Union, we believe that the Ruling Council has a pivotal role to play in sensitizing every Onitsha adult to be a card carrying member of the Union. Other towns favour the use of sanctions and penalties where their townsmen fail to be members of their Town Unions. We cannot run away completely from such penalties. We have requested National Executive of the Union in Onitsha to seek the approval of the Ruling Council to fine tune what is best for us to ensure that our people participate in the Union.

With all these fostering, we can address the setbacks that have marred our competitiveness and distinctions. As the saying goes, Team work divides the efforts and multiplies the effects. Let us all together put our best foot forward.

Your participation in the End of Year Get-together will be highly appreciated.

Thank you.
OKEY AGUNYEGO
Organizing Committee.
18th September, 2015.

NB. OIU Lagos branch holds monthly meeting at Ado House, 22 Alawode Street, Ikate, Surulere, Lagos.

Onowu Iyasele, Onuiyi.

**Ajie Ukadiugwu, Idejiogu.
Onya Nyaka, Ukanagboji.**

I salute you.

Agbalanze Ogbuefi Ogbuefi, Umu nwanyi Omu Omu, Iregwu nnonu, Onitsha Ekenemunu. Distinguished guests,I have a great pleasure to welcome you to Onitsha Improvement Union Lagos Branch year-end banquet. We give thanks and glories to God Almighty Father whose goodness has no comparison. We thank Him for making this event be.

Let me here acknowledge some reforms instituted by Agbogidi and the Ruling Council. I can tell you too that we have done much towards rejuvenation of the union. The unpleasant truth is that it is not yet Uhuru.The decided advantages and singularity that placed Onitsha as a front line city has waned considerably.It would appear that we rested on our oars and lived on past glories. Could it be that we did not expect challenges and competitions from other quarters too soon? Reflecting, one is at sea that despite our leading edge, we became earth bound for too long.

We deny ourselves benefits from self-help. We fail to marshal fund for development but will go extra length to provide for socials and pageantry. The late sage, Owelle Nnamdi Azikwe warned that a community that relishes in festivities without creating wealth is bound to slide.It is a matter of deep concern that our youth consider the work done by artisans as menial. By so doing, we deny ourselves the huge work opportunities that abound for artisans. It is not only parents that take the blame for not sensitizing the youth on the importance of Tradesmen, the town is also culpable. We must note that tomorrow's world will be shaped by what we teach our children.We resist any attempt to raise dues in many of the town's associations. It is rather worrisome and incomprehensible that some associations still pay monthly dues of one hundred naira.

There are also other mitigating issues against us. The case of Trans Nkisi is pathetic. Clawing back this land will be great but this ought to have been done over twelve years ago. Acquiring this land by the government and later allotting it mainly to non-indigenes to my mind is a grandiose scheme to whittle our fame and distinction. Yet we did not tackle it as expected, given its importance.With these retrogressive attitudes how can we reclaim our distinction?

Let us note that the race/competition is not between Onitsha and any particular town in the State, but a race/competition between Onitsha and other towns in the state. Naturally when a group has a commanding role for a long period, it is visited with resentment by other groups. That is our situation but this contempt is rarely disguised. Selling off the heartland of Onitsha on free hold as against lease is another huge error and setback. Frankly, this scenario has greatly affected our rating.Little wonder, a great friend of mine ascribed that 2/3 of our predicament can be traced in-house. Where we are able to tackle this debacle head on it will most likely generate passion, drive and vigour in addressing the remaining 1/3 that is externally induced. Somehow too, you find out that selfish attitude of some us also aid these external factors.

Every hill in life is too high if we think we must climb it all at once. But no hill is insurmountable if we consistently take it one step forward at a time and with God's help – David Banon.As we celebrate this year get-together, let us contemplate a bold way forward. Together we can re-conceptualize our mindset, propagate healthy attitude and zest for the town. Let us heed the clarion call in rejecting habits that cripple our aspirations. Let us also diplomatically embrace entente with our neighbouring towns.An earlier write up enclosed in some of the invitations examined the role of Union, setbacks and remedial. We are circulating this for general awareness. The pith of this address is to systematically retrieve the situation. We will be better off reframing, restaging and reshaping our visions and strategies. It is not a one-off thing. It demands continuity.

Furthermore, the pursuit of these aims cannot bloom in isolation. It therefore calls for your participation. I hope that this brief stance will strike a responsive chord.

"The past is but cinders of the present, the future smoke that escapes into the cloud-bound sky" Kwesi Brew.

In the light of the above quote, it is relevant to acknowledge past leaderships, particularly the post civil-war Presidents, and their efforts:

Ononakuobi C. Motune
Ojinnaka R. I . Chukwurah
Odinigwe Onuorah Nzekwu,
Mr. Damian Oguno,
Chief Benedict O. Adibua, Ajie Ukadiugwu.
Mr. Sunday Osegbue,
Mr. Law Akosa,
Mr. S. L. Ojekwe,

In the manner the mantle of leadership was handed over to successive executives, this current executive shall do our damnedest. We shall put our best foot forward and ensure cordial hand-over to the next executive.

Thank you for your attention. We are also grateful for honouring our invitation.

May the light lit by J.A Agusiobo (aka Penniless)- co-Founder Friendly Society 1920 and P.H. Okolo and Associates, Co-founder Onitsha Improvement Union 1924 keep glowing.

Long live the Union
Long live Onitsha Ado N' Idu
Long live the Monarch
Igwe Alfred Nnameka Achebe

Chinyelugo Chudi Oranye
President Onitsha Improvement Union.

ONITSHA
Quest For Reinforcing & Sustaining Pre-eminence
OZANZEDIEGWU
Ancestry & Progenies

Okey Maduegbunam Agunyego

ONITSHA: QUEST FOR REINFORCING

AND

SUSTAINING PRE-EMINENCE

OZANZEDIEGWU ANCESTY

AND

PROGENIES   2007

TABLE OF CONTENTS

ONITSHA:
QUEST FOR REINFORCING AND SUSTAINING PRE-EMINENCE.
OZANZEDIEGWU: ANCESTRY AND PROGENIES.

ABOUT THE BOOK

The compendium on Ancestry and progenies is not only meant for tracing the author's larger family pedigree and by extension the knit affinity of Onitsha families, but is also an attempt to reinforce the efforts of our forebears and many indigenes that have in many ways championed the growth of the town.

Part of this consolidation warrants jettisoning some ethos, societal values and attitudes that may no longer provide competitive advantages. It is directed in remedying many ills that have overwhelmed the families, villages and the town.

It sues for conciliatory spirit. It calls for planning and

executing strategies today based on modified past performances and aimed at better development of the town and her people.

As such, the compendium is not restricted to Ozanzediegwu family. It is recommended for all Onitsha people and non-Onitsha people that value its concept.

OKEY MADUEGBUBAM AGUNYEGO

TRIBUTES

GLORY BE TO GOD FOR CONTEMPLATING AND PERFECTING THE CREATION OF THE FOREBEARS OF ONITSHA ADO N' IDU.

TO OUR FORBEARS AND NUMEROUS INDIGENES; DECEASED AND ALIVE THAT HAVE WORKED HARD FOR THE CAUSE OF THE TOWN; I SALUTE YOUR COURAGE.

SPECIAL TRIBUTES ARE PAID TO CHIMA, CHIMAEVI, AROLI, CHIMEDIE, OZANZEDIEGWU, OZONWANSIALI, OZIZIODIA AND MORA FROM WHOM THE FAMILIES OF MOLOKWU, EDEOGU, NZEGWU, ISIMA, AGUNYEGO AND OSAJI TRACE THEIR ROOTS.

FOREWORD I

I deem it a special Honour to be requested to write the foreword to this book; Ancestry and Progenies of Ozanzediegwu and Quest for Reinforcing and Sustaining the Town's Pre-eminence, by Okey Maduegbunam Agunyego. This is not the first time Mr. Agunyego has delved into the history and development of Onitsha. His first compendium; Onitsha names and phrases teased out was a bold attempt in demystifying Onitsha names and phrases. The afterword section of the book concentrated on how to remedy the ills of the town.

Ozanzediegwu family is from Ogbeoza Village in Onitsha where the author and my humble self-belong. Surviving nuclear families include Nzegwu, Molokwu, Agunyego, Edeogu, Osaji, Chukwuma, Obiefuna and Obeleagu. The major import derivable from this genealogy is the close relationship of Onitsha families.

I find the various articles under the chapter, A Wedge to abyss taut and timely. Given the breakdown of basic social infrastructure, it is of pressing importance that we embark on communal development to complement that of the Local and State Government. Both the title of this chapter and that of the book are apt. The chapter catalogues things that divide us and reduce our competitive edges and also proffers solutions to them.

He ventured into the idea of discarding some ethos that is no more relevant. It may sound difficult, but it is not impossible as we live in a dynamic world. The author who has painstakingly researched these topics of interest is not motivated by political needs or material interests rather, he sees it as his contribution to the community and for posterity.

I find also the inclusion of songs of Muo Avia with their poetic interpretation in both the first and present compendium, very inspiring.

In conclusion, I would like to commend the taxing efforts put by the author in this book. The book provides joyance. It is an invaluable addition to Onitsha literature. I would like to associate myself with the book and recommend it to all Onitsha people and to other people that are interested in ancestral genealogy and social development.

Nnabuenyi Henry Nzegwu

FOREWORD II

This latest addition to the previous books already written by the author on Onitsha affairs is a welcome development. It is partly an answer to the clarion call by all lovers of Onitsha people to dig deep into the family history of our people and document same for the generations yet unborn. When the manuscript was presented to me to read and make contributions, I had no hesitation in doing so, believing that I would in my own little way encourage the author to make more research in the project he believes will benefit his people.

There are many ways in which one can demonstrate love for his country, town or village. Some out of zealous love are prepared to risk lives for the sake of their country; others can manifest this love by donating financially or otherwise, greater part of their earthly possession. By embarking upon the publication of this book, I believe the author Mr. Okey M. Agunyego has sacrificed his time and money to delve into the history and lineage of a very important and indeed large segment of Onitsha community. He has therefore displayed great sense of patriotism of his people and stands to be commended by all who may have the opportunity of reading the book.

The book basically is in two principal sections; the first section tries to identify where and why Onitsha town and its people, once the envy of all other people located across the great Niger has now been relegated to the background in the scheme of affairs, particularly in the political state of its location. It is well known fact in history that empires come and go, but the author is very much worried that Onitsha which in every field of human and economic endeavor, such as politics, education, religion, judiciary, sports, manpower resources and administration has always been in the forefront should go down with such speed. This he feels should be a cause of concern to all lovers of this ancient town. Not only has he tried to identify the problems, he went further to suggest solutions which he considers capable of helping Onitsha people regain its lost glory.

The second part traces the history and family lineage of the various families that make up the powerful but tactful unit known as "Ozanzediegwu" of Ogbeoza quarters, Inland town Onitsha. I know from experience that it is not an easy task to write accurately on family lineage as there is bound to be one criticism or the other from people who may not agree with facts in the book, but this problem notwithstanding, I consider his efforts as the right step in the right direction and a beginning of the many inquiries/ searches necessary to be made to bring the history lineage to near perfection. The gain from his efforts must not be allowed to go down to drain; therefore the author is advised and encouraged in writing future editions of this book to make more in-depth inquiries and obtain more detailed information from our elders who are still alive because if facts are allowed to go extinct, they will be replaced by imagination.

Such additional information could be very useful in writing future editions of the book. It must be remembered that Onitsha traditions, local laws and practices are unwritten, and have been built up based on complicated and age long traditions which in his modern time can be manipulated to suit the whims and caprices of people who wish to take advantage.
In concluding the FOREWORD to a book, I would proffer for the benefit of authors and readers alike, to remember always that in our quest for knowledge, power and earthly wealth, people form varying attitude and ideals; which they need and often use to confront problems and seek their solutions. It is therefore necessary always to bear in mind that in all our dealings, we must first seek the guidance and

direction of our Father in heaven because it is through these quest and subsequent actions that helps us to embark on heroic endeavors that may eventually lead to making life long decisions.

Things may not have gone well as one would have wished, but all hopes are not lost. Onitsha has always been a great town favored by our Creator, and what I may consider as "temporary" set back which all of us have been witnessing since after the last civil war, must be seen as a chastisement resulting, most probably due to our failure to appreciate God's love for us and return enough thanks to Him or due to our inability to quickly adapt to the ever changing situations of modern world. I therefore hope that the contents of this book will arouse historical interests and encourage more positive actions on the part of our citizenry to disentangle facts from fiction and thus reconstruct the social and cultural background of the age in which we now live in. I wish the author huge success in his endeavors and the book wide circulation.

Ogbuefi Nwakibie P.O. Egbuniwe
London 1st January 2007.

PREFACE

The urge to undertake this project stemmed from the unfinished stenciled work on Chimedie family tree by my father. Unfortunately some relevant parts of it could not be traced after the crisis of 1966/70. The urge became stronger after the reprint of my publication; Ancestral Voices Onitsha names and phrases teased out. In the compulsive books; Know Onitsha families by Eke-Prince P.O Ekwerekwu and Chima Dynasty by Onuora Nzekwu, the families of Molokwu Edeogu, Nzegwu, Agunyego and Osaji are shown as children of Ozanzediegwu. This may not be completely wrong but for better historical recordings, it is exigent to note that the direct children, sub families of Ozanzediegwu were not listed in these books. In the case of Molokwu and Edeogu, there are three sub families between them and Ozanzeigwu, in Nzegwu two, in Isima that is not listed in these cited works, two, and in Agunyeogo and Osaji one subfamily. Such error of omission may have arisen because of the magnitude of the task treated by the above mentioned authors or perhaps in not knowing about them. I find the latter applicable even to some members of the family.

In tracing the pedigree of Molokwu Edeogu, Nzegwu, Isima, Agunyego and Osaji to Ozanzediegwu, Chimedie Aroli, Chimaevi and Chima, this project seeks to validate the places of Ozanwasiali, Oziziodia and Mora who are three immediate children of Ozanzediegwu, and other families that are hardly mentioned. Under Ozanzediegwu family members I tried to include details of fathers, mothers and children spanning over three generations, whereas the family tree is based on patrilineal method.

The project also attempts to bring to focus the roles of the forebears of Onitsha Ado N'Idu and many other committed indigenes that were instrumental to our past glories. Their undeniable commitments and unsurpassed well-thought-out plans to settle in a peaceful and fertile grounds carry out heartfelt thanks, unbound admiration and undying gratitude. It is strange and worrisome that not much is on ground to immortalize them. A good number of the treasures bequeathed to us have not been put in commensurate perspective while some others are neglected. These glaring oversights, the prevailing incubi that have dulled our competitive edges and the way forward are tied to a chapter titled; A Wedge to Abyss. It is about a grand design; a challenging quest to reinforce and sustain our distinction.

This article is designedly brought forward before Ozanzediegwu family members and trees because of its general concern all Onitsha indigenes.

I believe that we can immensely benefit from the past by amplifying strengths, capitalizing on successes, reducing weaknesses and playing down on failures. This strategy will ultimately lead to the creation of more treasures and purposeful leadership. The impact in many ways will generate sobering effects on our youths as good number of them at present are drifting aimlessly. I am aware of the controversies that visited the outstanding publication of Eke Na Ubene The big Tree by Nwakibie Orakwue Egbuniwe and Nweze Obiora Amechi, and likewise the sketch on Isiokwe family Tree by Kpajie Ikechukwu Ubaike. Obikporo village circulated amongst themselves their family Tree not long ago. This too attracted vehement rejoinders. While we cannot foreclose controversies/ criticisms, they can be managed with tact, delicacy and sincerity of intent. Even though that this project is restricted to one large family as against that of the above authors that treated theirs at village levels, it will be presumptuous for me to claim perfection. I would like to apologize for any error especially omissions in this compendium. On the other hand, I would hope that this project would serve as a platform to embrave others to carry out works on Onitsha; including family Trees. The salient information these publications will bring about would most likely prod our people in appreciating the physical and spiritual treasures that were bequeathed to us by our forebears, and in comprehending the affinity and bond in Onitsha families, and hence work hard to consolidate these treasures and bond with less rancor, schism and antipathy. I would reckon that the eclectic assortment of quotes cited this compendium and the lessons they portray will goad us on to achieve better development of the town and her people.

ACKNOWLEDGEMENT

As earlier mentioned, the unfinished work on Chimedie Family Tree by my late father, Mr. Alex Okwudili Agunyego inspired me. I remain in many ways indebted to him.

In carrying through this work, I discussed with some of the family members at home and abroad. I must admit that obtaining the information took longer time than I had expected. Nevertheless, their courtesy and cooperation enabled me sift through the information gathered.

I would like to thank Ezennia Akudo Molokwu, the family Head Diokpa Ozanzeiegwu family, Nnabuenyi Obianeze Nzegwu, Nnanyelugo C.Y Nzegwu, Akunwata Olisa Nzegwu, Orummili Amechi Osaji, Obiora Edeogu, Fano Osaji, Mrs Chinwe Okafor, Ogugua Edeogu, Chuka Agunyego, Ikechukwu Nzegwu, Ogoegbunam Nzegwu and Eddie Nzegwu and others for their efforts. The compulsive works; The Ground Work of The History and Culture of Onitsha by S.I. Bosah, Chima Dynasty by Onuora Nzekwu, Eke Na Ubene the Big Family Tree by Nwakibie Orakwue Egbuniwe, the Igalas of Onitsha by Tom Onono and others are refreshing any day. I would like to acknowledge the information gleaned from them. I also read various articles and lifted various quotes to portray our past enviable achievements, the pitiable derailment that followed and the counsels towards consolidation of the town's pre-eminence. The authors are duly acknowledged under footnote.

I remain grateful to Nnabuenyi Obianeze Nzegwu who obliged me with the foreword to this compendium, and to Nwakibie Orakwue Egbuniwe who read the manuscript and offered useful advices and corrections. He also obliged me with the second foreword.

Finally I would like to appreciate the support and encouragement from Dr. Nkiru Nzegwu Danjuma and Chike Agunyego.

DEDICATION

This compendium is affectionately dedicated to my late parents; Mr. and Mrs. Alex Okwudili and Rose Uzoamaka Agunyego, to my immediate family Melanie Nwando, Mark Obiora, Olivia Nonyem, Patrick Okey Jnr., Pat Mbenyego, Myra and entire Ozanzediegwu stock.

PS. Gabriel Nzegwu, Orummili Amechi Osaji, Mrs Ozoemena Agbu and Mrs Agaegbu Ibegbu passed on while in the making of this project. May their souls rest in peace Amen

A WEDGE TO ABYSS

Here is an attempt to provide an outline of the glorious past, the prevailing incubi the why and wherefores and how Onitsha can consolidate and sustain her pre-eminence and hence avoid the abyss.

There is no doubt that Onitsha is a city with unique culture and tradition since its existence. The people are liberal, self satisfied, generous and proud. It is common to hear the indigenes vaunt that they will remain Onitsha people come the next world. This is a fathomless amour proper which some non-indigenes consider as arrogance and up appity. Such bold hypothesis by our people is traceable to our past glories that propelled Onitsha into a front line city. Few quotes and comments are used to buttress the decided advantages and the singularity of the town and her people.

"The pre-colonial Ibo political system lacked a differentiated administrative structure and permanent elective or hereditary offices with certain local exceptions such as Onitsha Kingship .... the unique administrative structure was second to none" (1)

"Though parts of Inland town are now congested with buildings which obscure the majestic aspects of the Niger, it is still possible from many situations to appreciate the reasons which caused the people of Chima to settle in this area and make it their abode. These heights dominate the Niger, well-watered, forested and fertile, a land built by nature for herself. It is no wonder that there have gone out of this place of meditation and beauty statesmen and visionaries, the rich and the strong, and the proud and leaders of Africa" (2).

"The Dayspring and George arrived at Aboh on the Niger on July 20th 1857 and five days later they reached Onitsha. The latter place was destined to become an important centre for development of the county (3).

"Up till the Nigerian civil war - 1967/70, Onitsha was a reference point and standard for measuring development and civilization in Nigeria" (4).

The following facts also confirm the early decided advantages. Onitsha pre-war was a citadel of education reputed to have the highest number of secondary schools and vocational centres in Eastern Nigeria and second to Lagos in the country. Onitsha then was a home with many numero uno in various disciplines who held enviable positions at both Regional and at Federal levels.

Onitsha had the largest market in West Africa in the 60's. By 1905, Onitsha had telegraph lines. Onitsha became a township in 1917. In 1929, pipe borne water was installed. As it were, Onitsha was an acknowledged city.

Whence did the derailment come from? Some people would trace it to the waxes and wanes associated with old cities. That may not be wrong but there are also glaring lapses on the people's side for not sustaining the lead and in not warding off the activities of detractors. Again few quotes are used to portray the effects of these lapses.

"Today's Onitsha is an anomic city. Onitsha is dead and the worms are feeding on it. It is the activities of the worms, which palpitates the corpse that people see and think that life still trembles in this city. Onitsha's case is the result of civil war which destroyed this city and from its ruins nothing came other than brutality...... There is a quiet predatory mood that pervades the dirtiest, the most dysfunctional and most broken city" (5).

"We are galloping at a speed to severe every link with our past as if they were not the things that made us distinct, which made us object of envy among other Ibos". (6)

"Those we taught how to run are now in the forefront and those who found succour in our back houses are now buying us out (7).

"Patterns which previously would insult our ancestor's standards of propriety now receive wide glorification. Egotism has struck deep roots in our hearts, the pursuit of morbid self interest, self exaltation and deification is rife ... fathers and sons collude at shady deals, kinsfolk shelter criminal elements..... An evil foreboding blankets our town, villages, families and our lives and our institutions are in danger of atrophy" (8).
"Onitsha, the commercial nerve centre of Anambra State may succumb to the over bearing weight of refuse unless urgent action is taken. This is compounded by the breakdown of basic social infrastructure, poor funding and no will to muster a self help programme by residents (9).

"Onitsha metropolis in spite of being the largest city in the South East is now a failed city with mass of building lying in dormant and dead capital. The air is polluted and I will not be surprised if the town does not have one of the lowest life expectancy in Nigeria" (10).
The wanes must have been steeped to have stunted our ideas, thoughts and visions and made us bark the wrong trees. Be that as it may, options to correcting these ills abound. Accepted that evolution is a systematic error management, we must begin in earnest to correct the recurring errors and go extra miles to avoid set backs.

Therefore in the quest for better tomorrow we cannot avoid to discuss issues that divide us and stunt our competitive edges. Acting on decisions reached should be given a high priority "must do". I do agree that some of the issues discussed below have been raised in different forum and in different write-ups. Nevertheless I do not see them error management strategies as unnecessarily repetitive and as long as the issues remain prevalent, we would need redoubled efforts to address them.

In the words of Brigadier General Johnny Mbanefo (RTD) "Sentiments and prejudices will be done with……We would require courage, sacrifice, time, intellect, (money)….. We must not expect automatic transformation of our situation because we have neglected them for too long. Things might get worse but get better they must" (11)

LAND ACQUISITIONS AND SALES

In an article I contributed to Ado Focus magazine in 1998, I discussed some strategies that would enable us to claw back our farm lands that were acquired by Government and allotted to mainly non-indigenes. I figured that we had not effectively used our contacts in lobbying the appropriate Government authorities and the will to mobilize money for such exercise and other projects were glaringly absent. My considered opinion then was to send a formidable high powered Onitsha delegation to both State and Federal Government. This was during the military era and many towns and states that had lobbied had some of their requests approved. Lagos State at the time got two Director General (DG) positions after a visit to the then Head of State.

May be we did not push hard enough. Major General Gummel, Transport Minister in the Abacha regime had promised to dredge River Niger and to complete Onitsha Port, after a lobby by Igwe Ofala, which was facilitated by Akupueome Ozobia who was the helmsman at Niger Docks at the time. Had we pushed it to the Head of State, the promise would not have faded away the way it did.

On a happy and pleasant note, the position of Agbogidi Igwe Achebe on clawing back the farm lands is very encouraging and positive. As I write this piece in June, 2006, various villages are surveying their farm lands. The agenda is on an even keel. However the efforts of Igwe must be sustained and supported to prevent any reverse.

On a sour note, the increasing propensity to and penchant of our people in disposing lands for all sort of reasons; title taking, burials etc are not helping our cause. Inland town that used to be the preserve of indigenes is not spared. The case of Owelle Ebo layout is unforgivable. It is rather incredible that the agreement reached by the kindred not to sell any parcel of land in the layout to non-indigenes was flagrantly flouted. Even the allocation of the land was marred by greed, lack of transparency and accountability. It is unfortunate that the speculators and those that embezzled the land and funds are our own people; the young, the old, titled men and, spiritual heads. Women were also part of this debauched scheme. Is it a sign of times that most of us are venally inclined? How would you fathom the sales of a dead person's land with fake documents or the sales of the same parcel of land to three different people? I am at sea why such cases have not been brought up to Nigeria Bar Association to strike out lawyers that assist in faking land documents.

A non-indigene friend of mine once lamented that one of his cousins sold a property at Iweka Road and likened it to the manner Onitsha people stifle their birth rights by dispossessing themselves of their land with careless abandon. It was not difficult to detect the smirk on his face shortly after he made the above statement. His consolation was that the property was not sold to an Onitsha man. An Ex- Governor of Anambra State at one time called Onitsha, 'no-mans-land'. He made other insinuations concerning our ancestral link with Benin people and such guarantees us the liberty to go back to Benin. This idea is gaining currency and represents a master stroke by some of these people to buy us out at any cost and whittle down whatever power and authority we have enjoyed.

But why must we leave our guard unprotected? If we must sell, why not give preference to our fellow kinsmen or sell on leaseholds. I do not ascribe to myself the knowledge of all the remedies nor do I give myself points on saintliness. I have gone through various papers by well-disposed indigenes on land sales but it would appear that we are not fully ready to unlearn our old habits. Some counsels are expressed in the following quotes.

"We must suppress our inordinate ambition of 'Ugo' which has led to indiscriminate sale of our land. We must resist lining our pockets........We must stop exposing our underbelly to all comers......... We must make respect, discipline and accountability our watchword" (12).

"Gradually our people are selling the heartland of Onitsha to other Ibos who rarely disguised their contempt and hostility towards us" (13).
We must support the efforts of Agbogidi to claw back our farm lands and then guard them jealously. We must not repeat the blunder we made at Owelle Ebo and other layouts. We must also come up with severe, irrevocable punishments for those that default the laid down rules by the kindreds/town.

BALKANIZATION

If we had envisaged the knock-on-effects of Balkanization, perhaps we would have pursued other alternatives if not maintaining the status quo. Quite often dissensions that are not irreparable cause these break ups of villages, age grades and in Onitsha Improvement Unions in some cities. The behaviour of some of our people in authority is sometimes unhelpful and unbecoming. Their penchant for aggrandizement is spelt out in the following quote. It is no wonder that "a good number of us sacrifice truth on the altar of expediency, greed and money and so end up giving wrong advice and causing more harm" (14). As a result, there is a profound abyss of mutual distrust and lack of understanding. Perhaps only three villages have escaped this dismembering. Ogbeoza has now two groups; each meeting all the requirements of a village. Ogbendida is split into two, Umudei three, Umuaroli three, Odoje three, Iyiawu two, Umuikem two, Ogbolieke three etc. Yet each administrative ward, made up of groups of the original villages has each one Political Head- A first Class Chief. Adjudicating disputes under these divisions is likely to attract doubts from one quarter or the other.

My concern is that the manner these divisions are done is fraught with distrust, hatred, rancour, enmity and unnecessary rivalry. Such dismembering does not help to achieve our common cause.

Could it be pretence for example in Lagos, village meetings are attended by all the splinter groups but no sooner we crossed the Niger Bridge, it is to your tent to these various groups. Likewise when the case concerns sharing of lands we are in union but thereafter in pieces.

The rapprochement reached by the splinter groups in Obikporo village in the 90's is exceedingly commendable that one would have expected other villages to adapt the same reconciliatory spirits.

Agbalanze is not spared. Though the existence of its splinter groups Itiwa Ozo dates back many decades, its reoccurrence is high since the end of the 1966/70 Nigerian crises. Ogbeotu has joined the band wagon. With few exceptions of two villages, it is splinter galore in other villages. Ozo initiates are expected to seek spiritual strength from Ani-the village shrine, but as a result of the intensity of rifts in some villages, some initiates avoid the shrine. At a close distance the initiate and his people would wave and greet the shrine. Granted that this act can be backed by one reason or the other, the failure to kneel down at the shrine and seek spiritual strength debases the Ozo rites.

The schisms in Age Grades compound matters. How can one also fathom the existence of splinter groups in Onitsha Improvement Union in Port-Harcourt and in America. In America one group went as far as suing the other to court. Is it a case of a house divided? Some people would advance that what is happening outside is a microcosm of what is happening at home. "Ife Afulu nne ewu na oru ka aga afu nwaya"; a case of all tarred with the same brush and sharing the same characteristics. Usually the bad aspects. With these various splinter groups, we are gradually and deliberately taking irrevocable steps; a case of burning one's boat. As I said earlier, it is the negative effects arising from schisms that must be dampened down or avoided and likewise other issues that work against the development of the town. The interactive sessions Agbodidi has been having with Onitsha indigenes in various stations is a welcome approach to tell ourselves some home truths and seek means to readdress our short comings and then plan ahead. We would need to work at full throttle to bring back our distinction.

TURNING SWORDS INTO PLOUGHSHARES

On the anniversary of Igwe Achebe's first Ofala on 11th October 2002, I published an article; an open letter to Obi of Onitsha -That Onitsha may bloom again in Champion Newspaper. Vanguard Newspaper carried an excerpt of it. The condensed article was later included in the reprint edition of my compendium on Onitsha Names and Phrases Teased out.

The article was opened with a call for reconciliation. I noted that the schisms and polarization resulting from Obiship contest in 2001 is minimal when compared to that of 1962. However less, my humble advice was a call for fence mending that would guarantee a formidable Obi-in-Council. I then counseled that the dissenting and suspended Chiefs should embrace the Olive branch the fence mending would usher in and thence we would begin to tackle head-on, the multifarious development needs of the town and her people. So much has happened since then. I am reminded by a friend that what is on ground is a case of a majority and a tiny minority. A truism but I noted that if two is added to thirteen, the result would be higher.

One leading revelation in this compendium is the affinity of Onitsha people. We have uncles, aunts, nieces, nephews, cousins, 'Nwadiani' and 'Nnaochie' from various villages. One can relate to other families within his village beyond the genealogical relationship of the villagers. For example, I hail from Ogbeoza village. My Maternal Grand Mother came from another family in Ogbeoza. My Paternal Grand Mother has a sister that married an Ogbeoza man. My mother's sister also married an Ogbeoza man. The affinity extends to neigbhbouring towns as a good number of the harems of our Fathers, Grand Fathers and Great Grand Fathers came from these towns.

The upshot of this narrative is that we have close knit kindred and as such, it becomes necessary to dampen down rifts in the families, villages and in the town than damper them. Afam Ogbotobo, reminds us in one of the lyrics of his song that we are of one blood and umbilical cord 'Ofu Obala ofu elili'. The above counsel when extended to those that were suspended because of being relations friends and associates of suspended/ousted personalities would no doubt douse the heated polity. It may have been better to restrict such actions to the principal characters if imperative, while strategizing other necessary peace moves. Where a slew of these associates and relations are suspended the line of divide would widen and make reconciliation more difficult. It would amount to strengthening the other party.

One other note which I have echoed earlier is that we must as much as possible consider the knock-on-effects of our actions and as well as work out how to accommodate them. I believe that reconciliation starting from the families will pave way to that of the villages and the town. The dismembering of families is assuming a worrisome scale. To the extent that some of us hold extreme views on various causes of schism in the families of which some of them are predicated on falsehoods, deceit and half truths, to that extent shall peace elude the family. How soon have we forgotten the exhortation "Ana esi na uno amalu mma welu pua ilo". This is a counsel to manage what ever the crises you have at home before one goes to the public. The Bible also reminds us in Matthew 5:23,24 to make peace with our brothers before giving offerings to God.

Let us therefore prevail upon each other, that anger ventilated often hurries towards forgiveness, peace, unity and better relationships, whereas anger concealed and prolonged hardens to revenge, hatred, further conflicts etc.

The bottom line which must be stressed is that development growth thrives much better where you have unity than disunity. We must avail ourselves on these counsels and begin to think ahead of the knock on-effects of our actions before they are executed. This piece is about fence mending, closing ranks than pulling ranks. It is about rapprochement. It is about keeping faith with our kindred than breaking faith. It is all about turning swords into ploughshares and hammering spears into pruning knives (15) than crossing swords and spears.

That was the spirit that influenced Igwe Ofala Okagbue (late) after a protracted disharmony in Onitsha in 1986 to uphold the wishes and aspirations of the people by declaring general amnesty. The high point of this declaration is that there should be no more ostracism as it is the very ant; thesis of peace and unity in Onitsha. In no way does this support rebellion against the community but rather it is seeking avenue for repentance and forgiveness and above all justice.

May Onitsha sooner than later bloom again?.

Rites Ethos-Norms-Values

Another controversial issue that has dismembered much kindred is the contention of the succession of Diokpa - The Spiritual Head of The family and the Custodianship of the spiritual relics.

There is hardly any rite that does not generate one dissension or the other. The breaking of kola nuts and its order of distribution sometimes can be hotly debated to a stage that some people may end up not partaking in eating the kola nuts. Ika Ozu; the official burial announcement can sometimes be unnecessarily dragged. Could it be right that a second burial rite of a titled man is performed without performing the second burial rites of his mother that was also titled? How about a case where the second burial rite of a titled woman was performed by a member of the larger family who had a different mother and without the approval of the deceased grandchildren that survived their father and grandmother? I believe that these cases are aberrant. It is however unfortunate that those that flout and break such burial regulations are left off the hook. I believe too that where such dissension exits, it is the duty of Obi-in-Council to wade in and stop such performance or advise accordingly. People may not necessarily have the same contentions, i.e., ideas and visions and the contentious aspect which borders on disagreement may not be totally bad. What is ruinous is the falsehoods and deceit on which these ideas are predicated upon and in not yielding to superior arguments. It is this negative outcome that tends to disunity.

In faraway America, an Ozo titled man considered as an aberration the hosting of an Ozo man- "Ikwo aka Ozo- by a non-titled man. Could that be right? I doubt it but if so why is it still in practice? At what age will an unmarried deceased be treated as 'Ozu nwa ebe'. A man who predeceases his father is said to commit an abomination.

Amongst his 'punishment' is that his children can no longer aspire to the headship of the larger family. A person who dies in motor accident or drowns is not giving the same burial as a man who dies in his sleep. There are other numerous norms which some people may not be comfortable with.

As the dynamics of our society are continually gathering momentum, it becomes necessary to streamline the rites and norms that will guide and bind us and avoid unnecessary strains in the kindred. Although our traditions were orally communicated, we were fortunate to embrace modernity earlier and as result we have today many written works on Onitsha. Onura Nzekwu's latest publication; Faith of our Fathers provides a penetrating account of our customs. This and other notable works and past reviews and probably a new one on burials and marriages can offer a platform for harmonizing our rites/norms. The call for further downward review of the cost of burial rites and marriages is not to dishonour the dead or make marriages cheap but rather is intended to stem the flagrant extravagancy and hence be in the position to provide for other needs. The late sage, Owelle Nnamdi Azikiwe counseled that a town whose past time is in festivities and which does not create and manage her wealth is bound to stagnate. It may be necessary to call for memoranda also from the village Heads and other knowledgeable people. The ratification of these works by Obi-in-Council will provide a workbook that will help in diffusing controversies/dissensions whenever they arise. It may not be out of place to set aside some norms that fail to meet the needs and acceptance of the people. In the case of contentious succession of family Headship, it would be necessary to stipulate the time frame within which the second burial of a deceased will be performed and hence stop people who deliberately postpone such burials to preclude other family members from aspiring to the family leadership. This would go a long way in dousing its contentions and wrangling that sometimes attain scaring heights. For those who seek and attain various positions of leaderships, their primary job ought to be directed more in reconciling their families, standing by truth, sincerity and other qualities that leadership demands than the trappings of their positions.

COMMUNAL DEVELOPMENT

One of the cited quotes by Mr. Lartey of Champion Newspaper harped on the total breakdown of social infrastructure in Onitsha and likewise the absence of poor funding and the will to muster self help programme. One would posit that our nonchalant inclination to communal development might have arisen because we grew up with water, electricity, schools, good roads etc in place. That was a phase. At the present phase when what trickles out from Government purse can hardly meet the demands of the people, it becomes imperative for the community to tackle some of these needs. Often times we misconstrue the offers by some of our people. It is unbelievable that a benevolent indigene who wanted to give Ogbeoye market a face lift by constructing open roof and lock-up shops with water borehole, drainage and toilets at no fees was rebuffed. The market at its present state with rusted old pans is unsightly. The offer did not debar the owners of the market from collecting their ground rents. A plaque indicating that the edifice is a gift from the donor to Onitsha was all this benevolent retired Engineer had expected. The villagers blew this opportunity up and the church the man supported doubly gained. It is worth mentioning that late Engineer Theophilus Nzegwu was this benefactor that was rebuffed. May his soul rest in peace? May others with magnanimous hearts not be disheartened, and may our people shed their narrow outlook that constricts developments. Can somebody say a big Amen? I believe that it is within our reach to tackle these development projects that would include, waste disposal, construction of culverts, minor road repairs, school repairs, donations to schools, scholarship awards to indigent students etc. A compulsory levy of between two to five thousand naira a year from every adult may not be too much burden when compared to what it is to obtain/achieve for the generality of the people. This works in various other communities. No matter the difficulties that the funding might pose, it ought not to stall this idea, instead we should strategize on how it could be better achieved. It would require sensitization of our people. We must encourage benevolent individuals. We have many people with hearts of gold and with hearts in the right places. The point is that we have not put our act together. Clubs, Unions, Age Grades etc ought to be sensitized too. Someone who bank rolled the initiation of six people into 'Ozo' can further donate half the cost of one person's initiation fees to his village development project. Those who are willing to be committed to such projects would have their names written in gold. The culverts at Bishop Onyeabo by Ugwu na Obampka, Ojedi by Tasia and many others have been bad and neglected over the years. The village grounds that are used for various social activities are eroding without any check. There is hardly any village that is not littered with wastes. We should begin to place emphasis on what can be done to help our community rather than wait all the time for what is expected from the local and State Government. That is the pith of this write up.

Some exemplary efforts include the repairs of culverts and donation of the two existing gates to Obi's palace by Ado Amaka Age Grade, the construction of culverts by Christian Women Association, the clearing of unsightly huge waste by Onitsha Improvement Union in America. There are probably other efforts not mentioned but I dare say that they are few and far between when compared to the multifarious needs of the town. It is not a must for all the projects to be without charges. In Lagos accredited waste disposal companies levy households that require their services every week. Such can be planned for Onitsha for the cost of three bottles of beer per house every week.

Our aesthetic responses are unfortunately very poor when compared to what existed in the 60's. There was then hardly any household that did not have economic trees and other majestic trees dotted around the premises and in the village square. The environment was much cleaner. The shrine and village squares that were well wooded are now without twigs. I reckon that tree planting does not take so much time. Elsewhere, I figured that it may not be out of place for Igwe to flag off tree planting during world environmental day or at any other auspicious time.

We cannot afford further delays in rebuilding our household. Here again, we need the direction of every arms of governance to sensitize our folks on these needs and how to meet them. Management of fund is another area that we have consistently failed to achieve desired accountability and transparency. This issue must not be dogged if we are to succeed. Ethics and willingness to serve counts !!!

P.S. The recent major road-works with drainage and culverts at Akwa Road, Ugwu na Obamkpa Road, New market Road and others by the State Government is a welcome news.

OTHER DEVELOPMENT MATTERS AND WHAT TO DO WITH OKWUEZE

Sokoto Caliphate celebrated her 200 years in existence sometimes in 2005. It was a colourful occasion that was well attended by 'Who is Who" in Nigeria. The nearby Kebbi State which used to be part of Old Sokoto State celebrates the yearly Argungu Fishing Festival. This is another gala occasion that boosts tourism for the state. Onitsha at over 500 years old may not have showcased any event in recent times with same magnitude. My concern here is that places of cultural interests and events that attracted visitors in the past have been neglected. Another concern is that dignitaries that attend some events; cultural, political, religious and business most often retire to Asaba and Awka in the evening. This is as a result of insecurity of life and property and poor quality hotels. There is hardly any night life except beer palours. Sport Clubs are no longer what they used to be. Markets as a result of insecurity open late and close early. The negative economic effects have telling effects. Although the crime rate has considerably reduced from what it used to be in the 90's there is still the need to check our wards and support the police, the village vigilante groups but definitely not the mayhem that Bakassi, NARTO, AVS and other dissidents have perpetrated.

The planned face lift of Ime Obi to accommodate a palatial home for Igwe and guests is welcome news. The completion of Koobamo suites and spas by a son of the soil is welcome news. Just like Argungu festival, we need to package our festivals to international level, to attract tourists and as well as being a rallying point of Onitsha people. One recalls with nostalgia the Ofala during the reign of Obi Okosi II, with attendance of panalopy of community leaders, namely, Hausa, Nupe, Igala and Yoruba. Their chiefs arrive on decorated horses and attended by retinue of courtiers and musicians carrying gifts for Igwe. Government representatives, Chiefs from other towns dignitaries from all over the country and representatives of traders grace the occasion. The unique performances of late Anataogu Onowu Iyasele, late Isaac Mbanefo Odu II and others add splendour to the outing. Ofala was at its nadir in 1995. How disenchanting can be gathered from the roll call of those in attendance; about twelve members of Agbalanze and two incomplete age grade and three Red Cap Chiefs. This was as a result of strained relationship between Igwe and the people then. Things have tremendously improved for the better but there is still the need to make Ofala a money spinning venture and as well as show cashing our unique culture. It would not be out of place to use the various symbols of royalty in art forms; pictures woodworks, metal works and paintings of various sizes. These would be sold as mementoes. Special designs with Royal seals could be made for sales and as gifts for Igwe's special guests. These symbols would include; Abani, plumaged Cap, Odu, Okike, masquerades etc. The artwork of Mr. Akpabo, Ife Onitsha ji bili (1975) depicts some of these symbols. We can also create a flag for Onitsha using colours that depict the town. For example, one of the monarchs symbol can be superimposed on a white and blue colours denoting purity and River Niger respectively. These mini flags would be sold not only to the tourists but to Onitsha indigenes. The flag has the leverage of patriotic feelings. The bigger flag can also be hoisted alongside that of the country at Obi's palace. These symbols also could be fixed at the people's gates, walls and could be worn as badges and brooches. Further, two reputable fast food chains can be licensed at a fee to provide drinks and snacks. The same is applicable to other vendors. I am sure there are other avenues to make money during the Ofala.

When the facelift planned for Ime Obi is put in place and hopefully two likes of Koobamo in place, the town can boast of comfortable accommodation for various dignitaries and tourists that would visit Onitsha. When also other issues discussed are tied up, their totality will contribute to making Ofala and other festivals occasions one looks forward to; as rallying point for Onitsha people, a pride of the town capable of generating patriotic feelings and a money spinning venture. Every town is said to stamp her own value upon her self. The town becomes great or little according to the will of the town. The same counsel is applicable to individuals. With commitment, we can edge towards modest improvement in communal developments and it would not take long thereafter to attain higher heights.

WHAT TO DO WITH OKWUEZE

Open squares can hardly be seen in Inland town as most of the village play grounds have been encroached upon. One prominent square that has not been encroached is Okwueze that occupies the ground bounded by Saint Stephens, Umuikem and Bishop Onyeabo roads.

Historically this ground was the domain of Monarchs. The tomb of late Obi Okwudili Onyejekwe lies in there. The ground was once populated by original rainforest trees up to 1958, if I remember correctly when they were lumbered. The question concerns what to do with this ground in order to cause better development of the town. The first thing that comes to mind is planting of trees around the square and a row across the centre with necessary landscaping that will conjure up royal presence comparable to late Obi James Okosi's palace.

Half of the ground towards the upper section that is presently used as a football pitch can be upgraded to a mini sports centre, accommodating a football pitch with a simple pavilion, race tracks and indoors games like squash and table tennis. The turf can also be used for basket ball. It would not be out of place to have within this complex, a hall of fame for Onitsha sports men and women that have made their marks. Beyond the youths expressing themselves creatively when the sports centre is in place, sports is also good for general good health and leadership training. This call for a mini sports centre in no way detracts from the need of a stadium. The stadium planned in the 70's after the existing one was used as Onitsha North Local Government Headquarters is still on drawing board. Recently the Anambra Governor Peter Obi hinted on the plans to relocate the Onitsha Local Government Headquarters and revert the place to a stadium again. I am not comfortable with its contiguity to Obi's palace. I would think that the Trans Nkisi layout or Isi Afo would provide an opportunity to construct a modern stadium for Onitsha.

What about the other half of the ground? I seriously think that a construction of a Museum that represents our history would be appropriate on this ground. The museum stocked with murals, portraits, sculptors etc etc would add splendour to this show piece. The tomb of Obi Onyejekwe deserves some beautification too. William Shakespeare grave still gets fresh wreaths daily after 500 years. Same is applicable to Queens and Kings of Great Britain. An imposing cenotaph dedicated to our people that died in the Second World War and during the Nigerian Crisis of 1967/70 would also enrich this ground. It would be a great honour to dedicate this museum to Chima or Chimedie. When all these are put in place Okwueze would become a beehive of activities for students, youths, visitors, and tourists in general.

How would the villagers be compensated? How would it also be financed and managed? Okwueze as a heritage land cannot be prized. Any compensation can be seen as a token. I would like to think that a percentage of the rents and fees be put aside for the villagers. The financing part may require a Think Tank, but I remain confident that a good campaign and launching of this project would attract tremendous support from the town, State, Central Government, Foreign Embassies and well-disposed individuals. This is another opportunity to use our contacts wisely. The signals should be sent to Onitsha Improvement Unions worldwide. I would bet that they will give their right arms to ensure the success of this project. The support from Age Grades, Societies, Professionals and various clubs would also add to the success.

Here again, we would need the attention of Obi-in-council to have this project in their agenda. Let it represent another beginning, another chapter that will help in consolidating and sustaining our pre-eminence and showcasing our unique culture. This is another "must do" by Onitsha people. The fund realizable would be used in the maintenance and further works on this ground.

SPIRITUAL DEFICIENCY

"Onye ma ebe mmili si bana opi ugbogulu". Who knows how water got into the stem of melon. This is an expression of doubt when things go wrong. These wrongs are now in legion. Most of our covenants have been broken. The ark bequeathed to us by our progenitor has been despoiled. Almost all the sacrosanct grounds are befallen by the same pillage. Our faith has dithered and our attitudes are laden with insincerity and divisionary tendencies. We hurt ourselves and often deny ourselves the opportunities to consolidate our past enviable records and glories. Our spiritual content is a far cry from what our ancestors held.

What has happened to Ani Onitsha, Otumoye, Anigbalute, Uto, Nwine, Ogwugwu, Urai, Ojedi etc? What about Udo the Coronation Ground and how is it managed to have relevance it deserves. How many adults/youths know the location? The village shrines that were surrounded by grove are now threadbare.

How much can our youth identify with these heritages? It is our collective fault in denying the young ones from not learning enough of our history.

That God favoured the final settlement of Chima kindreds in Onitsha cannot be faulted. How much have we thanked him? What is on ground to commemorate this important cradle of the town?

Obviously our social anthropology cannot be complete without the treasures that were bequeathed to us. Their likes in Europe are well preserved and appreciated. How would you explain that ancient treasures of Africa displayed in European museums are appreciated by Europeans more than the owners? Call it sheer neglect and I will agree with you completely.

Take the case of the ancient pyramids of Cairo, Egypt. They were built over a thousand years ago, much before the country was Islamized. At the height of religious tension, the nose of the sphinx was slashed. Today the pyramids and the sphinx are seen and cherished as great heritage. Tourists in multiple of hundreds visit the pyramids everyday and generate tremendous foreign exchange. We may be miles away in achieving such status as a town but we must begin somewhere. A journey of one thousand miles is said to begin with a single stride. We must first, free ourselves from the conundrum, the paradoxes we allowed ourselves to drift into and hence begin to rediscover our cultural values and institutions. There are obviously pathways through the paradoxes if only we can understand what is happening and are prepared to be different. Knowledge withheld has very limited advantage. Part of the rediscovery would warrant passing down our history to our children. A lesson from Deuteronomy in the Bible harps on God message through Moses to the Israelites to love God with their hearts, souls and strength for the great things he did for them. They were mandated to write God's rules on their doorsteps, and wear them on their foreheads in order not to forget. Much effort must be made to thank God all the time for his benevolence in giving us Onitsha. For our various lapses, neglects and failures, time to propriate cannot be delayed. We must be our brother's keeper and make truth, sincerity, candour and accountability our watchword, without which we cannot aim at spiritual realm. Time to commemorate the important cradle of our town can also not be delayed. I would further suggest that before or by the year 2010 that we should celebrate 550 years or is it 600 years existence of Onitsha. We have adequate time to plan this very important milestone that would encompass symposium and cultural displays. There are positive cornucopias of good things we can benefit from this celebration. I would particularly like Obi-in-council to consider the idea of celebrating 600 years of the town and have it in their agenda.

NON REPRESENTATION IN LOCAL GOVERNMENT

We are reminded in the following quote of a lingering unresolved conundrum. "In going downhills, Onitsha has bagged the distinction of being the only native town in Nigeria, where local government has consistently been headed and dominated by non-indigenes" (17). If other cities with overwhelming non-indigenous residents have their people heading their local government, we must begin to learn their tact. First we must seek for a credible consensus candidate and not the disparate candidates we had in the past, which led to the splitting of our votes. Elections involve money and in our dire situation, more money would be required. We must therefore have the will to generate money for this exercise. It calls for serious lobbying and offers. It is high time we used our contacts effectively and wisely. We must also have the will to countervail the activities of black sheep and quislings within us and clutch at every straw to achieve the desired results.

Last line ....How To Tackle The Dent On Onitsha Image By **MASSOB, NARTO, AVS** And Other Dissident Agents.

As I write, Onitsha is under curfew, monitored by a joint command of soldiers and mobile police. This is as a result of the mayhem carried out by these dissident groups. The media has not ruled out political schemes for this self destructive act. Not long ago the country home of Late Owelle Nnamdi Azikiwe-Inosi Onira, was burnt by **MASSOB** members. One cannot forget too soon the activities of Bakassi Vigilante Group during Mbadinauju's governance. It was bloody, barbaric and sometimes vindictive. Most of the killings were carried out in Onitsha. The reprisal attacks and killings of northerners was as a result of the killings of Ibos in the Northern states, usually start from Onitsha; a maelstrom that is now too many. Another bad news coming out of Onitsha concerns the seething war between fake drugs marketers and NAFDAC. According to the Agency Onitsha is the major supplier of these fake drugs and besides many deaths have been linked to such drugs bought or supplied from Onitsha.

Hardly do people outside South East know that most of this ruination are not perpetrated by the indigenes. Agbogidi's reaction on this mayhem that visited his dominion was swift. He denounced and discredited MASSOB and their ilk. I would like to suggest that the publicity outfit in Igwe's palace should from time to time educate the general public through media about Onitsha and the stand of Onitsha people. Such redeeming strategy can also be handled by Onitsha Improvement Union. For long term planning, the urgent need to strategize how we can reclaim our authority and respect cannot be delayed.

STILL ON AREA BOYS DEBACLE

Areas boys can be described as urban malcontents and they are mostly youths. The provenance of the concept may have come from Lagos but these boys are now in all the big cities. As such, Onitsha is not left out. Their other names include Omonile, Oluani, Talibans, militants etc. etc. To get even they demand for commissions from Business Organization, those that embark on new buildings, transporters and sometimes individuals. In many occasions, their demands end up in extortion. There is no law backing them; in other words they are illegal. They are often used by Politicians as thugs. Given their modus operandi they are unfortunately malevolent. Unemployment obviously has in many ways swelled the ranks of the Area Boys. Interestingly they make good money to enable some of them buy jeeps and other expensive cars. The matter on ground concerns the disruption of works on Globacom telecommunication mast in Onitsha by our Area Boys. I understand the boys made a demand of two million naira. Igwe's intervention was timely but unfortunately the project is still on hold at time of this write up. An examination of the Business Organization's vision and mission statements reveals the Organization's commitments to shareholders, the workforce, the communities, which would include, employment offers, scholarships, training, environmental sanitation etc. etc.

How many of us remember the Federal Government

employment regulation which gives priority to local indigenes which includes other neigbouring communities to be placed from level one to seven? How much has Onitsha benefited from the above mentioned commitments? I strongly believe that we can put a stop to both Business and Government unkept promises and offers that short changes our community. It behooves on us to bring up the unkept commitments to the attention of authorities concerned, and to ensure that in future such opportunities are discussed and firmed-up before the take off of such projects. If adequately tackled, the activities of the area boys would be checked.

On the other hand, we are reminded that the greatest cheat/fraud is the one which you cheat/defraud yourself. We cannot afford to rob ourselves further from the development benefits to the town especially when most other towns and States are gunning for the best for their people. The area boys are our sons and brothers and therefore they must be checked and countermanded by the family, the village and town. There is no doubt that a decrease in such entropy will in turn pave way for peace and development.

ON RAPPROCHEMENT BETWEEN INDIGENES AND NON-INDIGENES.

Open door policy may somehow sound contradictory to the earlier preference sought for Onitsha people. It need not totally be. Although we have detractors and spoilers from outside, we do also have lapses, spoilers and quisilings from within. Those that spike our guns are many and likewise those that put kibosh on our agenda, but there are many beneficiaries turned supporters and friends of the town. Each of these groups would require strategy to contain them. Acceptance of the inevitable is like knowing where you are before plotting your next strategy. That Onitsha is urbanized is realism. A strategy for peaceful co-existence with non-indigenes would not take the skin off our nose.

We should remind ourselves that power stems from the ability to combine other people's knowledge with your own and that may lead to open collaboration with your competitor, so far that the end result is satisfactory. As earlier mentioned we need to strategize on the ways and means to regain our authority and respect and from that position begin to influence the non-indigenous residents and the chance of having more of the beneficiaries turned friends of the town would be much. Disclosure in this respect has compelling currency.

On Honouring Our People And Other Nigerians.
Just like in Benin Kingdom, Obi of Onitsha does not confer Chieftaincy to people that are not from his domain. In line with this tenet, Vice President Dr. Alex Ekwueme of the Second Republic was initiated into Onitsha Age Grade. When you remember that some of

our illustrious sons and daughters have been honoured outside Onitsha, you will begin to think of other ways we can recognize proven excellence of other Nigerians and especially those that may have contributed to the cause of the town in different ways. There are also those that are well disposed and with hearts of gold and hearts in their right places. What comes to my mind is golden key, table plaques, medals, sculptured symbols of the monarch etc, all embossed with royal seal. I believe that there are also other ways. Our people deserve such honours as well. It has the leverage to boost patriotic services and higher aims by our people and especially the youths. One would expect that such honours list should be restricted to a manageable number. The ceremony can take place every year or every two years. It can be performed alongside other festivals or on its own. Which ever way, the benefits to the town are great. I would therefore suggest that this opinion be looked into.

Last line……….. Other Remedial Quotes
The following quotes may prove useful in our quest to consolidate our pre-eminence.

"One of the best ways of preventing, avoiding or dealing with man made conflict and misery (and oversights) is knowing when and how to start, when and how to change tactics, when and how to review and take fresh approach when and how to heal and if the matter has gone too far and is out of control, to know when and how to stop one's actions dead in their track".

Patrick Ellis Who Dares Sell 1991

"Today is tomorrow yesterday"
Patrick Ellis.

"To look is one thing.
To see what you are looking at is another thing.
To learn from what you understand is a different ball game.
What matters most is to Act on what you have learned"
Anon.
"Not all actions might bring in success but the biggest mistakes; the fatal mistake, is to do nothing.
Lan Morrison

"What we call the beginning is often the end.
And to make an end is to make a beginning.

T.S. Elliot

"Anger ventilated often hurries towards forgiveness, peace, unity and better human relations, whereas anger concealed and prolonged hardens to revenge, hatred and conflict.

"We must realize that being an Onitsha man without any (noble) means of sustenance is worthless" Arthur

Osaka.

"Chance favours the prepared mind".

"The worst of all fraud is to cheat yourself".

"Mature people feel confident but not arrogant"
Jack Welch

"To sin in silence when people should protest makes cowards of men"
Abraham Lincoln.
Foot Notes

1.   Audrey C. Smock Ibo Politics 1971
2.   R.W. Harding Harding Inquiries 1963
3.   E.T. Basden Among Ibos of Nigeria 1921-1966
4.   Arthur Osaka. A paper presentation: Impact of Urbanization of Onitsha 1967/1997. 1998
5.   Obi Nwakama. Onitsha: Death in the social of a city. Vanguard Newspaper April 25th 1999
6.   Arthur Osaka Op.cit
7.   Okey Agunyego: Onitsha Names and Phrases Teased Out.   1998
8.   Chike Osegbue: Rethinking Strategies for a sustainable community driven development 2003.
9.   Olamilekan Lartey: Punch Newspaper Tues 18th May, 2006.
10.   Prof. Charles Soludo: Central Bank of Nigeria Governor. Punch Newspaper 26th May, 2006.

11.   Brigadier Johnny Mbanefo RTD.-Onitsha Yesterday, Today and Tomorrow. Paper Presentation to 1st National Seminar of G36 Onitsha 1998

12.   Odigwe Onuora Nzekwu: Onitsha At Cross Roads Thoughts towards Rebirth and Resurgence. This is the Main article in 2002 Onitsha Day Celebration Brochure.

13.   Arthur Osaka op.cit

14.   Odigwe Onuora Nzekwu op.cit

15.   Isaiah 2.4

16.   Odigwe Onuora Nzekwu op.cit

17.   Odigwe Onuora Nzekwu op.cit

THE GREAT TREK

Accounting on what triggered off the exodus of Chima and his kindreds out of Benin and journey itself are replete in various Onitsha literature. As such, I will have to contend with its summary and tie it to Ozanzediegwu ancestry.

The exodus which took place about 1550 during the reign of Oba Esigie spanned over fifty years. At some sojourn stages eastward, Chima and his kindred fought their way through and in many others they interacted and intermarried with their hosts. Given this affinity, it is not difficult to comprehend the spread of Umueze Chima to Obior, Onicha Ugbo, Onitsha Olona, Isele Azagba, and Isle Mkpitime and later in Ugwuta Aboh and Obosi. They were instances of ill-health, old age and other reasons that prevailed upon some of the kindred to stay back at these various sojourn stages. There was the passage of Chima to continue its ruling house Ezi, one of the daughters of

Chima also could not continue the journey because of her pregnancy that was due. Interestingly the town she bore her baby still bears the name Ezi.

Oreze led the group that crossed over to Onitsha Ado. Their crossing of the River Niger was facilitated by the progenitor of Ogbeotus; Okomanya and Ogbodogo.

Dei established the ruling house in Ugwuta, Ogwueshi in Aboh, Oleigbo in Isele Ukwu and Daike in IIIah. It was in lllah that Chima married a second wife, Enubi thar begat Aroli and Olosi.

Aroli begot six children, Agadagba, Chimedie, Omozele, Usse, Olisa and Daike Anyo.

Chimedie had eight children; Orezeobi, Olodiowowo, Orowa, Nwazago, Akazue, Ijelekpe, Ozanzediegwu and Ajagba. Out of these children, Ijelekpe, Ozanzediegwu, Nwazago and Ajaba are from the same mother and are known as Umu Nwomi.

OZANZEDIEGWU FAMILY MEMBERS

OZANZEDIEGWU HAD THREE MALE CHILDERN NAMELY: OZONWASIALI OZIZIODIA AND MORA

OZONWASIALI BEGAT NWOKOLO, ONUMONU AND OSEMENAM. NWOKOLO BEGAT OKWUAGU AND OKWUAGU BEGAT MOLOKWU OMODI.

ONUMONU BEGAT OBIUDUNWA 1783-1848 OBIDUDUNWA BEGAT NWALIE EDEOGU,OKOLOMA AND MRS. EMEGOKWUE.

OSEMENAM BEGAT TWO FEMALE ISSUES;OKWUENU AND AGBAIZU.

OZIZIODIA BEGAT ANYAFULU AND ANUYAFULU BEGAT NZEGWU, ISIMA CHUKWUMA EXTINCT AND NNASO EXTINCT.

MORA BEGAT OSAJI AND AGUNYEGO. THEY HAD A SISTER MRS OFOEDU THAT BORE THE

GRAND FATHER OF THE OFOEDUS OF IYIAWU VILLAGE.

EZE AROLI DYNASTY

CHIMEDIE TONY
MOLOKWU
OBIOGBOLU

EZENNIA   AKUDO

LATE DIOKP

LATE MAJOR THEO
NZEGWU

LATE ODIZIAKW ORAME
MODEBE NEE AGUNYEGO

NNA BUENYI OBIANEZE
LATE A.G. ACTING DIOKSPA

NNNYELUGO MOSES
EDEOGU

LATE MADAM IFEDIABA AGUNNIEGO 1891-1976

LATE ORUMILI AMECHI OSAJI 1926-2006

LATE CHIKE EDEOGU AND LATE WIFE BEATRICE EDEOGU

LATE OFOEDU NZEGWU
V.I.E
GBOSA OBI 1

LATE   ONOENYI

EDEOGU 1885-1948

LATE L.N NZEGWU

LATE ENGR.THEO NZEGWU

GBOSA   OBI   G.H.N.   NZEGWU   BARR.NKIRU   NZEGWU
DANJUMA
AND ELIZABET NZEGWU OF BLESSED MEMORIES

LATE FRANCIS OKWUDILI
OSAJI

LATE MONSIGNNOR
WILLIAMS ETUKA

L.N.NZEGWU,SAM JIDEOFOR, AKUNWATA, ENEGOKWUE,OCHLIME NZEGWU, MRS AGBOWA EJOGU, AND MRS.IFENEME UMERA OF BLESSED MEMORIES

MESSRS MOSES, ALEX,AUGUSTIN AND IKEM AGUNYEGO
ALL OF BLESSED MEMORIES

LATE FRANKLIN MANWU
     CHUKWUMA NEE

LATE MADAM NNE

"EKWUIFE EKWEOGWU

S.K. NZEGWU   L ATE MR. NABOUTH
                                  EDEOGU

LATE ENGR.NNANYELUGO ALEX NZEGWU & WIFE MRS.
LILANN NZEGWU

LATE MR.ALEX OKWUDILI AND LATE MRS ROSE AGUNYEGO

MUO CHIMEDIE

CHIMEDIE HAD EIGHT CHILDREN

- *Orezeobi* - *His descendants inherit (under special arrangement) Muo Chimedie.*
- *Orowa* - *His descendants inherit Muo Chimedie*
- *Olodi Owowo* - *His descendants do not inherit Muo Chimedie*
- *Nwazago* - *His descendants inherit Muo Chimedie*
- *Ijelekpe* - *His descendants do not inherit Muo Chimedie*
- *Akazue* - *His descendants do not inherit Muo Chimedie*
- *Ozandiegwu* - *His descendants do not inherit Muo Chimedie*
- *Ajagba* - *His descendants do not inherit Muo Chimedi*

OZANZEDIEGWU DIOPKA

Ozanzediegwu had three children; namely
- *Oza Nwasiali*
- *Ozizi Odia*
- *Mora*

The family headship rotates between Oza Nwasiali and Ozizi Odia.

Mora is excluded because he predeceased his father.

PRAISE FOR SOME OF THE ARTICLES

I have gone through your write-ups on Strengthening

Onitsha Improvement Union and Related Matters. Thanks for the insightful thoughts and suggestions proffered. I hope that the message will sink and further stimulate us to positive developments Bravo. Sir Law Nwokedi.

Your open letter to Governor Obiano is a beautiful piece. Keep up the good work. Henry Onukwuba.

Thank you for the two articles sent to me, Pathways to Paradoxes and open letter of Governor Obiano. It couldn't have been said better. I heartily congratulate and applaud you…. Nnebolisa Arah.

Your letter to Governor Obiano is very apt and timely. The decadence in our beloved town is worrisome. Thanks for highlighting the problem. I hope the Governor will note and give the matter the attention it deserves. Sir Law Nwokedi.

I have gone through your thought provoking letter to Governor Obiano. It is beautiful piece. I hope it reaches the Governor. Aduba Okagbue.

I have gone through the thought provoking letter to the Governor. New broom they say, sweeps clean. Let us hope that the Governor will tow the right path. Keep it up and may your ink never dry. Nwachi Eche Chukwuma.

Good job, I have sent your letter to Governor Obiano to Riverside news for circulation. Jide Kaiji Afam Ofoedu.

NB. The open letter to Governor Willie Obiano of Anambra State was published by Daily Champion Newspaper on May 23 2014. Ado Sentinel also published the Letter.

CHIMEDIE FAMILY

OGBENDIDA QUARTERS

OREZE OBI: Diokpala Chimedie died before Chimedie.

Orezobi begat:-

Ugbelede:- Ochei

Aguzani:- Achebe, Ibisi, Anyakwo, Aniemena, Belu, Molokwu, Onuora and Edu.

Osuma Amalinze

Anyaso: Uyanne, Obanye, Chude

Bachi:-

Akah:- Oranye

Isagba Okwuona:- Chukwurah, Moutune, Okolonji, Nkpuluma, Achutaobe and Ebosie.

Obi:-

Enendu, Osegbue, Mazeli, Onwuazo Onyechi, Affa, Iwobi, Boardman,

Okafor: Anyeaegbunam

Umu Okwuma:- Enwezo, Akaya, Emodi Oti, Andrews.

Adele: Anyamene, Nwokedi, Achike

Nwachie

Osowa Onumonu: Aniweta, Obechie

Agu Owowo: Areh, Egbunike, Chuka Alias Mustapha and Onwuatu

Ojiabo Owowo:- Onuwalu, Okwuosa, Ndulue, Chima, Okaka Ibeziakor, Ajeh

OGBEOZA QUARTERS

a) OROWA: Agbakoba, Akosa, Onyejekwe Irekwu,

Egbuche

b) NWAZAGO: Obiogbolu, Emodi, Nwurai
c) IJELEKPE:
   i. Osodi Emneagwali: Nwike, Okolo, Ononye, Oguno, Anierobi,
   ii. Obi Udogwu:
a) Akazue:-
   i. Odili, Odita, Mbanefo, Odukwe, Ezeadigwu, Ejoh, Oreadiwe,
   ii. Diali: Onyenyionwu, Molokwu
   iii. Anazonwu: Anazonwu, Obiozor, Chuke Ilukwe
   iv. Agbakoba: Nwabo, Agbakoba,
b) Anyakora-Odua: Egbuji, Nwabuzo, Nwagbolugu, Uzo,
c) Umu Okeke: Ofodile, Nwoche, Nwosa, Azuka, Onwuma, Obanye
d) Sonuba: Ubili
e) Ozoma Ononye: Anamma, Ikeomu, Ejembonye, Okolonji Osameka, Akanya
f) Chiewena: Ejiamike, Arima
g) Onyekoso:
i. Edeogu: Obiesie, Ibemesi
ii. Nsommuo: Nzeche
h. Inyieze: Anakwe, Ndaguba, Egbuniwe
iii. Ezumezu: Emodi, Egbuniwe, Areh, Akosa, Chuma, Chude and Achebe
iv. Onwudachi: Unokando

a. Okwusogu, Chuke
b. Emeta, Anyaegbanma, Ojiba, Ikeme (Akukalia) Iwobi, Chukwufo, Osuagbadi, Emeter.
c. Achukwu: Akpali
v. Olisa: Oramali, Ozo Ezugo
vi. Ozo Osuma:

a.   Nzekwu (Osuma) Ofodile, Ibelum Ralum

b.   Onukwuba: Onwora   (Odigwe)   Edozie, Okonkwo (Manyaike)

c.   Orakposim: Okechukwu, Ononye

d.   Agusiobo   Mazeli: Obiogbolu,   Oranefo, Otanlpologu

        Note: Umu Nwanyiama Onudachi, Olisa and Ozo Chuma

vii.   Tabasni: Anyaduba

viii.   Uyole (isitor): Ikwueme, Asika, Ndiwe, Okafor, Anierobi Isitor (Onoye)

D.   Ozanzediegwu: Ozanzediegwu   Begat Ozonwasiali, Ozizidia and Mora

I.   Ozonwasiali:

a.   Nwokolo, Okuwuagu and Molokwu Omodi

b.   Onumonnu: Obiudunwa: Nwalie   Edeogu, Okoloma and Mrs. Emegokwue

c.   Osemenam: Okwuenu and Agbaizu

2.   Oziziodia begat Anyafulu and Anyafulu begat

a.   Ofoedu Nzegwu: LN. Nzegwu, Sam Jideofo, Akunwata Emegokwue, Gilbert, Nwachukwu, Izuchukwu.

b.   Isima:- Obiefuna, Chukwuma, Orefo, Obeleagu

3.   Mora: begat

a.   Agunyego: Esesue Akonobi, Enyi Orame and Ogbuko

b.   Osaji: Chuke, Sam Okoye, Jacob, Ojiakeado, Martha, Nwaku, Umebe.

E.   Ajagba begat

a.   Isitor: Osadebe, Anyeaegbunam Afoaka

b.   Atula: Oburota, Inoma, Chukwuma, Anikamdu

and Akaigwe.

TRIBUTE TO LATE ALEX OSITA AGUNYEGO
FEB 22 1952 – JAN 12 2013
COMMITTED TO MOTHER EARTH ON FEB 8 2013

Birth is death begun. In an articulation by George Santayana in soliloquies in England he commented as follows: "There is no cure for birth and death,save to enjoy the interval". A great counsel for the living in borrowed time but we must acknowledge that only God, our Creator determines the interval and hence knows our expiry dates. It is only Him that can disprove death.Osi my brother, as the family mourns your demise, I reflect on many experiences that remind me of you. A few of them would do for this tribute. I was four years and you were two when we followed a local brass band parading our neighborhood in Port Harcourt. There was overcast that evening and we had some difficulties finding our way home. Someone who identified us called out my name but I told him that my name was Maduegbunam. We were so young to know the inferences. I believe that an angel guided us to the house safely. The man who identified us narrated the circumstances to our parent.

In your third year at Father Joseph College,Aguleri you came home with your school fees. We were worried about this development but your reflected your preference to Technical school. This choice was later manifest in your career. You joined OTIS, an elevator company in 1974 and you were in the team that constructed the first building with elevator in Onitsha. At Kano you joined AIS Cargo and later became the Cargo Manager. You also worked for NACHO and Base Aviation. On my various visit to Kano I was delighted with the ease you maneuvered the lever of the high loader while loading cargo pallets or off loading cargo and stacking them. Your ground to air communication is crisp, clear and splendid and with this you were able to mobilize your staff for effective aircraft handling.I must not forget your involvement in show business after the war. You got most of the Bills circulating contracts and you were also a delight doing Mutaba and James Brown shuffles.

Six days to your demise, I brought a photograph you took at 22, wearing bell bottom trouser and tough suede shoes. My intention was to animate you and it worked. You shook your head and laughed. I wished I had a camera to take your picture. Your daughter, Ifeyinwa thought the portrait to be Zubi, your second son. You did not eat much but on same day you were able to savour the Amala dish and after which you asked me if you have not tried. That was the last meaningful conversation I had with you. The ailment in the last five days took a toll on you. You were to see the doctor on Monday 14 January with the results of the test the doctor had recommended and I was to go with you and Nnamdi your son. Little did we know that the reaper whose name is death will snatch you away with its claws on Saturday 12th January 2013. As you join your wife, our parent's grannies aunties, brothers, sisters, cousins and nephews in the world beyond, I pray that our Lord Jesus Christ will provide you a room out of the many rooms His Father, our God and Creator has. May He forgive your sins and those of us that mourn you. Adieu my brother Osita, Nwa Mama.

OKEY AGUNYEGO
His Grace Lodge
Lagos.
2/2/2013

EPILOGUE

The main theme that runs in this compendium is about how to erase our pitiable derailment and in its place promote competitiveness for the development of the town and her people.

Vision and strategy; two components, that go together are essential in charting the course of any organization. Where the goal is not desirable, the organization concerned will have to reframe, restage and reshape its vision and strategy.

Jean – Marc Dru, in his book on Disruption – Changing the rules in the market place – defines disruption as dismantling the status quo and replacing them with what is bold and new. Some of us may think that this concept concerns only corporate bodies. Even churches have visions and missions and same is applicable to associations and communities. It would not be out of place for the Ruling Council to work with a Think Tank that will study various aspects of our community and fashion out the town's vision and strategy.

It is not as if things are standstill. Who would have believed ten years ago that vigil could be stopped? In Onitshaness – Reviewal 2008, I discussed shitting the vigil – Ikposu Ozu – to the following morning if there are no serious spiritual implications. See page...... The Otu Odu has few years ago monetized some aspects of their requirements in burials and during initiation of new members. This, no doubt is convenient and beneficial to their members. I understand too that the new executive of Agbalanze has begun on a new foot in engendering some positive changes. These are fine, but the problems that have dulled our competitiveness are huge and it is important for us to be aware of them. Much of these are discussed in the main text. As I cited earlier in one of my write –ups, the competition/race is not between Onitsha and other towns in Anambra State, rather it is a race between Onitsha inland Town against twenty one plus Local Government Councils. I hope that this drift is clear. We will need a serious commitment, a quantum leap strategy to bring back our pre-eminence and more so when others may not be aloof.

We have much wastage in burials and pageantry. This could now pass as our hallmark. It would appear that we celebrate death more than life. A person who receives little or no comfort in his/her lifetime is given a stupendous burial. Most times money is borrowed for this exercise. Even in cases of well –to-do people wastage abound. The major drawback of such practices is such that the purveyors of the materials required for burials and pageantry are non-indigenes. A good number of them have little or no commitment to Onitsha. The fines for contravening burial and marriage regulations were intended to check the excesses in entertainment, hence reduce the burden on the family. What is obtainable these days is that people are not worried about the fines. The initial objective can no longer be met, hence there is need to reshape the strategy. Another noticeable disadvantage is the yawning gap between indigenous artisans and that of other towns. Not having commensurate artisans amount to others exploiting the huge market provided for artisans. The instances cited above constitute serious financial haemorrhage in our community economy.

It is sad that the two skill acquisition centers cited in Onitsha North and South over two years ago are not functional. No equipment has been installed all this while. I believe that those of us with hearts in the right places can for example build a mechanic yard where our youths can undergo practical and theoretical classes at a reasonable fee. The mechanic yard could also accommodate service centre as well as car painting. It may not be out of place for the Ruling Council to assist in locating a piece of land for this project. The fear and doubts about our youth's willingness to become artisans can be doused with intense sensitization. Nobody has the preserve for trading or becoming artisans. You may recall that our grandmothers were successful traders and likewise many of our grandfathers were reputable artisans. We will be compounding our problems by not exploiting this profitable profession. Germany has so much commitment in turning out rated artisans that complements their workforce.

Considering the disruption principle we would have to jettison some of our ethos, societal values and attitudes that may no longer provide competitive advantages.

Take the case of 'Igbu ewu izu'. It is built on pretence. It entails the elders asking after the health of their titled brother and to be told that he is very sick. Thereafter invocation for healing and protection is sought by the family members. A goat is sacrificed and shared out raw among the numbers of 'umunna' kindred who are present. No sooner they stepped out than they are recalled and given the bad news of the death of their brother. What follows next is an outburst of disingenuous lamentation. Yet, that would not stop them from the entertainment; drinks and money all borne by the immediate bereaved family. Before all these sympathizers had thronged the bereaved family house and most likely the clearance date of the burial from Ime Obi would have been secured. These facts underscore the point that the death was publicized before the 'Igbu ewu izu'. By tradition the victim is treated as though he were alive but ailing. Here again, I will suggest a re-examination of this practice and many others to ascertain their relevancy in today's world. I think we can engage ourselves in something better.

Scores of ideas, projects and counsels have been expressed throughout this work, all designed to achieving Onitshanness. Let me take one or two more cases. It is paradoxical that we can muster fund for anything than for self-help. In addressing this issue, I reckon that we can generate N200, 000,000 yearly if every adult Onitsha person estimated at 40,000 pays N5000 every year. Census is another important project. It is the beginning of planning. I believe that the family Diokpas – Spiritual-Heads will be useful in extracting and updating the family roll call. We must begin to rise above fears and doubts that most of the times stunt our efforts.

The following quote is credited to Jack Welch. 'When the rate of change inside an organization is lower than the rate outside, the end is near. It is frightening but it is clarion calls to double if not quadruple our efforts – meeting Onitsha dreams. I would like our people to think boldly, sell brave ideals and create dramatic results (Clow).

Finally, I would like the Ruling Council, various arms of governance associations and individuals to study these various articulated ideas projects and counsel not only in this work but in other people's works and then use what are of prime consideration in developing our community.

To those that will drive the various projects, may God strengthen you?
To all, if God is prompting you to help the needy, your community etc, do not hesitate because time is short and tomorrow cannot be guaranteed.
To look is one thing
To see what you look is another
To understand what you see is another different issue.
To learn from form what you understand is still something else,
But to act on what you learn is all that matters.

Success and glory await those who dare to act
God bless you all

Okey Maduegbunam Olisa Agunyego
Feb. 2015.